CAPITAL INSTINCTS

Life As an Entrepreneur, Financier, and Athlete

Richard L. Brandt

with contributions by Thomas Weisel

WILEY

John Wiley & Sons, Inc.

Published by John Wiley & Sons, Inc., Hoboken, New Jersey.
Published simultaneously in Canada.

For general information on our other products and services, or technical support, please contact our Customer Care Department within the United States at 800-762-2974, outside the United States at 317-572-3993 or fax 317-572-4002.

Wiley also publishes its books in a variety of electronic formats. Some content that appears in print may not be available in electronic books.

For more information about Wiley products, visit our Web site at www.wiley.com.

Library of Congress Cataloging-in-Publication Data
Brandt, Richard.
    Capital instincts : life as an entrepreneur, financier, and athlete / Richard Brandt with contributions by Thomas Weisel.
        p.   cm.
Includes bibliographical references and index.
    ISBN 0-471-21417-5 (cloth : perm. paper)
    1. Weisel, Thomas.   2. Capitalists and financiers—United States—Biography.
I. Weisel, Thomas.   II. Title.
    HG172.W38 B73 2002
    332.1'092—dc21   2002155479

Contents

Thom Weisel has played a remarkable role in my life and in my career. It's not as though our relationship over the last 12 years has always been easy. In fact, there have been peaks and valleys, frank conversations, and tough times. But, in the end, it has given our relationship tremendous depth and color, and we have gained a strong appreciation for each other. In many ways, he's been something of a father figure to me.

Our relationship started when I spent 1990 and 1991 on the cycling team Thom put together, the Subaru-Montgomery team. At the end of 1991, I decided to leave the team. I was ambitious and the Subaru-Montgomery team just wasn't a great team. I was offered a chance to ride with one of the top 5 or 10 teams in the world. It was the old 7-Eleven team, although now it was sponsored by Motorola, and it was legendary. When I was growing up, it was the Dallas Cowboys of American cycling. It's where you wanted to end up.

I will never forget when I decided to leave the Subaru-Montgomery team. I had to call Thom and tell him. Let's just say he didn't like the idea. Here I was, 20 years old, and I had Thom Weisel on the phone telling me what a bad idea it was. For one of the first times in my life, I had to defend a choice I had made to a really serious and powerful person, someone I really respected. It was a painful conversation.

But I made my points, and Thom gave his moment of silence, like he does as he thinks things over. And then he said to me, "You know, Lance? I really respect your candor, and I support that decision." I just about dropped the phone. I didn't think I would get that kind of support. Because of that conversation, because of the way we left it, we maintained a relationship for the entire time that I was on another team. I would occasionally come out to San Francisco specifically to ride with Thom.

There have also been some tough, straightforward conversations. In 1998, after my cancer, I wanted to start racing again, but had trouble finding a team to take me. Thom had started the U.S. Postal Service team by then, so I called him to see if I could get a place on the team. But Thom not only turned me down at first, he told me why, in no uncertain terms. He thought I hadn't been the leader I should have been, hadn't lived up to my potential, and didn't think I would fit on his team.

That was probably the most brutal conversation I have ever had. He just put me in my place. But in the end, I think it was healthy for someone to tell me that. Thom expects people who work with him to be the best they can be. Thom was totally honest and straight with me.

Not long after that, my agent, Bill Stapleton, talked to him again, and walked through the reasons I could be good for the team. They agreed to a base salary, way below what I had been used to making, but just didn't have the money in the budget for the bonus Stapleton asked for: up to $1,000 for every ICU (International Cycling Union) point I earned in races over the next year. That's when Thom decided that he would personally cover my salary. It was an extraordinary gesture.

I have no clue as to why Thom changed his mind about having me on his team, but once he did, he stuck to his word. I'm sure he expected me to get maybe 40 or 50 ICU points. Ironically, I got so many I ended up making more money that year than I ever had before! Over $1 million came out of Thom's pocket to pay my salary. These days we laugh about it, and he calls me an SOB for costing him so much.

Thom is one of the toughest guys I've ever met. In fact, he's probably the toughest. He's also probably the most competitive person I've ever seen. This is a guy who likes to win all the time, at everything. Absolutely everything for him is a competition, in every part of his life, whether it's business, bikes, wine, art, or just driving from his office to home. To Thom, everything's a deal. Everything's a prizefight, a contest. He gets fired up about it. He's hard-charging, passionate, and extremely disciplined.

Thom is an emotional person. Anybody with the kind of drive and spirit he has shows how deeply he feels about things. He can be very lively, and he can be very heated and intense.

I remember one time Thom got really mad at me. I had let another rider win an important stage of the Tour de France. Sometimes in cycling you help somebody else out, and sometimes they'll help you out. But this was a tough and legendary stage of the race, over Mount Ventoux, 6,000 feet high. It's too important, too famous to just give away. Thom was furious. "Why give away one of the most legendary stages of cycling to a guy that's not your teammate, not even your friend?" And again, he was right.

But Thom doesn't meddle with the team's strategy or training. He wants to show up at the race, see his team prepared, see us execute our strategy properly, and be a spectator with the best seat in the house, riding in the pace car. There are times when he's riding shotgun in the car, and I'll gain two minutes on the next rider climbing a mountain. He'll pull up alongside me, hanging out of the car, beating the side of the car, just screaming at the top of his lungs. That's his bliss. I love it when he's there.

I wish he would throttle back a little on his insane pace. I've argued with him about this plenty of times. His pace isn't healthy, and he's done so much with his life already, I wish he would just slow down a little. But he can't do it. It's part of his flesh. But I guess I'm like that, too. It's one of the reasons we get along so well.

Thom has probably invested more in American cycling than everyone else combined. He has invested time, he has invested money, he has invested relationships, and at the end of the day, he has created the greatest professional cycling team ever. American cycling just wouldn't be the same without him. I doubt if the investing world would be, either.

I personally will never forget that it was Thom and the U.S. Postal Service that stepped up and gave a cancer survivor a second chance as a bike racer. If not for Thom's generosity and vision, there would be no Tour de France titles behind my name.

Lance Armstrong
Winner of the Tour de France, 1999, 2000, 2001, 2002
U.S. Postal Service cycling team

Acknowledgments

The authors would like to thank the following people for their help and perspective:

Lance Armstrong, Dick Barker, Erik Borgen, Terra Brusseau, Susie Dean, Amanda Duckworth, Paul "Red" Faye, Irwin Federman, Chuck Ferries, Dick Fredericks, Brad Freeman, John Gruber, Ed Glassmeyer, Mark Gorski, Kip Hagopian, Tim Heekin, Warren Hellman, Mark Higgins, Ted Johann, Blake Jorgensen, Robert Kahan, Jack Kemp, Tim Koogle, Dick Kramlich, Terry Lee, Derek Lemke, Jack Levin, Glenn Lowry, Peter Lynch, Jerry Markowitz, Karl Matthies, Jessica Miller, Dick Moley, Leonard Harvey Nitz, Jim Ochowitz, Ken Oshman, Joe Parkinson, Diana Sangston, Ken Siebel, Tom Siebel, Paul Slivon, Bill Stapleton, Allan Stone, Otto Tschudi, Mel Tuckman, Jack Wadsworth, Will Weinstein, Byron Wien, Dick Weisel, Bill Wilson, Ken Wilson, Governor Pete Wilson, Steve Wynn, and a few others who prefer not to be mentioned.

Richard Brandt also offers special thanks to Kim and Leila Brandt for their love and support.

Thom Weisel wishes to thank his wife, Emily Carroll, and all of his children for their support over the years.

Introduction

The spirit of the Wild West of more than a century ago still lives on in Silicon Valley. It's a place of pioneers, daredevils, and risk takers. Instead of pioneers moving into a lawless land, acquiring property, and building homes, farms, and ranches in a harsh and untamed environment, today's western pioneers acquire high-risk capital and build companies within a harsh and untamed business environment.

It's a risky ambition. Pioneering a new industry requires intelligence, creativity, guts, stamina, a strong sense of adventure, and luck. The regulations governing today's entrepreneurial businesses are still being written. For example, the phenomenon of a flood of young companies hitting the public markets in a massive wave, creating instant millionaires, is a new one. As we have seen in the last few years, it also has its perils.

But those who can tame this environment have managed to amass phenomenal riches, inspiring new generations to make the trek. Just as risk takers from Europe settled the eastern coast of America and then risk takers from the East settled the West, these days risk takers from all over the world have moved to Northern California to adopt and nurture the unique entrepreneurial business culture there. The wiser, more sensible types sit back and shake their heads at the brash ones who move west to risk their fortunes and careers on this relatively dangerous endeavor.

Even among this group of successful entrepreneurs there are those who stand out. A very few become the leaders of their industries. They are the ones who create new paths and change the business. Thom Weisel is a true entrepreneur and leader.

The thing is, Thom Weisel likes to lead a lot. As if dealing with the growth of his own companies were not enough, he is driven by an apparent need to set himself new challenges, then teaching himself how to master them. He has not only built an impressive bank, he has excelled at sports, created sports teams that win worldwide competitions, reorganized national sports organizations, influenced national politics, and put together an extraordinary collection of modern art.

He's not perfect, but he is an interesting, controversial, and highly accomplished individual. He is, in other words, one of the characters who make Silicon Valley what it is, for better and for worse.

Until recently, the general population has not been as fascinated by investment bankers as by the entrepreneurs and venture capitalists that start the entrepreneurial process rolling. But the investment bankers play a critical role in keeping the process going, in elevating the status of entrepreneurial companies and providing them with a long-term source of capital through the public markets. As we have seen more recently, they are also in a position of huge influence in the stock market, they face enormous potential conflicts of interest, and some have been part of the biggest series of scandals to hit U.S. business since the Great Depression.

Weisel is one of the people who stand out in a crowd of leaders. He's respected by colleagues, clients, and competitors. He's admired by athletes and top politicians. But he's also demanding, blunt, and sometimes controversial. The work environment he creates is as intense as he is. Some people say they would never work for him. Some competitors have accused his firm of overly aggressive business practices, and some dislike him as intensely as others love him. Weisel bristles at some of the accusations of his detractors, but his admirers far outnumber his critics.

Weisel has been working with entrepreneurial companies since the age of the modern entrepreneur began. He has had to figure out how to structure his business, targeting entrepreneurs, as he went along. He relies on instinct to take him from subject to subject, pursuing only those he develops a deep passion for. He also studies each topic, from cycling to banking, deeply and intently. Many people study and practice their professions and hobbies, but there are probably few who do so as rigorously as Weisel. Fewer still succeed as spectacularly as he does.

Perhaps his greatest instinct is for finding people who can teach him what he needs to know. He has the rare ability to find people who can handle demanding tasks, even if they have little or no experience for the job. And he has the sense to back—or follow—them without hesitation and with little interference, as long as they continue to perform.

The Taoist philosopher Lao-Tzu said: "The wicked leader is he whom the people despise. The good leader is he whom the people revere. The great leader is he [about] whom the people say, We did it ourselves."

People who have worked for Thom Weisel for any length of time *know* they did it themselves.

Most of all, Thom Weisel is a survivor. While other investment banks have been shaken by scandal or merged into oblivion, he remains standing. He managed to walk away from a disastrous merger and start over again. The ruthless recession has battered his young company, as it has battered some of the giant banks, but he has managed to shift direction, positioning his firm to outlast the downturn and thrive when business returns.

In a way, he may be the last of a generation. He is one of very few entrepreneurs left in a business now dominated by superconglomerates. His company is by far the most successful and influential of the entrepreneurial investment banks left. It's a testament to his tenacity.

As I wrote this book, the investment banking industry was in the middle of the worst business environment it has ever seen. Every investment bank is suffering. The flow of capital on which they rely has been largely dammed up. The investment banking industry is at ground zero of the financial scandals that are destroying several companies once thought to be stars of the Internet-induced business boom. And all of business is depressed by the nervous uncertainty of investors as America enters the age of terrorism.

All those issues are unfinished business. We don't know how it will end, either for the investment banking industry or for Thomas Weisel Partners. We do know that both will be changed by the battle. Doing the reporting for the book, I was able to observe some of the maneuvers Thom Weisel took in order to avoid disaster. We'll know how well these moves worked in a few years, and perhaps readers will learn from the experience as well. Learning from others is, after all, the nature of a good entrepreneur.

Our Approach

This book was commissioned, paid for, edited, and published by John Wiley & Sons. The book contract was signed several months before we convinced Weisel to cooperate. It would have been written with or without his assistance. Once he agreed to participate, he put an incredible amount of effort and thought into the book.

This is, therefore, an authorized biography, but one with a twist. The information in the book is based on research, dozens of interviews with Weisel, and dozens more with people who know him—both friends and competitors. I was allowed to write whatever I could come up with, but Weisel was allowed to argue his case over any disputed facts or opinions and to delete certain things he felt were wholly untrue or inappropriate. The majority of those changes were of a personal nature, in order to protect friends and family.

My goal was also to provide context to the story. This is not a dispassionate telling of a story, but an opinionated one. Therefore, it includes observations based on my 20 years as a journalist as well as valuable, topical commentaries and essays contributed by Thom Weisel. Weisel's essays appear at the end of all chapters except Chapter 1.

The final chapter, looking to the future of growth business and the stock market, is all his. Predicting the future is always a hazardous profession, especially if the prognosticator writes down the predictions, leaving the evidence behind. You'll be able to judge the accuracy of Thom's foresight as things unfold over the next few years.

Now, how many times are you made an offer like that?

Richard L. Brandt

Never Underestimate Thom Weisel

The great pleasure in life is doing what people say you cannot do.

—*Walter Bagehot*

It was December 1998, and the famed Internet bubble was growing like a virus at the peak of flu season. I was editor in chief of a technology business magazine called *Upside,* chronicling the evolution of the business world into what we thought would be a New Economy rife with new possibilities, exciting new companies, and seemingly limitless growth.

Late one afternoon, I sent an e-mail to one of my sources, a research analyst named David Readerman, who worked at a San Francisco investment bank called NationsBanc Montgomery Securities. It was a routine query. Research analysts probably talk to reporters more than they talk to their own spouses. The main use (and overuse) of investment banks by journalists is to contact the banks' research analysts for comments, quotes, and insight on the companies they cover. The main job of the analyst is to evaluate companies and their stock prices, primarily for their firm's investment clients. But they like talking to the press in order to see their name in print or their face on the air, theoretically adding prestige to their firm at the same time. A clever and lazy daily beat reporter could get an entire story by calling a favorite analyst and asking, "What's new?"

I no longer recall what I had contacted Readerman about (other than to ask, "What's new?"), but the response I found on my computer the next morning was unexpected, terse, and enigmatic: "Can't talk now. There's something going on here. Call me in a couple weeks."

Now that sounded intriguing! It might turn out to be nothing more than another defection in the investment banking business—another analyst scooping up an absurdly rich offer from a competing firm. That was common enough at that time. In the late 1990s, everyone wanted in on the technology feast. Bright young people with expertise in technology (and some without it) were flocking to new opportunities like ants to a picnic after a watermelon fight, and there were plenty of very ritzy picnics to choose from.

MBA students were starting dot-coms out of their dorm rooms. Top executives at blue-chip firms were trading six-figure salaries for stock options from tech start-ups. Day traders were speculating more wildly than the most addicted Las Vegas gamblers. And Silicon Valley start-up companies were rushing to go public, cashing in on the frenzy as though this incredible bubble were about to burst. The standard three- to five-year time period for a Silicon Valley company to go from start-up to public offering had been reduced to as little as one year.

The investment banks are the firms that take those companies public, and they were thriving. It had become the new glamour field. It wasn't as legendary as the high-profile venture capital business, but it was (and is) no less critical a component of the Silicon Valley financial machine. Some of the technology analysts at the investment banking firms, like Mary Meeker at Morgan Stanley, Jack Grubman, formerly at Salomon Smith Barney, or Henry Blodget, formerly at Merrill Lynch, had become media stars for recommending (often to reporters calling to ask, "What's up?") technology stocks that seemed to have invented a cure for gravity.

Montgomery, a San Francisco "boutique" investment bank, was much smaller than the New York–based giants of the industry like Merrill Lynch or Goldman Sachs. It took companies public and helped them issue stock after the IPO, but it did not have a brokerage business to help individuals speculate in stocks, focusing instead on acting as a broker for institutions such as money management firms and pension funds, the professionals of the investment business. It was also firmly nestled in the industry's hot spot. Montgomery, like its San Francisco rivals Robertson Stephens & Co. and Hambrecht & Quist, specialized in just a few fast-growing markets, and technology was the fastest in the world. Although relatively small (with revenues of roughly $1 billion, compared to Merrill's revenues of nearly $18 billion in 1998), Montgomery had very cozy relationships with the entrepreneurs and venture capitalists of Silicon Valley.

Those connections were giving the company unprecedented new clout. Montgomery's annual investment conference in San Francisco, for example, was famous for bringing together the CEOs of some of the most promising technology companies, who made their pitch to institutional investors that controlled trillions of dollars of assets. Stock prices of presenting companies often jumped during these conferences.

Thus, just as tech start-ups like Amazon.com and Yahoo! were threatening "Old Age" companies, perhaps the tech-focused investment banks—entrepreneurial organizations themselves—began to look like a threat to the Old Age investment banks. No bank could afford to miss out.

Add to that the fact that the federal government was now rapidly deregulating the banking business, and merger mania in banking began to resemble nothing so much as a great white shark feeding frenzy. Most of the New York (and international) banks had always been something like pelagic sharks, feeding across the entire ocean of industries, specializing nowhere. They had now decided to settle into Northern California for an extended meal.

The major banks were as wild-eyed and free with their money as any day trader. While stock speculators were buying up shares of any company with a name that ended in the phrase *dot-com*, the great financial institutions of the world were buying up any investment bank whose executives could spell the word *silicon* without an e.

That had already happened to Montgomery Securities. Just a year earlier, in 1997, NationsBank Corp. of North Carolina had announced a $1.3 billion acquisition of Montgomery, giving the southern bank a key trade route to the hip young companies of Silicon Valley. That same year, BankAmerica Corp. bought Robertson for $540 million. Hambrecht held out until September 1999, when Chase Manhattan (after buying Chemical Bank and Manufacturer's Hanover but before merging with J.P. Morgan) snapped it up for $1.35 billion.

Things got really interesting when NationsBank bought BankAmerica Corp. (the legal name), commonly known as Bank of America, in 1998 for $60 billion. (NationsBank later changed its own name to a slightly altered version of the name of its acquired bank, taking Bank *of* America Corp. as its legal name. It must have decided that spelling out which nation made for a better name.) That meant NationsBank owned two rival San Francisco–based, technology-focused investment banks— Montgomery and Robertson. So it sold Robertson to BankBoston Corp. for $800 million—a nice profit in one year. Fleet Bank Corp. later bought BankBoston, while Chase merged into J.P. Morgan.

The leading technology specialists, independent for decades, were now suddenly tiny subsidiaries of enormous conglomerates. It wasn't unusual for executives to jump ship in this environment.

But when I finally talked to David Readerman a couple of weeks later, it turned out the news was much more interesting than I had imagined. His boss, Thomas W. Weisel (pronounced WIZE-ell), the powerful and mercurial CEO who had headed Montgomery for nearly 20 years before orchestrating its sale to NationsBank, had walked out the previous September and was now creating a new bank.

It was a full-fledged coup against NationsBank CEO Hugh McColl. Not only had Weisel left after a dispute over control; many of his top executives and partners were now bailing out to join him, including Readerman. Even more incredible, the defectors were not being sued by their former employer—usually the immediate response when high-level defectors leave a company for a competitor. (Bank of America, nee NationsBank, did end up filing a lawsuit later, however, as the flow of talent continued.)

And not only that, the defectors were being allowed to cash their checks from the sale of Montgomery much sooner than they had expected. When the original deal was announced, $360 million of it was in the form of "golden handcuffs"—stock to be paid out to Weisel and his partners over three years, as long as they were still with the firm. But instead, BofA was forced to hand the final $240 million over to Weisel and his co-defectors immediately, in one lump payment. Most astounding of all, some of that money would be used to help launch a brand-new company that would directly compete with their old one. (These last two occurrences are definitely *not* common at any time.)

The coup became a big story in the banking business and in Silicon Valley. It turned out that McColl was apparently very fond of telling executives at companies he bought that they would play key roles in the new organization, only to replace them all with his own loyal team. It happened to the original BankAmerica. Although McColl adopted the name, it was soon clear that Bank *of* America was being run from North Carolina. At the time of the merger, the press reported widely that McColl had assured

BankAmerica's former CEO, David Coulter, that he would be next in line to head up the merged conglomerate. Coulter lasted but a few months before being pushed out. (One observant publication later noted that Coulter's contract only said that he was *expected* to become CEO, not that he *would* become CEO.) One by one, other BankAmerica executives also left, replaced by folks from North Carolina. I believe some of the old BankAmerica tellers still have their jobs.

Usually, displaced executives in this situation find themselves in early and unexpected retirement. Most of them are wealthier, to be sure (Weisel himself reportedly netted $120 million when he sold out to NationsBank), and a few executives decide, and manage, to find new jobs elsewhere.

But if negotiating transactions like these can be considered duels, Weisel had thoroughly skewered McColl. Weisel, his partners, and other senior executives at the firm were $1.3 billion richer, and a critical core had regrouped to start over. They once again had an entrepreneurial company with all its old contacts in Silicon Valley, Manhattan, and places in between. For his money, McColl ended up with a gutted, demoralized, and leaderless group of employees, a ghost of the former Montgomery. It wasn't one of his best investments.

In one bold move, Weisel had opened a fissure in the shifting landscape of the Silicon Valley financial scene. This was not just a split between two headstrong CEOs: It was a huge reshuffling of business relationships.

The process of funding a start-up company depends on an intricate web of relationships. The venture capitalists (VCs) start the process by throwing in the high-risk early money. The VCs also maintain strong relationships with several law firms, marketing experts, consultants of all sorts, and investment banks, and call on them for help as a start-up works its way along the path to an initial public stock offering.

The investment banks are deal makers. They introduce companies that need or want cash to investors with money to spend, and help to negotiate the terms. They also negotiate, and sometimes initiate, mergers between firms. They play a key role in setting the initial price of a stock when a company goes public, and in determining who gets to buy stock at the IPO price.

Each investment bank maintains its own critical list of industry contacts—both institutional investors, such as pension fund and mutual fund managers, and companies that at least have the potential to become great investments. The San Francisco investment banks, plus a very few others, had spent decades cultivating these relationships with Silicon Valley entrepreneurs, VCs, and institutional investors mesmerized by the visionary magic of the likes of Bill Gates, Steve Jobs, and Jeff Bezos.

The entrepreneurs preparing to go public will often employ one of the large New York banks in order to add name-brand prestige to their deals. But many are very fond of bringing in the specialty banks as well, either to take charge of the offering or to help out as the secondary bank, because of their proximity, deep knowledge, and experience in the industries in which they play.

Now, with all the buyouts, these relationships were splitting apart, walking out the door with important executives of the *nouveau grand* banks, who were jumping from one firm to another to find the best postmerger place to work.

Weisel, the consummate deal maker, was creating a brand new bank built partly with executives from his old firm and partly with executives who might not like their new bosses after their own firms were acquired. He was trying to consolidate the best talent, the best technology connections, and the best investors he could find into one new specialty bank.

The result: Thomas Weisel Partners, one of the few independent investment banks of its size in the world. Two other surviving San Francisco start-up investment banks, Wit Capital (now Wit

Soundview after its own acquisition by, unsurprisingly, Soundview Corp.) and W.R. Hambrecht, have been trying to make names for themselves by pioneering new techniques for taking companies public. Wit wants to take companies public by offering shares over the Internet, while W.R. Hambrecht has pioneered a method of "dutch auctions" for IPOs, which allows average investors in on the IPO process for the first time. The concepts, however, have been slow to catch on and will likely continue at that pace for years.

It was a bold move for Weisel, yes, but that wasn't unusual for the investment banker. He had long been a controversial figure. Some people describe him as ruthless and cold. Others say he's passionate and possessed of the highest integrity. He had taken over Montgomery after a famous battle for control with one of the company's founders, Sanford (Sandy) Robertson, two decades before. Robertson had then gone on to start a competing investment bank, Robertson Stephens, setting up a bitter San Francisco rivalry that outlasted the banks themselves.

Weisel was also an astounding athlete. He had just missed making the U.S. Olympic Team as a speed skater in 1960. He's known for having hired many Olympic medal winners to work at his firm, whether or not they had any financial experience. He used to be in charge of the U.S. Olympic Ski Team, and, most famously, had created the U.S. Postal Service cycling team and helped save the career of Lance Armstrong, the incredible cyclist and cancer survivor who keeps winning the Tour de France. Plus, Weisel loves modern art, and is on the boards of the Museums of Modern Art in both San Francisco and New York. Weisel began to look like a bookworthy character to me.

Still, I had to wonder: Could anyone really build a new investment bank in this environment, when everybody else was moving the opposite direction, toward bigger and increasingly more ambitious mergers? The question became particularly compelling as

the tech balloon deflated, bringing on recession and rapidly con-
tracting business for all investment banks. Just who was this
Thomas Weisel anyway?

So in January, 1999, the month that Thomas Weisel Partners
was officially launched, I began asking my own sources in Silicon
Valley this question. What did they think of Weisel's odds of success? Could he really pull this off?

I got an impressively consistent answer. Several people reacted
with almost exactly the same words: "I wouldn't want to underestimate Thom Weisel."

Life on the Edge of a Precipice

I think it important to try to see the present calamity in a true perspective. The war creates absolutely no new situation: it simply aggravates the permanent human situation so that we can no longer ignore it. Human life has always been lived on the edge of a precipice. Human culture has always had to exist under the shadow of something infinitely more important than itself. If men had postponed the search for knowledge and beauty until they were secure, the search would never have begun.

We are mistaken when we compare war with "normal life." Life has never been normal. Even those periods which we think most tranquil, like the 19th century, turn out, on closer inspection, to be full of crises, alarms, difficulties, emergencies. Plausible reasons have never been lacking for putting off all merely cultural activities until some imminent danger has been averted or some crying injustice put right. But humanity long ago chose to neglect those plausible reasons. They wanted knowledge and beauty now, and would not wait for the suitable moment that never comes. Periclean Athens leaves us not only the Parthenon but, significantly, the Funeral Oration. The insects have chosen a different line: they have sought first the material welfare and security of the hive, and presumably they have their reward.

Men are different. They propound mathematical theorems in beleagured cities, conduct metaphysical

arguments in condemned cells, make jokes on scaffolds,
discuss the latest new poem while advancing to the
walls of Quebec, and comb their hair at Thermopylae.
This is not panache: it is our nature.
            —*C.S. Lewis, sermon preached at*
            St. Mary the Virgin in Oxford,
            September 1939

Thomas W. Weisel's office is pretty standard fare for the CEO of a substantial financial firm—a 37th-floor corner office with a multi-million-dollar view; large, polished wood desk; one Bloomberg and one Bridge terminal with stock listings floating down the screens; a computer; a few modern art paintings from his collection; bookshelves filled with neatly arranged books and awards; framed pictures of his wife and kids; a small conference table with a speakerphone.

But the walls are dominated by several poster-sized framed photographs of his friend and protégé Lance Armstrong in various stages of winning the Tour de France. One of the photos is of Armstrong and Weisel side by side on bicycles, circling the Arc de Triomphe, Armstrong waving an American flag, Weisel with one hand on Armstrong's shoulder. Framed and hanging high on the wall right next to Weisel's desk are four yellow jerseys Armstrong won in the world's most famous cycling event, all signed by Lance in felt pen.

Armstrong is probably the man Weisel admires most. The fact that Lance Armstrong posters adorn his office like photos of a rock star in a teenager's bedroom shows just how much he admires the guy. Sure, Armstrong is a star athlete—in a sport that's still pretty obscure in the United States. And Armstrong rides on the team that Weisel created. But the thing that really sets Lance Armstrong apart is his extraordinary story.

When Armstrong was diagnosed with testicular cancer in 1997, almost everyone, including his doctors, thought he was going to die. The cancer spread to his lungs—never a good sign for an athlete who competes in long-distance, grueling events. But he overcame the worst of odds, and, two years later, with Thom Weisel's backing, won the top event in the world for his sport for the first time.

What really impresses Weisel is the fact that Armstrong not only overcame the ultimate crisis, he thrived. The illness changed Armstrong's life so much that he describes it as the best thing that ever happened to him.

Weisel likes people who are tough, physically, but mostly mentally. He likes people with the right stuff. That's telling, because it's the ideal Weisel strives for in his own life. Weisel's career has not been a smooth ascent to the top. He has faced many tough situations: difficulty getting his career started, a losing battle for control of the first investment bank he joined, a single trader who cost his company $10 million when it could ill afford it, a scandal at one of the companies he took public, losing control of the company he had run for over three decades, recessions, and an avalanche or two. He has generally—sometimes literally—managed to land on his feet.

Weisel and Armstrong, in fact, like each other so much because they are so much alike. Both are extraordinary athletes, obsessive about their passions, competitive to death, and two of the hardest-working people imaginable. They took different paths, most likely the best choices for themselves and their impressive talents, but they understand, love, and admire each other like the best father-son relationship one can imagine. There is nothing that either individual enjoys more than a triumph against nearly impossible odds.

Weisel has a huge number of admirers, as well as a few detractors (mostly competitors). The one thing that almost all friends agree on is that he is one tough SOB. He thrives on adversity.

One of the primary ingredients contributing to his success is the fact that he enjoys taking on tasks that most people feel to be absurdly difficult, and often succeeds at them.

Weisel looks like a former athlete, which he is, although the pressures of creating a brand-new company have cut dramatically into his time for exercise and training over the last several years, adding a few pounds to his frame. He stands at average height, a little over 5 feet, 10 inches, but he leaves one with the impression of being much taller. He looks at least 10 years younger than his actual age. With a long and narrow face, he's not movie star handsome, but he has a steady gaze that seems to always be evaluating what he sees with quiet self-assurance. When he was younger, he actually bore a bit of a resemblance to Warren Beatty.

Weisel denies it, but during his college years, those qualities seemed to attract women like teen fans to a Backstreet Boy. "Women loved him," says Brad Freeman, a Stanford classmate. "They were crazy about him, because he was very strong mentally. He was very self-confident."

Weisel's response: "He's pulling your leg." Of course, he does confess that for two years at Stanford he dated a girl named Nancy Albert, possibly the prettiest girl at the university. And that her father, Frankie Albert, was a legendary quarterback who had led Stanford to a Rose Bowl victory and later joined the San Francisco 49ers. Oh, and her sister played tennis at Wimbledon. Weisel always did like athletic people. Nancy herself was a pom-pom girl.

In fact, that self-possession is not only what attracts women, but business admirers as well. Steve Wynn, the hotel and gambling king of Las Vegas, owner of Treasure Island, the Golden Nugget, and the Mirage, has been friends with Weisel for years. Wynn met Weisel on the ski slopes in the mid-1970s, and they became ski buddies. "We would go up the mountain, ski together, and spend time with the ladies together," quips Wynn.

Weisel doesn't like to boast about himself. He's an overkiller of understatement, hugely concerned about the appearance of arrogance. Michael Bloomberg, in his autobiography, tells an anecdote about a ski trip in the Bugaboo mountains in British Columbia with Weisel and some other friends in the 1970s. This is the kind of place where you drop from a helicopter and have a grand time trying to get to the bottom alive. An avalanche swept away one of the skiers, a man named Bob Brandt (no relation to one of the coauthors of this book). Bloomberg was the one to locate Brandt buried under the snow, and helped rescue workers to dig him out, shaken, frighteningly blue, but unhurt.

When asked about it, Weisel recalls that he and Brandt were skiing together when he heard this "big *kahoon!*" from behind them. He turned and saw the avalanche coming, and veered off to the nearest ridge to get above it. But Brandt continued down the slopes and was caught. Weisel's comment: "One of many avalanches I've avoided in my life."

He then mentions one day, on a break from college, when he got caught in an avalanche while skiing in Alta, Utah. He struggled to swim on top of the avalanche when it hit a road and shot him up in the air like a champagne cork. He landed on top of it as it settled.

Gambling magnate Steve Wynn recalls another incident when he, Weisel, Jack Binion (who owned the Horse Shoe casino in Las Vegas), and a young man named Tommy Thomas were helicopter-skiing in the Monashees in British Columbia. They ended up sitting in the lounge at the Mica Creek Hotel playing cards, minding their own business, when a group of construction workers who were working on a nearby dam started to drunkenly harass them. They made fun of the city slickers, asked for some of their poker chips, and became increasingly louder and more obnoxious. At first Weisel's group ignored them. But after a while, Binion told young Thomas to go back to his room.

These city slickers weren't your normal desk jockeys. They started planning. The trio started quietly dividing up the group, deciding who could take whom ("I'll hit this guy on the head as hard as I can with a ketchup bottle . . . "). "We were gonna have a Blitzkrieg, give these guys a real migraine headache lickety-split," says Wynn. "It looked like we were gonna end up in jail. But we stood up, turned around, and they saw we had business in our eyes. And if you've ever seen Jack Binion's eyes, you'd know what I mean. They changed their minds and said, 'OK, we don't want any trouble.'"

The workers left. "But it was real exciting for a minute," says Wynn. "Just making a plan [of attack] was chilly enough." Weisel is really at home with businessmen like these. "Weisel is afraid of nothing," says Wynn. "He's a bull. He's a jock."

None of Weisel's friends would be surprised to hear this story. "When things get tough, you can always count on Thom to get tougher," says Kip Hagopian, a venture capitalist who has known Weisel for decades. "I've always said that when you're pushing the bar stools away from the bar, Thom is someone you want to have on your side."

But ask Weisel about skiing with Wynn and playing cards, and he describes a different day on the same trip: "We were skiing in the Monashees, but the wind was blowing so hard that we couldn't get out of the helicopter. So Steve Wynn, Jack Binion, and I end up playing seven-card hold-'em at the Mica Creek Hotel. I never won so much money in my life."

The investment banking industry may not be as physically demanding as a bar fight—unless you're making bids on the trading floor mosh pit. But even in San Francisco, it's just as ruthless as it is in New York. In many ways, it's more New York culture than San Francisco. It's the only West Coast business involved in technology where the executives regularly wear suits and ties. It's also an industry of ruthless ambition and frequent backbiting, where rumor and innuendo may be doled out like stock options to win customers or employees from competing firms.

Thom Weisel is controversial, a man who tenaciously goes after what he believes is right, whether it's a bid to take over control of a company, fighting for an unpopular political cause, or taking control of sports organizations and shaking the inefficiencies out of them, no matter who he might offend. Weisel is often described as a natural leader. Irwin Federman, one of Silicon Valley's premiere venture capitalists and a partner at U.S. Venture Partners, puts it this way: "Thom seems to breathe bounce and energy into his team. He has surrounded himself with very good people. But neither of his companies would be a shard of what they are (or were) without him. He'd be a leader in any crowd."

There are several people, both former colleagues and competitors, who do not like Weisel. He's demanding, competitive, practical almost to a fault, and successful. Some dislike the aggressiveness with which he does business. Some people find him to be very cold. In part, jealousy may play a role. Says Ed Glassmeyer, another friend and venture capitalist, "You'll find people who don't like him. He oozes success." In an industry recently rocked by scandal, his companies have actually come through with surprisingly little taint. Although aggressive, he has always insisted on a corporate culture that puts integrity above everything else. "He's totally transparent," says former congressman and vice presidential candidate Jack Kemp, another friend. "There's no guile there. Sure he's got his critics, but if somebody doesn't get along with him, it's generally their problem, not his."

Weisel is a guy who can intimidate the hell out of just about anyone. He's smart, and he's calculating. He seems to treat everything like a chess game, studying the different angles, calculating his moves several steps ahead. Anger him and he'll respond. Let him down and he'll castigate you loudly. Stand up to him and you'll earn his respect. In these ways, he's just like most of Silicon Valley's (maybe the world's) top executives.

Criticism seems to bounce off him like sticks off steel armor. His wife, Emily Carroll, says: "It's not a shield. He really is that tough. He has very high expectations of people, and if they don't deliver, he can be very hard on them. But he gets over it quickly—whereas the other person is probably in therapy a month later."

But, says Emily: "Under that big, hard surface, there's a soft side, too. He has passion. He can watch a game on television, when somebody he admires is winning, and get tears in his eyes."

The state of investment banking at the time this book was published was rough enough to make a grown CEO cry. Weisel was fortunate to start Thomas Weisel Partners before the dot-com revolution imploded and the U.S. economy slid into recession. It gave him the opportunity to build some revenues and tuck some successful deals under his belt before business went into hibernation, or perhaps a coma, after September 11, 2001. (Fortunately, TWP did not have any employees working in the World Trade Center.) But the business climate did become extraordinarily harsh, and TWP suddenly faced layoffs, a dead IPO market, and investigations into business practices amid an industry filled with scandals (although Weisel's company has not been specifically accused of any wrongdoing).

Weisel slices through it with fierce determination, like a hockey player dodging opponents all the way across the ice. In October 2001, even as the recession slid into a hole so deep it was hard to see the light above anymore, Weisel convinced Japanese bank Nomura Securities to invest $75 million in return for 3.75 percent ownership of his company, as well as to commit $125 million to Weisel's private equity fund. That comfortably padded the company's cash reserves—its equity capital currently stands at $240 million—and created a cross-Pacific relationship that will allow both banks to expand into new territory. It also set TWP's total valuation at $2 billion, an astonishing figure for a company yet to reach its third birthday—especially in a recession—and close to twice what Weisel sold Montgomery for a few years earlier.

Still, despite his success as an athlete and his extraordinarily competitive nature, Weisel confesses to his own moments of doubt: a long-standing tendency to get the jitters before a race, worrying about achieving the near perfect performance required to win.

Not many people would expect that from him, a man who seems about as insecure as General Patton. "That surprises me," says Lance Armstrong, when told about Weisel's confession. "It's probably that minuscule amount of insecurity that keeps you training hard, keeps you competing hard. I think that question mark is a healthy thing. Although *insecurity* is a word you don't want to attach to yourself."

Does Weisel think he's at all insecure? "That's just an adjective," he says. "I don't know if it applies."

Weisel loves people who overcome their own demons to succeed. When they succeed where he cannot or has not—including anyone from Olympic athletes to accomplished artists—he displays unabashed and sincere admiration.

But don't expect him to pine for missed opportunities or shortcomings in his own life. The closest he has ever come to that is when he looks back through the decades at his failure to make the Olympic team. He knows he could have done it, and the thing that probably grates on him the most is the fact that he has to explain why he failed to make the team, one of the few outright failures of his life.

Ultimately, he dealt with that the way he deals with everything— a full frontal attack—becoming, for a couple years at least, the best cyclist in his age group in the country and perhaps in the world, while running his own company at the same time.

If anything, though, it's a small chink in his armor. He likes who he is. That's probably not too difficult, considering his success and wealth.

But more than likely, the success and wealth came second.

Crisis Management

Thom W. Weisel

I'm sometimes asked what it takes to be a great entrepreneur. There are several requirements, but one of the most important is an ability to deal with crisis. When you're trying to build a company over a matter of decades, there will be many moments of crisis. Those are the times when you're really tested, when you're really judged.

It barely matters what you've accomplished before. Just like an athlete in the final event of a decathlon, you're only as good as that day's event. No one cares what you did in the past. It's today that matters. I kind of like that. It keeps one humble. It keeps life in perspective.

I've been pretty good at going through crisis periods. The worse the situation, the more difficult it is, the calmer I get and the more resolve I have. It seems to just be the way I was born. I figure when things get really tough, you have to just suck up your gut and go.

In 2001 and 2002 we faced probably the most difficult business environment I've ever seen. The economic slowdown, especially in Silicon Valley, has been more dramatic than any of us have ever experienced. What we thought was going to be a huge new business on the Internet, the seed of an enormous new economy, just blew up, and nobody really anticipated the enormity of the crash. Then the country was hit with the terrorist attacks on

September 11, a terrible and unprecedented tragedy for Americans. Sometimes it has seemed as though things couldn't get worse.

And then they did. The collapse of Enron and Global Crossing, the alleged accounting fraud of WorldCom and other companies, and insider trading scandals have all combined to bring down investor confidence, weakening the economy and the stock markets even further.

During times like these we all need to keep a balanced viewpoint. We live in a great country with a great future. (I'll discuss my views on the future in Chapter 14.)

From my perspective, one should have a realistic but optimistic outlook. There will always be problems in the world. After the terrorist attack, I had a conversation with my friend Glenn Lowry, the director of the New York Museum of Modern Art. He sent me a quote that someone had given to him. It was written by C.S. Lewis in 1939, just as the German war machine was starting to crank up. It talks about continuing the search for knowledge and beauty in the face of tragedy. It makes you think about how bad things were then.

I agree with that sentiment. Life has always been uncertain, we've always been in crisis, we've always been on the edge of the precipice. It just seems tranquil for a while. That's life.

But it's human nature to go on in the face of crisis. Out of adversity comes opportunity. A new world order comes in cycles of 5, 10, and 15 years. Those who are able to adapt quickly will succeed. Those who are patient during more tranquil periods will be rewarded.

When I started my current company, at 58 years old, I approached it a little more conservatively than I would have 20 years ago. This time, I came in with the awareness that there are going to be potholes in the road, and I tried to plan accordingly. We're incredibly well capitalized, and we have a very flexible compensation system. All the partners in the firm make money depending on how profitable the company is, so when business declines our expenses do as well. Employee compensation is roughly 50 percent of total expenses.

You don't have to actually be an athlete in order to survive crisis, but it helps to have the athlete's attributes: perseverance, discipline, dedication, optimism, and a strong desire to win.

Nobody knows that better than Lance Armstrong. After his cancer, he refocused. He tried to figure out what's important. When he joined our team after his recovery, he still had to work some things out. A few months after joining, on the third day of the Paris-Nice race, he quit. He was going to quit cycling altogether. But he went home to ride again and recommit himself to cycling, to renew his enthusiasm for the sport. Then he came in fourth in the Tour of Spain, which is almost as tough as the Tour de France, and fourth in the time trials and road race in the World Championships, and he was back.

After his cancer, he completely retooled how he cycled. He changed his training regimen, the way he climbed mountains, his cadence, everything. He became a better leader: more empathetic, with a better understanding of the needs of the people around him as well as what they needed to do in order to help him. He turned outward, instead of inward as a lot of athletes are prone to do. He transformed his personality. Lance is a totally different individual than he was before going through the terrible adversity of cancer.

And it's not like he lost a lot of competitions before. He was already a world-class athlete before his cancer. But afterward he became an even better athlete and an amazing human being. His higher calling now is to help others get through cancer, using the Lance Armstrong Foundation as his primary vehicle.

That's not to say that maintaining a tough attitude will overcome anything. Another very good friend of mine, Jimmy Stack, contracted throat cancer in 1996, although he had never smoked. He underwent grueling, intensive, painful radiation therapy. He lost 40 pounds. For a while, it looked as though he was beating it. He was disease-free at his two-year postdiagnosis checkup.

Then, two months later, he was diagnosed with leukemia. He went through several chemo sessions, went into remission a couple times, but it returned. He underwent a stem cell transplant. That failed as well.

Jimmy and I were very close friends for a very long time. But in the last six or seven years I've been so busy with my companies that I hadn't seen Jim as much as I should have. In May of 2000 he called me from his hospital bed and said, "Weis, I'm not that far from leaving here, and I just wanted to chat." I went to see him that afternoon. There was a line of about a dozen people outside his room, waiting to see him. I was talking to his wife, Barbara. He heard my voice and said, "Hey, Weis, get in here!"

He was totally alert, as ill as he was. We talked for five or six hours—about old times, about life and philosophy. Then he looked at me and said, "Weis, I'm through. They've tried everything. My immune system is going to shut down here soon."

He died the next morning.

This was a really special guy, just a phenomenal individual and a great athlete. I first saw Jimmy competing in the Olympic trials at Stanford in 1960. He ran the 800-meter in the trials in 1:47.8. He didn't qualify, but that time remains a record for Yale University (where he went to college) to this day. He was the only American to ever outrun the famed Australian athlete Herb Elliott on American soil. Later on, when I started running competitively, he became my training partner. He eventually came to work at Montgomery Securities.

Jim had a friend write down a message he wanted read at his

funeral service. It was amazing. Half this essay was unbelievably self-critical. In his own eyes, he hadn't lived up to his full potential in many areas.

And yet, this guy was a wonderful human being, the kind of person any of us would like to be. He was one of the most well-read, interesting individuals I've ever known. He was a walking encyclopedia on sports, the Second World War, politics in the 1940s—he had the most diverse intellectual pursuits of anyone I've had the privilege of knowing. He just loved his kids, loved his family. And yet he was able to look at himself and review his life in a critical way. I don't know if I would be that strong.

Unfortunately for Jim, although he had the right stuff to get through most crises, he couldn't beat his cancer. He was not as fortunate as Lance. That kind of strength can help get you through almost anything, but it can't get you through everything.

In sports, in business, and in life, luck always plays a major role.

3

Of Midget Boys and Men

In the long run men hit only what they aim at. There-
fore, though they should fail immediately, they had bet-
ter aim at something high.

—Henry David Thoreau

It was January 1952, when Tommy Weisel, weeks from his 11th birthday, raced in a statewide speed skating championship in his home state of Wisconsin. As one of the youngest entrants in the state championships, he was competing in the diminutive division called Midget Boys.

Weisel had taken up the sport almost by default. He's an expert skier, something he has done most of his life, but, as he recalls it, about the only competitive winter sports available to a kid in Milwaukee in those days were basketball and ice skating, and he wasn't very good at basketball. He found speed skating to be a "decent sport," and started skating competitively when he was seven.

Now he had worked his way up to the state championships. Nearing the end of the race, he was holding on to a third-place position when chance intervened. About 50 yards from the finish line, the two leaders collided and fell. Tommy Weisel was able to simply glide past the fallen skaters for the win.

This was nearly half a century before Australian speed skater Steven Bradbury won a gold medal in short-track speed skating at the 2002 Winter Olympics in much the same way. It's one of the quirks of the sport: Weisel figures that he fell in about one-third of his speed skating races. But to 10-year-old Tommy Weisel, his win was probably just as thrilling as winning Olympic gold. After all, he was now the 1952 State of Wisconsin Midget Boys speed skating champion! Even better, the feat got his picture into the *Milwaukee Sentinel,* right alongside Nina Roberts, the Midget Girls champion and "the best looking lady I'd ever laid eyes on," he recalls.

Becoming top Midget Boy was something of an epiphany to him. Unlike Bradbury's win, this wasn't a once-in-a-lifetime golden opportunity. It was a first-in-a-lifetime opportunity, and it got Weisel to thinking: Could he win the big races even if the leaders *didn't* fall? Did he have the potential to become a truly skilled athlete? "I started thinking that if I really trained for this sport and worked hard at it, I could make something of myself," he says.

If you really want to understand Thomas Weisel, you have to understand his passion for the world of competitive sports. The word *sports* goes with Thom Weisel as *adventure* goes with Sir Richard Branson or *seclusion* went with Howard Hughes. It's not his main job, and may not be the thing he's most remembered for, but it's an association that naturally comes to mind any time his name is mentioned. Typically for Weisel, he doesn't just go with the popular American sports like baseball and football, but has dedicated himself to the more iconoclastic sports of speed skating, ski racing, and cycling. He never was much of a conformist.

In his day job, he's a highly successful entrepreneur. For over three decades, most of it as CEO of the San Francisco–based investment bank Montgomery Securities, he has carved out for himself a position as one of the leading figures of the financial scene that blossomed in San Francisco right alongside Silicon Valley. In late

1998 he walked out of NationsBank, which had bought Montgomery a year earlier, and in January 1999, approaching his 59th birthday, he started over again.

But considering the amount of time he has spent in competitive sports throughout his life, one might have thought he'd become a professional athlete. He began skiing at age two and hasn't missed a season on the slopes since. Every weekend of the winters through his teens he was on a bus to ice skating competitions in Wisconsin, Illinois, and Minnesota.

Pretty soon, getting his picture in the papers for speed skating wins became old hat. At 13, three years after winning the state championship, he won his first national speed skating championship, setting a national record of 19.9 seconds in the 220-yard Junior Boys division. He then went on to win four more national competitions in a row, setting four other national records and seven state records in the process. With his impressive record and competitive nature, he looked like a natural for the Olympics, and local newspaper articles began describing him as a shoo-in for the Olympics—right up until the actual event.

In the summers of his youth, he was active in the typical sports of boys his age, including baseball, football, and track, and he enjoyed canoeing and swimming at summer camp. But aside from speed skating, he was also one of (he estimates) three cyclists in the entire state of Wisconsin. He wasn't, however, the type to take leisurely bike tours through the countryside or even marathon road trips. He much preferred the stark precision of track riding. It just so happened that there was a cycling track, called a velodrome, only a mile from his house. Unlike Lance Armstrong, who is a distance rider, Weisel is a sprinter. Riding on a track was more like speed skating, he says, because, "You get on a track and for short periods of time you go really fast."

He used cycling as a way to stay in shape for speed skating, and didn't really compete in the sport, although he seemed well suited to it. In July 1958, at 17 years old, he joined in a bike race in Milwaukee, a one-miler on a 400-meter track. There happened to be top cyclists from all over the world entering the race, preparing for a national cycling championship coming up in Chicago the following week. These were professional racers, some a decade or more older than Weisel. He was the only one without a team uniform, just racing for the hell of it. But he kept up with the leaders, and on the last lap he poured it on. "I caught 'em all sleeping!" he recalls gleefully. He won the race and a 6 1/2-foot trophy, and got his picture in the paper again. He also broke three state records in speed skating that year, in the 440-meter, 880-meter, and one-mile races.

He has continued to compete in athletics, and seems to take up a new sport every decade or so, repeating the experience of winning national and international amateur championships. He took up competitive skiing himself after becoming chairman of the governing body of the U.S. Olympic Ski Team, the organization that sends American skiers to the Olympics. He also reorganized the entity in the process. He took up competitive cycling in the late 1980s, became a national champion, and is now spearheading a major reorganization of USA Cycling, the domestic organization that governs competitive cycling. He built and is the largest investor in Tailwind Sports, which operates what is probably the greatest U.S. cycling team ever to exist, led by its star rider Lance Armstrong, who has seriously offended the French by daring to win the Tour de France four years in a row (as of publication date of this book). Before Armstrong, the only American cyclist to win the Tour was Greg LeMond, who won three times, in 1986, 1989, and 1990. Armstrong's team, the U.S. Postal Service team, is the only American-based team to ever win the Tour on American bikes. He's the fourth person in the 100-year history of the sport to win four times in a row. One person,

Miguel Indurain, has won five consecutive Tours. Armstrong plans to tie that record in 2003, and he may just beat it in 2004.

Weisel's self-identity as an athlete colors with fine detail his approach to business. The primary trait that spills over from his sports to his business career is his overpowering competitiveness. Describing Thom Weisel as competitive is like describing Albert Einstein as smart. Says Terry G. Lee, now president of Bell Automotive, a spin-off from Bell Sports (most famous for the Bell cycling and motorcycle helmets), who has known Weisel for many years: "You can probably find Thom's picture next to the word *competitive* in the dictionary."

Weisel complements that competitiveness with a level of self-discipline and training that could make Harry Houdini look like a slacker. He has earned the respect of many business leaders across the country, as well as a few enemies. Many people who have worked for him look up to him and try to emulate him. His psychological makeup is titanium-tough, dedicated to success without doubt, and highly demanding. Like speed skating, not everybody should try this at home.

He not only loves sports, he loves athletes. He identifies with them and surrounds himself with them. He's addicted to the camaraderie shared by elite athletes in a sport—that feeling that one belongs to a very exclusive club, set apart from everyone else. He tries hard to duplicate that comradeship at his own firms, and more than a few of the people who worked with him at Montgomery Securities speak nostalgically of the firm that no longer exists, although he has also hired a few star players over the years who have been notably difficult to deal with (and some people put Weisel himself in that category). He has hired many athletes to work at his investment bank. Some are former Olympians; many are people he met through his own sports activities. He seeks them out for their personality, competitive spirit, discipline, and just plain toughness. By the late 1970s, Montgomery Securities was known as the Jock House of investment banks. It was also known as possibly the most aggressive and ambitious in the business.

Weisel doesn't like being second at anything. In business, he has only briefly had to suffer the compromise and lack of control that come from reporting to a boss, and he mostly chafed. At the beginning of his career he was impatient to become the boss, and moved quickly to become a partner, then became CEO seven years after joining Montgomery Securities. More recently, he had to report to NationsBank/Bank of America CEO Hugh McColl for one year, between the time he sold Montgomery to the giant banking conglomerate in 1997 and when he walked away from it all in 1998. He's quick to add: "If they had kept their end of the bargain, I would not have had a problem," but some of his closest friends say they could never see him reporting to someone else for long. The rest of his professional life has been spent in the role of CEO.

His drive and independence are part of his heritage. He has never paid much attention to his family background, but his brother, Dr. Richard Weisel, has traced the Weisel family's roots back to a farming region north of Frankfurt, Germany—a stolid, hardworking region known as the birthplace of the Lutheran Church. In 1850, Weisel's great-grandfather's family emigrated to New York City, where there was a thriving community of German immigrants. They immediately realized, however, that Manhattan was not the best place for farming. So they moved to Alexandria, Nebraska, and started the Weisel farm, which still exists today. Thom actually inherited and still owns a 1/19th share of the farm. It loses money every year.

The primary influence on Thom Weisel was his father, Wilson Weisel, by all accounts an extraordinary individual. The elder

Weisel had a photographic memory and graduated first in his class at the University of Wisconsin when he was just 18, the age when most people are just entering college. He got his Master's at Harvard and went on to medical school there.

Wilson Weisel was also a dedicated and innovative athlete. He worked his way through college playing semipro hockey and held track records as a miler. An expert skier, he was even involved in the development of safer ski bindings to replace the old bear trap style.

He was a surgical resident at the Mayo Clinic when the United States got involved in World War II. Thom was born at the Mayo Clinic in February 1941, just as his father went off to fight the war. Wilson Weisel became a front-line surgeon and participated in the D-Day invasion of Omaha Beach in Normandy. He was part of the third wave (fortunately) and flew over the front line in a glider. He evidently became the ranking officer because all the officers in the first two waves were wiped out. He also survived the Battle of the Bulge and marched into Berlin after the Russians.

He proved to be no less impressive when he returned home. He held positions as chairman of thoracic surgery at Marquette Medical School and chief of surgery at four other prominent hospitals in Milwaukee. He wasn't around a lot, but, says Thom Weisel, "I liked and admired my dad a lot."

Thom Weisel's brother Dick believes that their father's motivation for this outrageously difficult schedule was the desire to provide a relatively lavish lifestyle for their mother, Betty Amos Weisel. Betty was a southern belle from a wealthy family with roots in England and a fortune made from the hardwood lumber business, and then plastics, in the United States. She met Wilson when he was at Harvard and she was attending a finishing school in Boston. "At the beginning of their relationship he was a struggling surgeon and academic. She was not happy with that," says Dick. "He had to compromise his academic career in order to meet his financial goals. His academic expectations for himself were higher than he achieved." That infused a strong aversion to compromise in his children, whether indulging their personal passions or their professional ones.

Wilson expected a lot from his kids, and they delivered. Thom was always an A student in school. Wilson was not a man to cross. In those days, nobody thought anything about smacking a child for misbehaving, and Wilson Weisel was a particularly harsh disciplinarian. "He kept a stick handy for the purpose of beating the shit out of us," Thom recalls. If the two brothers horsed around at night instead of sleeping, their father would walk into their bedroom and whack them across the legs with it—at least, until Thom adapted. "I was smart enough to suck my legs up under the covers," he says. "I'd still cry like crazy but I didn't get hit."

As a youth, Thom clashed with his parents at times. "My dad was such a disciplinarian, and I was interested in a more balanced life," he says. "He did not like me going out and having fun on Friday nights. I like fast cars, and all speed sports. He was just so by the book."

Thom had his moments with his mother as well. His father may have done things by the book, but it seemed as though his mother had the book memorized. Used to a well-heeled life, she was big on formality and decorum and expected her children to know how to behave in polite society. At dinner, Thom knew how to properly set a table and hold a fork. Miss Manners might appreciate it, but Thom couldn't stand it.

Still, Thom seems to have inherited from his mother an easy comfort with his own wealth. His home is extraordinary, comfortable and immaculate, with wonderful works of modern art on the walls and sculptures in the garden. When he throws a big dinner for friends, he may not expect them to know how to correctly hold a fork, but he's very fond of setting an impressive, formal meal with fine linen, china, and silverware.

From his father he inherited discipline, a rock-hard work ethic, and a charmed athletic ability. Dick Weisel, 2 1/2 years younger than Thom, was athletic enough in his own right, and became captain of his high school football team. But he couldn't keep up with his brother. "It was tough for me, because I was always second," says Dick. "No matter how hard I tried, I was second. He's always aimed at perfection. We've been amazed. When he sets his mind to it, he seems to be able to do anything."

Thom was the starting quarterback for his high school football team, but his brother says he was too much of a nonconformist to be interested in becoming team captain himself. "Those were his days of alienation," says Dick. "He was going to find his own way. I had the feeling he lived the life of Jack Kerouac. He was separate and different and he enjoyed that."

Thom thought of himself more like James Dean's character in *Rebel Without a Cause.* In high school in Milwaukee he felt apart from those around him and could not relate to Midwestern parochialism. His classmates didn't seem intellectual enough for him. Sports were his primary pastime.

But he wasn't a shy and retiring school geek, either. As a kid, he got caught throwing snowballs with rocks in them—at police cars. He was hauled off to the police station, and his sentence was stiff. In fact, there were 300 of them. That was the number of times he had to write a long sentence about being a good boy and not launching low-level comets at cops.

And he was prone to showing off. Once, a mentor and teacher at his junior high school, Mr. Hannel, called him into his office to castigate him for his unsportsmanlike behavior during an ice skating race. He had been so far ahead of everyone else that he had turned around and finished the race skating backward. "I was a pretty egocentric kid," he confesses.

He was something of an iconoclast even within his own family, always the odd man out. Dick Weisel, like his father, ventured into academics and medicine, and is now chairman of the Division of Cardiac Surgery at the University of Toronto. Their sister, Amy, the youngest of the three siblings, took after their mother, whose career was running her household. Amy even took over the family homestead after their parents died.

Thom, however, wanted to make his own footprints. He decided at the age of 10 that he wouldn't cut it as a surgeon. At that age, he went to see his father perform open heart surgery. What he remembers mostly is all the blood. "I was revolted by it," he says. "I just about threw up."

As far as career choices go, he was more inspired by Papa Amos, Betty's father. Roy Amos was an entrepreneur. From scratch, he built Amos Thompson Corp., which became one of the largest companies in the country producing hardwood lumber veneer. Recognizing, long before Walter Brooke whispered the secret of success to Dustin Hoffman in *The Graduate,* that much of his product line might be displaced by plastics, he expanded the business and created one of the largest injection molding plants in the United States. He owned a bank and several racehorses that won prestigious trophies, including the Hamiltonian. Edinburgh, Indiana, 30 miles south of Indianapolis, near the Kentucky border, was a company town, and Roy Amos was the company.

Weisel spent many summers stacking lumber for his grandfather. He was no more interested in a career in hardwood veneer, plastics, or even horse racing than Hoffman's Benjamin Braddock, but Papa Amos provided him with a strong role model as an entrepreneur.

By 1958, Weisel had focused his goals on the 1960 Winter Olympics. However, he ran into a couple of roadblocks. In the fall of 1958, the start of his senior year, he shattered the cartilage in his knee during football practice. Weisel sucked in his gut and worked his way through this setback. After surgery and months of rehab, he was in good enough shape to make it to the Olympic trials in Minneapolis in February 1959. Despite the recent injury, he placed third in the 500-meter speed skating competition. It looked like he would be one of the youngest skaters to ever make the U.S. Olympic Skating Team.

He was also very anxious to get away from home. That fall, he entered Stanford University, and his life took a new turn. For the first time, everything seemed to click—everything, that is, except the thing he had trained most of his life for: the Olympics. He was at Stanford for just one quarter, then took the winter quarter off in order to train for the coming event. The problem was that most of the athletes had been training all year long, rather than taking a quarter off to get into college life.

He exercised with his buddies in the gym several hours a day through the fall, staying in great shape, but he didn't practice on ice, working the particular muscles necessary for the sport. He figured he could make up for it when he went home for the Christmas holiday, but the weather was bad, keeping him off the ice. He headed up to Squaw Valley, California, where the 1960 Olympics were to be held, several months before the final Olympic time trials. But the ice-making machine at Squaw was broken for a month, and he got little practice.

The result was that he could not make it through the Olympic skate-offs in 1960. He was more than a second behind his time from the previous year, and placed behind people he had never lost to before. Even worse, two people he had beaten in the 1959 time trials went on to win Olympic medals: Bill Disney took a silver in 1960, and Terry McDermott got the gold in 1964. Weisel spent the rest of the winter as a ski bum, working as a handyman in the Russell Lodge in Alta, Utah, a place where he had used to ski with his family as a child.

Surprisingly, Weisel claims that missing out on the Olympics wasn't as devastating as losing out on the opportunity to play football in his final year of high school. At the time, that may have been true. It's telling, however, that he never again in his life let such small obstacles get in the way of his goals. In the end, the 1960 Olympics was his once-in-a-lifetime opportunity, and this time he blew it. It may have been a factor behind his extreme competitiveness later in life.

But he was young. He was ready for new challenges. And he found not only intellectual challenges at Stanford, but great friends and a lot of fun. He joined a fraternity and partied with his fraternity brothers, many of whom went on to become prominent businessmen themselves. Weisel finally felt like he fit in. He could do as he pleased without the disapproving scorn of his father.

They worked out in the gym and ran the stadium stairs and track on a regular basis. They rode motorcycles all over the hills of Palo Alto. They would strap pistols to their belts and shoot at targets among the apple groves near Stanford. One favorite target-shooting spot was later paved over and turned into Sand Hill Road, now the home of Silicon Valley's most prestigious venture capital firms and one of the most expensive pieces of business real estate in the world. "We all started off as young guys full of piss and vinegar," Weisel says.

And, of course, there were the mandatory frat pranks, the type of stunts that would have fit easily into the National Lampoon film *Animal House*. Weisel and his fellow pledges schemed for four months in order to get back at their older classmates for the torture of pledge week (all in good fun, of course). One night when their brothers were at a toga party, they removed the distributor caps from every one of their upperclassmates' cars, ensuring a very long walk home and plenty of time for the young guys to execute their plan. Weisel had cow-napped a heifer from a nearby farm and hidden it in a barn at Stanford, and now walked it up three flights of stairs to the top floor of their frat house. Being from Wisconsin,

Weisel knew that you could get a cow to walk up a steep slope, but it's almost impossible to drag it back down again. They topped off the scene by releasing 100 chickens in the house.

Then they left before the partiers could return. In fact, Weisel and his buddies didn't come back to their house for several weeks, and skipped a lot of classes where they might run into their victims, in order to give them a chance to cool off, primarily from having to clean up the mess. The cow was removed with a crane.

These days Weisel likes to think of himself more as a family man than anything. He's been married three times, always to very athletic women. He married the first time just after graduating from Stanford in 1963 (with honors and distinction in economics) to a girl he knew from high school, Carolyn Gebhart. She moved with him to Cambridge while he attended Harvard, then relocated with him to Northern California while he started his career, but the marriage lasted only seven years. "We fought like cats and dogs," he says. "She was just too much of a hippie for me." That's not surprising, considering he was a young Barry Goldwater supporter.

He has three children from his first marriage, all now over 30, and two from his current marriage (his third and, he insists, his last). Many executives from Silicon Valley claim to be dedicated family men in the same breath they use to boast that they work so hard that they haven't seen their children for three months. But Weisel has remained close to all his children, always opening time in his schedule to be with them. He not only spent a lot of time teaching them sports or playing with them, he now works with them.

His oldest son, Brett, is a partner at Thomas Weisel Partners. His oldest daughter, Heather, now has a Ph.D. in psychology, and her husband has also become a partner at TWP. Weisel's third child from that marriage, Wyatt, has also worked for his father as a block trader, but decided to go back for an MBA. He recently graduated from Dartmouth's Tuck Business School and went to work for a Northern California real estate development firm.

Weisel is now married to Emily Carroll, an artist and athlete and, by all accounts from friends, a thoroughly charming woman. They have two small children, a seven-year-old boy and a three-year-old girl. He loves teaching them sports, among other things.

Weisel's philosophy is that success in sports lends success to life. Throughout his career, he has made his own mad and intensive forays back into competitive sports. When he gets involved in sports, he's as intense and dedicated to it as he is to business.

While his athletic career has been off and on, it's been most often on. His reputation in sports these days is mainly due to his sponsorship of the U.S. Postal Service cycling team and Lance Armstrong. Weisel is still a strong cyclist himself, and took up the sport competitively in the late 1980s. He became a huge devotee of the sport and won several impressive championships (although his wife Emily, about 25 years younger, says she can beat him in an uphill bike race these days). He's still a fanatical skier, and took up downhill ski racing for a while in his forties.

His first sports comeback of sorts was in 1973. He was 32 and a partner at his investment bank, then called Robertson Colman Siebel & Weisel, in San Francisco. A group of local bankers and brokers there got together and organized what they called the Summer Rally Olympic Games, or SROG. They swam, ran both the 100- and the 880-yard dash, raced bikes uphill, and competed in chin-ups, broad jump, and shot put. It was a great excuse to get back into shape. The first year, Weisel won the 100-yard dash, the 880-yard run, and a bicycle race, and claimed first prize overall. The second year he got second place.

Weisel found the SROG so much fun that he decided he might like to do some serious training and get back into real competition. While at Stanford, he had met a spectacular runner named

Jim Stack. Stack's brother, Chris, was one of Weisel's frat brothers at Stanford. Stack went on to Harvard Law School, but ultimately ended up at UC Berkeley as assistant athletic director. Weisel decided Stack would make a good running coach, so he called him up.

They ran together and became friends. Stack taught Weisel how to run competitively, and Weisel ended up hiring Stack to work as personnel director at his company. They built a corporate running team at Montgomery, which won a number of national championships over a span of 10 years. Weisel himself won several quarter mile and half mile regional races. He also ran half-marathons, 10Ks, San Francisco's huge Bay to Breakers (a combination professional race and moving party that draws up to 100,000 contestants), and the famous and grueling Dipsea race over Mt. Tamalpais, just north of San Francisco.

His love of sports and of competition became part of a major pattern in his life. He thrives on taking on new challenges. It's not enough for him to win; he wants to win again and again—in different sports, in business, and in new disciplines like politics and art collecting. His life is fulfilled by taking on new challenges, a trait he describes as seeking diversity in life.

Although he studies like a scholar and trains harder than a Roman gladiator, Weisel's approach to new challenges is simple: Whatever he happens to develop a passion for, he does. From the profession he adopted to the sports he has taken on throughout his life, he likes things that are slightly offbeat, paths that he has to navigate without a road map. He does so boldly and aggressively, impulsively, almost without fear. He makes mistakes, but the path he follows is equal parts impulse and logical progression. When he does something, it makes sense—at the time, anyway.

A famous story about Weisel recounts the time in the early 1980s that his company placed ads in running magazines for women runners interested in a career in financial services. The idea was, in part, to help fill out Montgomery's women's running team for the Runner's World Corporate Challenge Cup races. Weisel later laughed about the approach, conceding that running magazines weren't the best place to find promising stockbrokers. However, the ad did have impact: One of the women who answered it ended up as Weisel's second wife. For several years, the story became a favorite aside in newspaper articles about Weisel and the spectacular rise of his unusually athletic company.

But his biggest races were yet to come.

The Influence of Sports

Thom W. Weisel

I've gotten a lot of the definition of who I am through sports. It has given me the drive for diversity in life and brought me perspective and balance.

It started with my parents. As with most people, the example that my mom and dad displayed rubbed off on me. My dad was a hardworking, extremely focused, dedicated, and passionate individual. His pursuit of excellence was just off the charts. I look at my kids now, and I see those traits in them as well.

Back in the 1950s, my mom and dad used to pack the kids into the car and drive west to Aspen or Alta or Sun Valley once or twice a year to ski. I spent my 10th birthday at the Sun Valley Lodge in Idaho.

It was incredible. I remember it all very clearly. Sun Valley in the fifties was one of the most attractive areas in the country. It was like a European town in nature and flavor. Ernest Hemingway had a house there. For a kid, it just doesn't get any better than that.

What I really enjoy now about skiing and cycling is that the environment is so uplifting. The mountains are grand and beautiful. There's nothing like waking up to three feet of new powder and getting on the mountain before anybody else. Or cycling through the Dolomites, or the hills outside the Napa Valley, or through Tuscany. There's sheer beauty in riding up mountains or through meadows of sunflowers. Even when you're racing, the streets are the arena—particularly in Europe, where everyone knows what's going on with cycling.

It has been important to me to stay close to my own kids, and sports has provided me with one means to do that. When my first marriage broke up, my ex-wife took our kids and moved to Oregon. I'd fly to Oregon every other weekend to see them and spend as much vacation time as possible with them. Eventually my former wife and I agreed to send the two older kids to prep school on the East Coast. My younger son, Wyatt, ended up living with me in California and attended the local grade school. These days, my family, including all my kids and five grandkids, has dinner together once a week. We still spend most holidays together.

When my older kids were young, they spent six weeks with me every summer. We created our own Olympic sports competition, with swimming, a 100-yard dash, gymnastics, and other events like that. Every summer they would compete against their own times from the previous year. I kept a big chart with their progress from year to year. I love sharing my own love of sports with them. My seven-year-old son can go from surfing in Maui to skiing at Vail, tackling two feet of fresh powder on the back bowls as if he owned them.

People find it surprising when I say I wasn't that upset about missing out on the Olympics. But it's true. When I went off to college, I decided I wasn't going to compete any more. I was ready for the next chapter in my life. In Milwaukee, I hadn't developed a lot of friendships and didn't have a lot of fun. I was really looking forward to Stanford and to taking a great new step.

Stanford was great for my social and intellectual development. Our group was very close. I studied subjects that I loved in political science and economics. It was a great era, a great part of my life.

Looking back, would I have liked to win an Olympic medal? Sure. But was I willing to sacrifice everything for the next four years in order to become a gold medalist? No. I had decided to move on with my life.

Competitive sport requires an incredible amount of time and work. It just consumes you. I've always had trouble with the isolation of being an athlete. I learned at the age of 11 or 12 that nothing else can go on in your life if you're going to excel in a sport. Anybody who's been successful in sports knows what it takes to win: discipline, focus, preparation, and dedication. In my case, I have been willing to dedicate a finite amount of time to focus on competitve athletics and then move on.

Look at Lance Armstrong. Lance works harder than any other athlete in the world, with incredible preparation and attention to detail. He trains harder, and he thinks about the sport more than anyone else.

He goes through a training regimen that most athletes wouldn't think about taking on. He can hardly take a vacation. He often sleeps in a low-oxygen chamber that simulates being on a 10,000-foot mountain, in order to keep his red blood cell count high. He's on his bike four to seven hours a day, every day, for nine months preparing for the Tour de France. He maintains a rigorously controlled diet. He practically starves himself. He lost 8 kilos (18 pounds) during his chemotherapy, and he's kept it off. It requires a lot of personal sacrifice.

I believe it's important to stay realistic about yourself and your own capabilities. I do that by continuing to engage myself in sports. It's one of the benefits of sports competition. But in order to be competitive, you have to accept sacrifices and develop the discipline to get your mind and body in a position to win.

It's also important to have a long-term vision and set of goals. Whether it was running or cycling, it would take me three years from the beginning of a serious effort and the establishment of goals to actually get to and exceed those goals.

In running, for example, I set myself a goal to run a 2.0-minute half mile and a 50-second quarter mile by July of the next year. I figured that would help me win the SROG and be a competitive force on the various relay teams that we were focused on in the National Corporate Running Challenge sponsored by *Runner's World* magazine. From the fall through the winter I laid the foundation. I would run longer distances, usually 10 to 15 miles, four times a week at a good pace. I'd run shorter distances the rest of the week. Then, in the spring, I started my track workouts, first doing short 220s at moderate speed and eventually running at race pace, but for shorter distances than the race objective. It gets your body used to running at the pace you want to race at.

Since the pace I wanted was a two-minute half mile, I would train by running a 60-second quarter mile, then walk 220 for about two minutes, then repeat the whole thing four times. I'd start out doing these interval workouts once a week, then twice, then three times a week until race season. During the race season, I was usually racing on a weekend, so Monday was a rest day. Then Tuesday I'd do intervals, Wednesday a long run, Thursday more intervals, Friday an easy run, and Saturday and Sunday compete again.

My goals in cycling were to set a Masters World Record in the kilo of 1 minute 10 seconds or below; to win the world sprint competition, which would require me to do the 200-meter flying start in 11 seconds; and to win the National Criterium Championship (a multilap one-day race).

Cycling workouts and preparations were very similar to those for running. I would start cycling longer distances, usually 60 to 80 miles, at moderate speeds in the winter, two times per week over varied terrain—both mountains and flats. This allowed me to build a very substantial foundation. Then, in the spring, road racing season would start, so I'd race on weekends and do two interval training workouts during the week. The interval workouts again simulated race pace at shorter distances. I would slowly close the gap in distance by the time the competition date arrived.

When I first met my wife, Emily, around 1990, I was in serious training for cycling. For a couple of years, I was gone every weekend racing, and most afternoons I was on my bike training. It was all business and cycling. Skiing and all other sports took a backseat. I had to forget about a diversified lifestyle for a while. I'm sure there was a period of time when Emily wondered what she was getting herself into. When I stopped racing, I was a totally different guy.

I enjoy training. I enjoy getting fit. You start to understand your body and what it can do. At the beginning of a training program, I would test my important physiology elements like my maximum VO_2 (ability of the body to transport oxygen from the air to the muscles for energy generation), maximum heart rate, and anaerobic threshold (the point where the body is no longer able to process oxygen and starts developing lactic acid in the muscles). This allowed me to train efficiently and effectively as well as to monitor my conditioning progress.

I'm lucky; I seem to have a very high pain threshold. I can take my body into the hurt locker and keep it there for a long time before I say uncle. It's almost like there is no pain. That doesn't mean I can fly up mountains, though. There are still physical limits to what a body can do.

One of the frustrating things for me is that when I was training, I was always getting sick from this arduous training schedule. Sitting on a bicycle isn't as hard on your body as the pounding you take running. I wasn't very injury-prone, but I was still prone to

illness. Then I'd have to stop training for a week or more. That
got very frustrating. I'd go through a few months of training, until
the national or international competitions heated up, and then I'd
constantly get off track because of illness.

Rest is as important as arduous workouts. Training requires a
balancing act between workouts and recovery periods. Knowing
your physical limitations and working within them is an important
part of an athlete's preparation.

I actually enjoy the preparation, the training, and the strategy
that come before a race much more than the race itself. I've never
been a guy who really enjoys the competitive act. I've always found
it hardest to deal with the pressure, the nerves, the whole psychology of being in a race. I used to get incredibly nervous at competitions, and I've had to get over it.

I'll never forget standing on the starting line for a skating competition when I was 13 and looking up at guys with bulging muscles and beards. I'd wonder what the hell I was doing there. These
guys were my age? It can be very intimidating.

It's difficult to master the psychology of competition. There are
a lot of nuances to competition that just aren't that straightforward, especially when you're 13 or 14. It has to be instinctual.

In a sport like ski racing, for example, one tiny misstep, a frac-
tion of a second, can throw you off the course. You've got to
maintain a certain level of concentration. You have to visualize
what you're going to go through. You need to anticipate what's
going to happen when you're in a race. If you're reacting, it's too
late. If you're not there when that split-second event happens,
you'll lose.

On the other hand, you don't want too much concentration, or
there's no instinct involved. You want a certain level of adrenaline,
but not too much. It's a delicate balance.

When I took up competitive cycling in the eighties, it took me a
while to get back into the sport. At my first national championship

kilo, in Texas, I fell off my bike on the first pedal stroke. They let me start again. As good an athlete as I thought I was, I had a lot to learn.

The fear of failure comes into play even more strongly once you've succeeded and need to repeat that success. There's always a tension between risk and failure. There's got to be some part of your mind that's almost outside of your body, telling you to settle down. You've got to be above the competition.

If you're a superior athlete and you know you've had really superior preparation, if you've been through the race before and know what to expect, and if you're on top of the competition, then the race can be an enjoyable experience. It's like Barry Bonds getting into the batting box on his way to breaking home run records. After 35 years of doing this, he wasn't really worried about hitting the last three or four home runs for a season record. He just stepped up and did it.

Lance Armstrong enjoyed his third and fourth Tour de France victories more than the first. He's more in control today than he was in 1999. He knows what to expect and can prepare for it mentally and physically. This is one of the benefits of sticking with a sport or a job over a long period of time.

Still, 99 percent of it was just a lot of fun for me. I've had the opportunity to get back into training at different points of my life and prove to myself that I could do it. You've got to compete if you want to see what you're made of. If you don't risk anything, you don't accomplish anything. It took a lot of training and work. Also, I had some of the best teachers in the world.

When I took up cycling, I got to know the racing techniques—everything from pedaling techniques to my position on the bike to strategy during the race. No race is the same. Every race is a movie you haven't seen before, although there are similarities to other movies you've seen.

But even if you're in control, things can go wrong. Once, when

I was at the World Cycling Championships in San Diego, I had just won the kilo and had the fastest time in the trials for the sprint, where you qualify for the seating in the competition. I was in the shape of my life, winning every race through the semifinals. After the semifinals, I went for a 30-minute ride just to cool down. My wheel got caught in a storm drain, and I planted my face in the road. I had 49 stitches in my face, which obviously took me out of the competition. All that training and preparation came to nothing.

But when you're really in command physically, you're ready for anything anybody can throw at you. After two or three or four years of training, after all your preparation, you're finally ready. You're prepared for attacks, counterattacks, a drag race, an endurance race, and tactical moves. You think you've got it handled. Then what do you do? With a little bit of luck, you win! That's just hugely rewarding.

Cycling isn't a sport where you can just come in one year and win. One year spills over to the next in power, endurance, and stamina. You have to know your own body so you can stay in the race until the final seconds and get yourself into a position to win. You have to conserve your energy so you can get the maximum output when the time comes.

Two of my most rewarding experiences in racing as a Master were against established past champions. I had to prepare especially hard for the inevitable major shootouts that would occur. For example, my first encounter with an established champion was against a guy named Jim Montgomery. He was on top of Masters cycling for at least a decade. For the first couple of years, I lost every major race to him, both on the track and on the road. I had his picture pinned up on my weight room wall so that, during the winter, it would remind me why I was working out so hard.

The first time I beat Jim was in a criterium in San Diego, in the National Championship. These are crazy races involving 50 or

100 guys. They're all diving in, beating on you, always launching attacks by pouring it on and pulling out ahead in order to try to tire you out. It requires both strength and strategy. When you're going 30 or 40 miles per hour, if you get out of the pace line and into the wind, you can get blown back.

If someone launches an attack, you have to cover it yourself— just go after him and don't let him get too far ahead. Jim Montgomery and others kept launching a number of attacks, and I had to keep covering him until the final lap. We rounded the last turn together, about three and four back from the leader. Coming out of the turn, I gave it everything I had. On the final straightaway, it was a drag race between myself and Montgomery for the lead. I looked over to my left, and there he was, right next to me. I beat him by a wheel.

When you've worked for three or four years for one particular moment, it's pretty satisfying when it happens. That was also the first national championship that I won in cycling.

When I turned 50, I moved into a new age group and met Joe Sailing, who, like Montgomery, had been winning races for decades. He was at the top of his class in the over-50 Masters. The first time I met him was also in a National Criterium Championship.

It came down to Joe, a partner of his, and me. Sailing had dominated his age category for so long, I thought he was over-confident. Sure enough, during the last lap at the National Criterium Championship, he made a calculated guess that he could just blow me off his wheel. In previous races, no one could stay with his pace on a final attack, so he thought he could just chew me up.

He was wrong. I was on his wheel, with him acting as my wind-break the whole way. It was like sitting behind a Mack truck for miles. I couldn't believe this guy was just giving me the race. He gave me a huge leg up, something nobody had ever done before.

I had all this energy left at the end, and I beat him by 30 or 40 meters. Talk about an adrenaline rush!

One of the reasons I like cycling is that it is a sport for the common person. You're really out of the limelight: The roads are the arena, and the spectators come to the event for free and play a major role cheering people on. I've really enjoyed the people I've met and the friendships that I've made. I was more of a track and criterium rider than a mountain rider. I enjoyed the early-season training rides with Andre Mogannam and Leonard Harvey Nitz. Andre is a local fireman who's very fit and loved to go out for a 60- to 80-mile ride and just beat against the wind. Leonard had been a rider on the 7-Eleven team, rode in five Olympics, and would share his many experiences racing around the world with us. Along with "Eddie B" (Eddie Borysewicz, the coach I trained with and then hired to train the cycling team I started), he taught me the most about racing tactics in the various track and road races. We would go to the Friday night track races in San Jose and race in every different event we could, which was an incredible learning experience for me.

The other great thing is the art of cycling. Particularly in stage racing over many days, there's almost a mystical aspect to it. There are men who can go 150 miles a day through several mountain passes. There's a real mystique about some of the older, famous riders. These guys had so many stories about their experiences racing, especially when the sport was first getting going.

I've always had a long-term plan about what I wanted to do, but I've enjoyed attempting to be as good as I could at an activity and then moving on and trying something new. In the late seventies and early eighties I tried to do well in running in the summer and fall and then win ski races in the winter. Currently, I am learning to wind surf, and am cycling for health.

Since I stopped competing in cycling, I've enjoyed cycling trips to Europe with many of my old friends from Stanford, such as Ward Woods, Jack Lowe, John Beaupre, Mark Gates, and Beau Bianchi, as well as weekend training rides with Andre Mogannam, Jerry Malone, Ken Carpenter, Mike McCarthy, and other members of our Masters cycling team.

The thing that I learned from these experiences is that life is a series of journeys, and that the journey is a lot more important than where you end up. It's not about *being* at the top of the mountain. It's about *getting* to the top of the mountain, and then repeating that experience as many times as you can. In the end, it wasn't the world championships that were most important to me. It was simply the process of getting there.

Breaking Away

*The marksman hitteth the mark partly by pulling,
partly by letting go.*

　　　　　　　　　　　　　　—Egyptian proverb

In the 1960s, Keynesian economics was the rage. President John F. Kennedy tried to stimulate a sluggish economy by lowering the capital gains tax and the marginal income tax rate. The assassinations of Kennedy and Martin Luther King Jr. and the police action in Vietnam launched a cultural revolution and violence on college campuses nationwide. The Nasdaq did not yet exist. The hottest chip company in the world was a pioneering firm called Fairchild Semiconductor, a company south of San Francisco run by a group of Ph.D. engineers including Bob Noyce, the co-inventor of the semiconductor chip. The picturesque valley dominated by apple orchards south of San Francisco, once dubbed by Jack London the "Valley of Heart's Delight," was just beginning its transformation into the glass and steel metropolis called Silicon Valley.

Thom Weisel spent the first half of the decade, protest-free, at Stanford University and Harvard Business School, building the background to become an investment banking tycoon. There's no seminal event that made him sit up one day and say, "I really want to be an investment banker when I grow up!" He didn't win any Midget Boys economics contest that led him to believe he could be a great financier if he just put his mind to it.

But he does recall his hardworking father bitterly complaining about the government confiscation of up to 90 percent of his income through taxes, fees, and the liability insurance required of surgeons. Weisel was fascinated with the stock market and its ability to make people very rich—if they knew what they were doing. Economics seemed like a good thing to know.

Weisel entered Stanford University in the fall of 1959 as an engineering student, but soon switched to economics. Despite the fact that he made a point of enjoying himself, friends recall him as a serious student, unafraid to speak up publicly, always challenging the professors. Weisel graduated with distinction and honors in the summer of 1963.

During Weisel's Stanford years, small electronics companies feeding the latest gadgets to the U.S. military were sprouting in the technologically fertile ground around Stanford University. This trend actually started before World War II, and was encouraged after the war by Stanford's visionary dean of engineering, Frederick Terman. The first major Silicon Valley company (although the term was not yet used) was Hewlett-Packard, founded in 1939 by two of Terman's most promising students, Bill Hewlett and David Packard.

The next major event in the creation of the Valley came in 1955, four years before Weisel arrived in California to attend Stanford. William H. Shockley Jr., a Stanford grad who led the Bell Labs team that invented the transistor in the 1950s, moved back to California to start Shockley Semiconductor. The transistors, made of silicon, replaced vacuum tubes in electrical devices such as radios, televisions, and computers. The transistors were smaller, cheaper, and longer-lasting than vacuum tubes, features guaranteed to ensure a large market for the devices.

In 1957, Shockley's team of brilliant engineers, tired of his tyrannical rule, split off to start Fairchild Semiconductor, also in the valley south of San Francisco, backed by Fairchild Camera & Instrument Co.

The creation of Fairchild Semiconductor was probably the single most important event in the extraordinary history of Silicon Valley, although no one knew it at the time. First of all, it may have been the most impressive collection of brainpower ever assembled into one company—at least until some of the top talent split off to form Intel Corp. in 1968. It also became the genesis of Silicon Valley's chip industry, as other top executives and engineers split off to start their own semiconductor companies. Many of these companies still exist today, including Advanced Micro Devices, National Semiconductor, and LSI Logic.

In 1958, Jack Kilby, an engineer at Texas Instruments in Texas, came up with a brilliantly simple concept: Instead of just making silicon transistors, what about creating several different components, such as resistors and capacitors, all on one piece of silicon? About six months later, Fairchild CEO Bob Noyce came up with the same idea and designed a way for the different components to be efficiently wired together on that single piece of silicon. Noyce called it a "unitary circuit." The name was later changed to *integrated circuit*, and Noyce got the first patent. The beginning of the 1960s saw the creation of an industry that would change the world.

The silicon chip became a booming business. But another seminal event occurred in 1965. Another of Fairchild's founders, Gordon Moore (who also became one of the founders of Intel), was planning a speech intended to show that there was indeed substantial potential for this fledgling semiconductor business. So he went back and looked at the increasing performance of Fairchild's own chips from one generation to the next. He discovered that the number of components that could be fit on a single chip doubled roughly once a year. Even better, the scientists and engineers would use the latest generation of semiconductors to create the next generation of chip-making machinery, which was used to create even better semiconductors. The result was that, although the chips doubled in power from one generation to the next, the cost of producing them did not. It's a process that engineers call a "virtuous feedback loop." And Moore didn't see any end to the trend in sight.

Although it was a simple observation of an existing fact, it also became a self-fulfilling prophecy. Once chip designers became aware that it was possible, they purposely tried to obey Moore's Law and make each generation of chips twice as powerful as the last. It required faith, because the design and construction of each new generation of manufacturing plants cost a small fortune (these days, a large fortune) in order to achieve the goal. Moore's Law, later modified to 18 months between generations, has continued to be in effect to the present time, and is likely to continue for at least another decade—probably two.

The power of this doubling in the complexity of chips is one of the most extraordinary phenomena of the modern age—in fact, of any age. It means that every 20 years, chips increase in power by a factor of 1 million. In the roughly 40 years since the invention of the integrated circuit, the power of a chip has increased by a factor of 1 billion, and 20 years from now, chips (and desktop computers) will be 1 million times more powerful than today's.

This capability has been the core behind the extraordinary growth of the chip business as well as every device that uses chips, including the computer. It's why giant computers costing millions of dollars a couple decades ago can't keep up with a $1,000 home computer today. The world has never before seen such an extraordinary phenomenon, the basis of all the technological marvels that permeate our lives today. And with several more decades to go, it's hard to believe that there isn't still an enormous future in technology companies and stocks—at least, once they get through the worst recession they've seen since Intel was founded.

As that potential became increasingly apparent, people and banks with a lot of money decided that giving money to entrepreneurs in order to create new companies exploiting this technology was a risk worth taking. Thus, in San Francisco in the early 1960s, the nascent venture capital business began helping to launch new technology companies. The investments weren't restricted to chips, but were also doled out to bright people creating new computer systems, storage systems, software, and other products that used those chips.

Venture capitalists didn't start in Silicon Valley. There have always been a few wealthy individuals willing to risk money on a wild new adventure. Probably the first of the modern venture capitalists was Laurence Spelman Rockefeller, the third son of John D. Rockefeller Jr. Laurence Rockefeller decided in the 1930s to start investing some of his inherited wealth in risky scientific ventures. In 1938, Rockefeller gave $550,000 to World War I flying ace Eddie Rickenbacker to revive Eastern Airlines. Rockefeller also invested $475,000 in James S. McDonnell Jr., who then started McDonnell Aircraft.[1]

After World War II, Rockefeller set up a formal investment group in New York. The goal was not really to grow his substantial wealth, but to see if it was possible to start new industries by investing in a few visionaries.[2]

One of the first, and probably most famous, of the professional San Francisco venture capitalists was a man named Arthur Rock. Rock started as an investment banker at Hayden Stone & Co. in New York, where in 1957 he helped the Fairchild team find the money to start that company. He also helped raise private money for another successful California technology company called Teledyne Inc. After these investments proved to be substantial successes, he decided to move to San Francisco and make a formal try at the business. He arrived in 1961 and teamed up with a California lawyer named Thomas J. Davis to start an investment firm called Davis & Rock.

Their first investment: a $1 million deal they put together in 1961 to help launch a computer company called Scientific Data Systems (SDS). Both Rock and Davis thought there were already too many computer companies, but Davis became convinced by the engineers' plans to create advanced scientific computers, and told Rock over the phone that he was interested in the company. Rock, who had not yet left New York, reportedly responded: "Jesus, I've gone into business with an idiot!"[3]

But Rock was soon convinced as well, and the pair included $257,000 of their own money in the deal. Seven years later, when SDS was sold to Xerox for nearly $1 billion in stock, the duo's investment became worth $60 million. The pair split up in 1968, but Art Rock went on to earn fame as one of the primary backers of Intel (in 1968) and as an early investor in Apple Computer (in 1978). Davis started the Mayfield Fund, now one of Silicon Valley's most prestigious VC firms, having backed such companies as Genentech, Tandem Computer, and LSI Logic.

But the process of starting companies with "risk capital," or money that individuals were willing to bet on a long-shot start-up with huge potential payoff, was still ad hoc and only occasionally successful. While the trend in technology was clear, picking the right teams and ideas is trickier. Another early attempt at professional venture capital in the San Francisco area, the firm Draper, Gaither & Anderson, managed to raise $6 million from the Rockefellers and other wealthy people, but by the mid-1960s had gone out of business.

Still another early investor was a man named Reid Dennis. In the early 1960s Dennis was working in the investment division of Fireman's Fund. Despite the risky and still experimental nature of the venture capital business, Dennis managed to convince Fireman's Fund to create its own VC fund, which Dennis himself then managed. He invested his own money, as well as investing on behalf of Firemen's Fund. Dennis put $15,000 of his family's money into Ampex, a Northern California company that invented a magnetic tape for storing computer data. The product would later be adapted to store video and sound, and Sony transformed it into a consumer product called videotape. But the computer storage business was sufficient to take the company public, and Dennis turned his $15,000 investment into $1 million in a few years.[4]

Weisel met Dennis at a friend's party in 1962, before graduating from Stanford, and struck up a conversation. He convinced Dennis to hire him for a six-month gig in the Municipal Bond department at Fireman's Fund in 1963 before he headed off to Harvard. Dennis' partner, Vic Parakeni, was a strong role model for Thom. Thirty-seven years later, Dennis invested in Weisel's new investment bank, Thomas Weisel Partners.

Working with Dennis gave Weisel his first glimpse at the process of venture capital, West Coast style. It's also where Weisel encountered the concept of actually doing real research on public companies before investing in them.

In the fall of 1964, Weisel left for Harvard Business School (after spending three months in Europe, including one month rock climbing in Austria with his brother). At Harvard, he learned to analyze the case histories of companies, still a staple of the university and its famous business publication, the *Harvard Business Review*. Among other things, Weisel wrote a paper on his own family's business—the rich side of the family, his mother's side. Weisel was inspired by his grandfather's abilities as an entrepreneur.

Weisel's Harvard colleagues also recall him as a student who liked to challenge the wisdom of his professors. "He was always trying to find a different angle on the case studies we discussed in class," says classmate Erik Borgen (who later became a client and an investor in Weisel's companies). Borgen developed a huge admiration for Weisel. "I've had the good fortune of having both Thom Weisel and Michael Bloomberg as classmates at Harvard," says Borgen. "Of all the people I've run into in my career over the years, those two individuals are the most aggressive business people I've ever met."

Borgen adds that back then, Weisel was already hugely competitive. One of the first times they met was when a group of first-year students at Harvard Business School headed out to the football field for a friendly game. Immediately, Weisel started dividing people into teams and calling plays. "It wasn't five minutes before Thom was running the game," says Borgen. "And he's been like that ever since."

Harvard business students are required to submit weekly lists of their career goals to certain professors. Despite his fascination with Wall Street, Weisel's list of goals started off with a simple idea: He wanted to live in California. The weather and countryside were really nice there.

One of his favorite professors, C. Rowland Christianson, an expert on corporate strategy, was furious that a promising student would have such an absurd priority. "What the hell are you doing?" he asked. "Don't you want to be where the opportunities are?"

Neither Weisel nor Christianson realized that the combination of technology breakthroughs and venture capital out west was about to create the most extraordinary opportunities for wealth creation since the discovery of oil. Weisel's fascination with entrepreneurship was still the driving force behind his business ambitions. As a major financial center, San Francisco was at this time more potential than reality, but linking up with the pioneering bankers and investors there was much more exciting than joining the management of Merrill Lynch. As a banker who also wanted to be an entrepreneur, Weisel seemed likely to be a perfect fit with the bright young engineers who were to create Silicon Valley.

Weisel once again made some valuable friends at Harvard, including Borgen, Jerry Bremer, and Michael Bloomberg, although his friendship with Bloomberg didn't really take root until later.

But as Weisel's Harvard days came to a close, he had to face the truth. He had no idea what he was really going to do next. He knew he wanted to be involved in the world of finance and investing, but he also wanted to live in San Francisco and be an entrepreneur. Exactly how he would reconcile those goals was still a mystery. Armed with that vague plan, in 1966, 25-year-old Thom Weisel and his wife set off for the West Coast, in order to become part of a financial industry that was almost exclusively based on the East Coast. Weisel barely even knew what investment banking was.

The profession of investment banking, in fact, got its start in America not long after the Revolutionary War. In the late 1700s, traders would gather on Wall Street in Manhattan to trade in tobacco, wheat, and, to a lesser extent, securities. Alexander Hamilton started using the exchange to sell government bonds in order to pay off debts from the Revolutionary War. The New York Stock Exchange was officially launched in 1792 (as the New York Stock & Exchange Board) when some two dozen stock brokers gathered under a buttonwood tree in New York and signed the Buttonwood Agreement, agreeing to trade with each other for a fixed commission.[5]

In the early 1800s, the U.S. government regularly issued bonds to finance things like wars, banks, and transportation. Loan contractors, auctioneers, and even merchants started selling securities and bonds along with their other wares. In the 1830s, commercial banks started adding investment banking services such as selling stocks and bonds to their original repertoire of keeping people's money in checking and savings accounts.

By the middle of the 1800s, professional investment banking houses had sprung up, selling shares in turnpikes, canals, and railroads to the public in order to finance the building projects. The banking houses spread throughout the country, but those on the East Coast, near the major stock markets, were the most successful, and the industry largely settled there. The investment banks sold bonds to the general public in order to help finance the Civil War, and the industry expanded along with industrialization.

Investment banking hit a milestone in the 1870s when a huge syndicate of banks from the United States and Europe teamed up to buy $50 million worth of U.S. Treasury bonds and resold them to the public. J.P. Morgan & Co. was founded in 1895. At the beginning of the twentieth century, J.P. Morgan put together another syndicate to reorganize U.S. Steel from an array of affiliated companies into the first billion-dollar corporation by trading shares from the smaller constituent companies for shares of the merged conglomerate.[6]

Today, one of the most important functions of investment banks is taking companies public. They do this by helping the companies provide all the necessary documentation for their new stocks, pricing the stocks, and taking company executives on a road show to introduce them to investors who might be interested in buying the initial shares when they go on sale. The investment banker has to help drum up excitement about the new stock, or the initial public offering could fall flat.

But Professor Christianson was right. In 1966, the investment banking industry was still concentrated in New York. Companies in Northern California were not exactly fighting over promising young Harvard MBAs then. Weisel spent his first year looking for a job. In the meantime, he took a job in the fall of 1966 at FMC, a food machinery company, analyzing potential investments for the firm.

Despite the slug-paced economy, there were a few promising signs for the region. The defense industry kept growing, semi-conductor companies were doing well, and Stanford was regularly churning out engineers for jobs at local institutions such as Lockheed, Sylvania, and the National Aeronautics and Space Administration's research site, NASA/Ames, in Mountain View. Hewlett-Packard, the pioneering electronics firm, was proving to be an innovative company in both technology and management techniques and was destined to become a prime training ground for managers who would become CEOs of many of Silicon Valley's early electronics companies.

In the summer of 1967, one of Weisel's college connections finally helped him land a job at a financial firm. A friend told him, "You've got to go see this guy Tommy Davis. He's a partner with Art Rock, but I think that relationship is just ending." Davis and Rock were indeed splitting up, but Davis didn't hire Weisel. Instead, he put him in touch with another friend, William Hutchinson, who was getting ready to launch a new investment bank in San Francisco, William Hutchinson & Co.

Weisel became one of the founding employees, but was not one of the firm's six founding partners (the senior executives who own a piece of the partnership). He was, however, the firm's first research analyst.

Some of the New York investment banks were over 100 years old by that time, but were still tiny financial businesses by today's standards. Hutchinson, even tinier, decided to specialize in studying West Coast companies, plus certain well-defined industries with high growth potential. Technology companies were now beginning to multiply in the region like California poppies in early spring, and the firm started focusing on those as well as other promising businesses.

It was here that Weisel learned the business. Then, as now, the main business of an investment bank was to help match up companies that needed money with people and institutions that had it. The banks might help link businesses to private investors or VC firms, sell large blocks of public or private stock to institutions, or help a company issue stock on the public markets, raising money from public investors.

Because Hutchinson was a West Coast firm, the bankers had to get started by 5 or 6 A.M. in order to be prepared for the market's opening in New York. Weisel would often hang out in the office until 10 P.M. in order to pick the brains of the other bankers, analysts, and salespeople. Then he would drive the 40 miles back to Palo Alto, where he lived. Or he just ended up sleeping in the office. It's probably another reason his first marriage didn't last.

This was the time he reestablished his relationship with Michael Bloomberg, who was then a trader at Salomon. In 1972, Weisel, Bloomberg, and later a few other friends, even chipped in together and bought a condo in Snowbird to make it easier to get away and ski.

Weisel loved the business, learning how to raise money for companies and making money for investors. He seemed to have an instinct for it. "I was born to do this," he says. He quickly discovered that he made a much better institutional salesman (as well as much more money) than an analyst and switched jobs, becoming an institutional broker at Hutchinson. Like retail stockbrokers at other banks, who help individuals buy and sell stocks, Weisel's job was to recommend to institutional money managers which securities to buy or sell, in return for a healthy commission. At that time, the stockbrokerage industry had a standard commission fee: 35 cents per share of stock, regardless of the stock's actual selling price. The advantage of being an institutional broker rather than a retail broker is that institutional brokers get to buy and sell huge blocks of stock. Sell 1 million shares of a company's stock—a big but not unheard of trade then—and your take was about $350,000. It was a good business.

Weisel made a name for himself by trading in the stock of a transportation and oil energy company called Natomas, located in Indonesia. Natomas also owned a large gas field, the size of which had not yet been established. Hutchinson had two research analysts following and recommending Natomas based on their analysis of the long-term intrinsic value of that gas field. The firm sent one of its partners, Paul "Red" Faye (who was previously undersecretary of the Navy under President Kennedy), to Indonesia to get better sources and information about the Indonesian plan.

Armed with this kind of data, Weisel could recommend to his institutional clients when to buy the stock and when to take their profits and sell it. He would fly to Manhattan to talk to his institutional clients, unrolling large seismic maps of Indonesia onto conference tables, explaining why certain drilling sites had the potential to become gushers. In the precomputer age, before instant communications and split-second buying and selling decisions, the stock markets were less efficient than they are today and information was harder to get, making Weisel's recommendations highly valuable.

Natomas stock turned out to be the Dell Computer of the late 1960s. Between 1968 and 1970, the stock rose from $15 to over $140. Weisel made his clients a lot of money, and was well paid himself. Within two years he had earned enough stock options at Hutchinson to become its second-biggest shareholder.

Some of Hutchinson's research analysts were also making names for themselves. John Gruber, for example, was one of the company's main technology analysts. In the late summer of 1970, he recommended buying semiconductor stocks, which seemed poised to take off. He was right, and people began paying attention to his reports. Of course, notes Gruber, "If I had written that report two years earlier, I would have been a schmuck."

At this point, other investment bankers decided to try out the San Francisco scene, primarily to tap into the growing ranks of the technology companies just to the south. Most notable was William R. Hambrecht, a New York investment banker who moved to San Francisco in 1968. He teamed up with George Quist, who came out of Bank of America's Small Business Investment Corporation (SBIC), an investment firm backed with money from the federal government. Hambrecht also developed extremely strong relationships with the new venture capitalists and with the underwriters at Morgan Stanley. That helped Hambrecht & Quist to become one of the country's preeminent technology-focused investment banks, taking some of Silicon Valley's most prestigious tech companies public.

In 1971, however, Hutchinson was the largest investment bank in San Francisco. As the person who brought in the most income for Hutchinson, Weisel naturally felt it was about time for him to run the company. As Karl Matthies, who was the restaurant analyst at the time, puts it: "Thom and Bill Hutchinson had a disagreement about who was more important."

One day, when Bill Hutchinson had gone to Europe ("which," says Weisel, "he did every six months or so"), Weisel decided to stage a coup. He went to the company's board and proposed putting himself in charge. The board agreed.

When Hutchinson returned, Weisel told him the good news. Hutchinson could move up to the chairman position, but would have no more say in running the company. Hutchinson said he would go off to think about it for a few days, and apparently managed to turn some of the board members back to his camp. He came back and told Weisel he'd have a proxy fight on his hands.

Weisel decided to leave. "The company was poorly run, was losing money, and wouldn't go anywhere with him in charge," says Weisel.

Now 30, Weisel again found himself unemployed for several months. He decided it was time to start his own company.

Getting Started

Thom W. Weisel

Creating and running a business like an investment bank isn't something you learn in school. You learn on the job, by working with great people. I've spent a lot of time, from Stanford on, learning this business from many different people.

Certainly, your education has an influence on you. When I started at Stanford, I was fascinated by political science, but more so by economics. I was really interested in the stock markets and capital markets. I studied under Edward Shaw, who was one of the great monetarists of the time. I'm not really a Keynesian. I was more interested in the fact that Professor Shaw, being a monetarist, could change the course of the economy through interest rates and the money supply. I was trying to get my hands around the banking system and how capital formation really worked, both from a macro and a personal viewpoint.

After Stanford, working with Reid Dennis was a great experience. Venture capital was a very small business at the time. The venture capital industry didn't really exist yet. This was when Art Rock was just thinking about investing in a company called Intel.

In the 1960s, stock investors had very little information to go on other than what the company provided. But one day, a very interesting report crossed my desk at Fireman's Fund. An investment bank in New York, Donaldson, Lufkin & Jenrette (DLJ), had put out a research report on General Motors. Unlike the short summaries that investment banks usually published on public companies, I believe this was the first independent, detailed report from a Wall Street company. It analyzed the finances, debt, cash flow, strategy, growth potential, risks, and, thus, the future potential of GM's stock. DLJ became famous for this idea.

After that, at Harvard Business School I was really interested in studying entrepreneurship. At that time, Harvard had only two classes on the subject. The capital markets courses were called "Finance." As I thought about graduating, I knew that I wanted to be involved in the financial business, but I had no idea how. I was intrigued with venture capital, money management, and brokerage, whether it was retail or institutional.

It might have been smarter to go to New York after my MBA, but I really fell in love with Northern California when I was at Stanford. I had access to these incredible physical surroundings, the oceans, the mountains, and this wonderful, mild weather. When I decided I would move back to the Bay Area after Harvard, I knew it could be difficult to find a job, and that it would probably take me longer to be successful. But a diversified lifestyle was just too important to me. It's much more sustaining than a maniacal one-dimensional focus on your career. I didn't think I could sustain myself for decades with that kind of focus. I'd get bored.

When I was at Harvard, Boise Cascade was the hot company of the time. I didn't want to move to Idaho, and I didn't want to move five times in five years for my career, as Boise would require. A friend of mine moved to Kansas after graduating, because that's where he found a job. I just couldn't do that. I wanted to be able to control my own destiny. Besides, at a big company, you get buried. You can't make much of a difference. I wanted to build, to be part of a community, to have roots that could really help me in the long run.

I was back at Harvard giving a talk recently. The students were worried about being able to find work in this economy. I told them how it took me a year to get my first job. I banged on the door of every brokerage firm, every money management firm I could find, and got zero offers. In this environment it will take longer to realize one's goals. Patience and perseverance are the watchwords.

At Hutchinson, I finally found what I wanted. I was there from day one when they opened the doors. I used to live in the office. My best mentors were Peter Bennett, Dick Griffith, and Bob Brown. The three of them were extremely important to my learning curve in the first several years.

They taught me the art of selling and interfacing with the various institutional clients: mutual funds, hedge funds, and investment advisors. I received a crash course on the analytics of research and the fundaments of how to relate them to stock prices of a company, as well as the technical aspects of the market. I learned the value of being a long-term investor.

They also helped me to increase my network by introducing me to some of the key players in the industry. Bob Brown, who was Hutchinson's head of research, had been a money manager at FIF in Denver and ISI in San Francisco, and was nice enough to take me to New York to meet some of the biggest institutional traders in the business, including the traders at Goldman Sachs and Salomon.

At Goldman, L.J. Tennenbaum took me under his wing and was very helpful. At Salomon, both Jay Perry and Michael Bloomberg were supportive of our efforts and acted as a counterparty to us on many trades.

One other talented individual was Will Weinstein, who was head of the trading desk at Oppenheimer. Will retired after May Day of 1975 to Sun Valley, Idaho. We spent a fair amount of time together, which was very beneficial in rounding out my knowledge of the block trading business and its overall positive influence in the institutional brokerage business, as well as investment banking. I really appreciate the opportunities I've had and the people I've been able to work with.

At Hutchinson, we were an institutional house, and the business was small. We were following growth companies on the West Coast. The technology companies were just starting to evolve, and we had several tech analysts. We followed energy and oil companies, restaurants, and forest product companies like Weyerhaeuser.

The whole industry was much smaller in those days. The entire exchange traded 11 million shares a day. By way of comparison, in October 2002 we traded 60 million shares a day just at Thomas Weisel Partners. The marketplaces weren't as efficient, and the research was more difficult because most companies' financials lacked transparency. If you did quality, in-depth research and talked to the management of the companies you were recommending, as well as their customers and suppliers, you could provide some real value to the institutional community.

At Hutchinson, we tried to find a few companies that we could stake our franchise on and make our clients money on a long-term basis. One of those companies was Natomas, a gas play in Sumatra and Indonesia. Our research had indicated high potential. As Natomas drilled additional wells, our initial thoughts were validated. We developed into the primary source for information on Natomas and all the derivative plays and were the primary upstairs market maker. We became so large in trading volume of the stock that on many days the specialist on the NYSE, Irwin Sloss, would call us before the opening bell in order to ask us where he should open the stock that day. Making our clients money was a sure way to build a client base that was loyal for a long time.

We tried to duplicate our success with Natomas with a few other companies. That's how I built a footprint, a franchise, so that when I moved across the street to a new firm, I had something to bring with me. My Rolodex was portable, and I brought the clientele with me. I had finally found something I could truly dedicate my business life to.

5

A Good Place to Be

Every exit is an entry somewhere else.

—*Tom Stoppard*

The 1970s were a time of dramatic change socially and economically. President Richard Nixon resigned early in the decade and the police action in Vietnam finally came to an end. At the start of the 1970s, the venture capital movement in San Francisco was heating up. By the end of the decade, most of the venture capital firms had packed up and moved from the city to Sand Hill Road in Silicon Valley in order to be closer to the growing community of engineer-entrepreneurs. Ostensibly this was to help the VCs find new ideas more easily; most definitely it was in order to keep a closer eye on what the entrepreneurs were doing with their money.

1971 was an important year, both for Weisel and for technology entrepreneurs. Intel was just a few years old when one of its engineers, Ted Hoff, invented the microprocessor, an integrated circuit with all the components necessary to handle all the logical computations a computer needed—essentially, the single-chip "brain" of a computer. Intel also went public that year (in an offering underwritten by C.E. Unterberg, Towbin & Co.).

It was also the year that a reporter for *Electronic News* coined the name *Silicon Valley*. And in 1971, the over-the-counter exchange was automated, becoming the National Association of Securities Dealers Automated Quotation, or Nasdaq. That transformed it from a second-class exchange for companies that couldn't meet the strict requirements of the NYSE into a dynamic market for high-tech and entrepreneurial companies, whose executives had a bias favoring an electronic exchange.

There were important milestones throughout the rest of the decade as well. Microsoft was founded in 1975, but would remain an arcane and obscure company until the following decade. In 1976, Steve Wozniak invented the first commercially viable personal computer, and Apple Computer was set on a path that would change the world—until Microsoft took over the task two decades later.

Although most of Silicon Valley was focused on electronics and the computer industry, there were other technologies to be exploited. Stanford University and the University of California at San Francisco, for example, had some extraordinary biologists who had managed to splice a gene from one organism into another. In January 1976, a 28-year-old Silicon Valley venture capitalist named Bob Swanson drove up to UCSF and requested 10 minutes with Herbert Boyer, a biochemist and one of the inventors of recombinant DNA. The discussion moved to a local pub for several hours, and Genentech, the genesis of a whole new industry, was born.[1]

While the venture capitalists were starting to get the hang of things, investment banks were still primarily focused on trading stocks of existing companies than on becoming IPO machines. Most of the venture-backed companies were still growing, working to gain the credibility that would allow them to raise money by offering stock to the public. In 1975 there were only five IPOs over $5 million in the United States. (Together, these five raised a total of $176 million.) Corporations didn't tap the public stock market to raise money as often as they do today. Investment banking was simply not a glamorous field—yet.

In the early 1970s, even the biggest New York investment banks were still small by today's standards. At the end of 1975, for example, the total market value of Merrill Lynch was $437 million. A quarter century later, its value reached about $41 billion, an increase of almost 8,000 percent. J.P. Morgan did even better, growing about 17,000 percent to about $73 billion in that time.

It wasn't hard to start a brokerage to help institutional investors decide where to put their money, charging them a fee every time a transaction was made. It required very little cash up front; all you needed was to be known and trusted by enough institutional investors. A lot of people figured they had the connections to do just that, and investment banks proliferated in San Francisco and elsewhere—mostly elsewhere. But the San Francisco bankers had now realized that if this new venture capital trend really took off and created more technology companies like Fairchild and Intel, there might be a lot of IPOs coming from Silicon Valley.

In 1971, Weisel started talking to people who might be able to help him start his own firm. The person he found was Sanford J. Robertson.

Sandy Robertson was a partner at Smith Barney. A few years earlier, he had moved to the firm's San Francisco office. Noting the success of companies like Fairchild Semiconductor, Hewlett-Packard, and Ampex, he decided there was promise in these New Age technology companies. He arranged a private placement for Spectra Physics, which made equipment that used lasers to help the new semiconductor industry carve its ever shrinking circuits onto silicon. The company became a leader in the business as circuit lines contracted into near invisibility.

But it was a real struggle finding investors. Robertson managed to convince Smith Barney to put in $100,000, but few in the company believed in this wild and futuristic stuff from California. When Robertson visited the company's New York headquarters, associates would say, "Hey, Buck Rogers, how's your ray gun company going?"

Still, in three years, "Buck" Robertson had increased the San Francisco office's revenues 15-fold. Rather than ensuring him a great future at Smith Barney, his success fostered jealousy within the firm. In particular, it made his former boss, who had run the San Francisco office before him, look bad by comparison. Robertson decided to start his own investment bank. His goal was to get to know the venture capitalists and create a firm that could both invest in new companies and help take them public once they were ready. He left Smith Barney in October 1969 and started a new company in the first few days of 1970.

Robertson teamed up with Ken Siebel, a former basketball player with the Baltimore Bullets who had decided to leave the NBA and get an MBA and had also ended up at Smith Barney. Robertson recruited another hot Smith Barney banker, Bob Colman, who was in the firm's Milwaukee office but wanted to move to California. Colman's fiancée lived in California, and while they were trying to decide where to live, Colman made the mistake of taking her to see Milwaukee in February. She wasn't into ice skating. They named the firm Robertson, Colman & Siebel.

Colman, a Milwaukee native, had known Weisel growing up, and became the next business connection to boost Weisel's career. In the fall of 1971 Weisel attended a birthday party for Colman's wife in the swank southern California beach town of La Jolla. Colman asked him how things were going with Hutchinson. Weisel replied that he had quit. Weisel was soon offered the opportunity to join up with the new firm, with the understanding that he would be made partner if he did well.

It seemed like a good partnership. At the time Weisel joined, RCS was primarily a small investment house. It had raised a small venture fund to invest in start-ups and was trying to help start-ups find other funding as well. Sandy Robertson became deeply involved with the venture capital community, meeting and developing friendships with most of the major players. It was Sandy

Robertson who introduced Eugene Kleiner to Thomas J. Perkins; the two teamed up to create the most prominent venture capital company in the world today, Kleiner Perkins Caufield & Byers.

While Robertson was establishing connections with the venture capitalists, Weisel was doing the same with institutional investors and other investment bankers. Weisel had built up a strong institutional brokerage business at Hutchinson, and he now set about doing the same at RCS. He also bought RCS a seat on the New York Stock Exchange so that it could trade stocks directly with the institutional investors.

Both Siebel and Colman also played the role of salesman, but couldn't keep up with Weisel any better than his brother could keep up with him on a racetrack or ski slope. "They just didn't have Thom's energy level," recalls Karl Matthies, one of the analysts who decided to follow Weisel from Hutchinson to RCS. Weisel brought in the most revenues by far, and became a partner. The firm was renamed Robertson, Colman, Siebel & Weisel in 1972, with each of the principals owning roughly 20 percent of the company's stock. Weisel bought a condo in Snowbird that year.

Weisel had managed to convince several of Hutchinson's best analysts to come with him, including Karl Matthies, John Gruber, Reb Forte, and Steve Mittel. By then, all the investment banks were trying to imitate the success with research reports that Donaldson, Lufkin & Jenrette had started in the early 1960s. But RCSW became known as a particularly savvy, research-focused investment firm. It maintained the basic strategy of William Hutchinson, focusing on emerging companies in technology, restaurants, health care, and energy. Says Matthies, "Hutchinson was a larger firm, but they weren't trying to move as fast as Thom was. We were young guys [Matthies was about 28] and we were eager to try something new. We were excited to get in on the ground floor." It turned out to be a good place to be.

The firm's strategy was to produce tough, no-holds-barred

analysis of public companies. Frank and opinionated research reports were valuable to Weisel's clients, who were buying stock. They also got the firm noticed by the venture community and the entrepreneurs whose firms were being analyzed.

The interesting thing about this business is that the investment banks maintain critical contacts with clients on both sides of the deal—buyer and seller. They may represent a particular company in a merger negotiation one month, and in another represent that company's opponent in a hostile takeover bid. They represent companies trying to sell their stock for the highest price possible, as well as large institutional buyers who may want to buy a large block of that stock at the lowest possible price. It's a business that's more prone to conflicts of interest than a lawyer in a one-lawyer town.

Their stock analysts are supposed to write unbiased opinions of the value of a company's stock price, preferably keeping both buyer and seller happy. Generally, any institutional investor will have its own research analysts (called *buy-side analysts* because they work for the stock buyer) to help it evaluate stocks. But many stock buyers also end up relying heavily on the investment bankers' sell-side analysts, whose reports are more widely distributed. Stock buyers love tough research reports, but stock sellers only like reports that make them look good. A sell-side analyst who pans a company is in danger of losing that company's underwriting business. That's why a sell recommendation from a sell-side analyst is still rarer than a carnival fortune-teller with bad news.

These conflicts made headlines after the dot-com crash, when everyone started losing money rather than racking up outrageous fortunes, raising complaints from everyone from the U.S. Securities and Exchange Commission to grandmothers with their pensions buried in Enron stock. Wise stock investors make sure they have a reasonable understanding of how this business works and which banks are representing whom. Not very many stock investors are that wise.

RCSW's analysts wrote reports that stood out from the thinly veiled love letters most firms were prone to producing. "Thom always understood that good quality research was the foundation of the business," says Matthies. Matthies believes that it may have been easier to resist potential conflicts in those days. For one thing, the analysts didn't command the million-dollar salaries they get today, but averaged around $35,000 a year, plus bonuses if the firm did well. They simply didn't have as much at stake. Generally, only very sophisticated investors read their reports.

The fact that RCSW, as a West Coast boutique, had very little underwriting business certainly helped. The company's main clients were stock buyers, not sellers, and the buyers wanted real evaluations on the stock they were trading. "When people wanted interesting new ideas, they would turn to us," says John Gruber, who was then head of the technology analyst team.

RCSW's research reports also earned the company respect. Entrepreneurs got to know the RCSW analysts, especially after they went public and the reports started to focus on them. Then the CFO would establish relationships with the analysts in order to help make sure they had "accurate" information by giving them "guidance" on the company's near-future prospects. Of course, the companies are only supposed to give the analysts information that's also available to the public. Anything else is inside information, and it's illegal to trade on inside information, making these relationships tenuous.

It can be done, though. Gruber points out that if you simply knew the CFO well enough, you could tell what a company's prospects were for the next quarter, even if the CFO didn't say anything substantial. For one thing, CFOs were always happy to report good news. "And then one day, you call them and they don't call you back," he says. "Or they just say, 'I can't talk about that,' or 'I don't know the answer to that.' Then you know margins might be under pressure, and you consider changing the recommendation on the stock."

If the company and the analyst got along well, other executives would also get to know the bank and might send it some underwriting business. That was sometimes when the CEO would get to know the executives at RCSW. It was a slow way to build the underwriting business, but the institutional sales more than compensated.

RCSW also came up with another innovative approach to building its visibility: the investment conference. Weisel and his team continued to develop relationships with institutional investors, visiting them personally, staying in touch by phone, and offering their research reports to help them find the most interesting investments in small companies. But Siebel came up with the idea of creating a conference to bring together a large group of entrepreneurs and investors for a few days. It would be a more efficient way to get the word out and give the investors an opportunity to talk directly with the management of companies in which they might like to invest.

In 1971, the RCSW conference became possibly the first of its type in the nation. It began as a conference to introduce some of the more interesting specialty retailers to potential investors. The first conference included presentations by seven or eight companies, including Levitz Furniture and Ponderosa Systems, a chain of family steak houses. About 30 institutional investors attended.

In addition to the company presentations, the conference left plenty of time for networking, lunches, dinners, and private meetings. It allowed the institutional investors to talk in detail with company managers they were interested in, as well as to spend time with their peer group, swapping stories and exchanging information. This conference model has become widely copied, to the point where, by the 1990s, the glut of conferences became a burden to investors wanting to keep up with their field. But the RCSW conference (later the Montgomery conference) maintained its prestige and popularity.

In 1973, one of the longest bear markets in history started, hanging around through much of 1974. The stock market in those days was far from the topsy-turvy get-rich-quick environment it became in the 1990s. In 1972, the Dow Jones Industrial Average hit 1,000 for the first time, and many people thought that was too high. Sure enough, 10 years later it had slipped back to 776. Weisel took the opportunity during the slow time to participate in the Summer Rally Olympic Games in San Francisco, to begin serious training as a runner, and to create his corporate running team.

Congress passed an important law in 1974 that was destined, if not necessarily designed, to give a huge boost to the stock market. The Employee Retirement Income Security Act (ERISA) of 1974, signed into law by President Gerald Ford, set up a list of restrictions and rules on the way company pension plans could invest money in the stock market and elsewhere.

Pension plans had been investing employees' retirement funds for a century. Railroad companies, one of the high-tech businesses of the late nineteenth century, were the pioneers in setting up private pension plans for their employees—notably the Grand Trunk railroad in 1874 and Railway Express in 1875. The Revenue Acts of 1921 and 1926 allowed employers to deduct pension contributions from corporate income and allowed for the income of the pension fund's portfolio to accumulate tax-free until the participants cashed in at retirement.

But there were flaws in the system. Although private pension funds were regulated by the Internal Revenue Service, and several disclosure rules were adopted over the decades, some companies abused the pension system. Some didn't fund their pension funds adequately, and some pension plans were shut down without enough money to pay the promised amounts to retirees. Some companies made employees meet certain age and other requirements in order to participate. Companies or unions (which also ran private pension funds for their members) diverted money into their own coffers.

ERISA created rules of conduct for private pension plans. It mandated vastly increased disclosure of where the funds were invested and how they were doing, both to the employees and to the government. ERISA also gave the government enforcement power and set up a federal insurance program (the Federal Deposit Insurance Corporation, or FDIC) to ensure that the funds are protected and that benefits are paid out appropriately. One restriction was to prohibit a pension fund from investing more than 10 percent of its money in the stock of the company sponsoring it, in order to avoid the temptation to use the funds to boost a company's sagging stock price. (Unfortunately for Enron employees in 2001, that didn't prevent employees themselves, even at management's urging, from voluntarily electing to put much or all of their own retirement funds into their company.)

With more disclosure and government protection, however, employees became more comfortable with allowing their funds to go into riskier investments, including the stock markets. This has steadily increased the amount of money pouring into public, and more recently private, stocks over the years. That trend has created an ever growing investment banking business, particularly for institutional brokers who help pension funds decide where to invest their money.

The first big break for RCSW's stock underwriting business was a restaurant chain called Victoria's Station. A group of entrepreneurs in San Francisco, headed by a man named Dick Bradley, decided to create a restaurant chain with a theme, a fairly unusual approach at the time. The theme was more station than Victoria: The group bought old railroad cars, refurbished them, and turned them into restaurants decorated with railroad paraphernalia.

In the early 1970s, the chain had fewer than a dozen restaurants but was growing at a good clip. It was the kind of place you went for prime rib, a baked potato, and a salad bar, and its quirky theme (and full bar) became popular with the Yuppies of the day. Bradley decided to do a public stock offering. It was too small a deal for the major banks, but RCSW had developed a good reputation following restaurants and was based in San Francisco, and Bradley had come to know Sandy Robertson. Victoria's Station tapped the firm to lead its IPO. The company's strategy of making contacts through various doors was beginning to pay off.

The offering was a big success. The stock was priced in the teens, and for several years grew nicely as the chain expanded. But Victoria's Station didn't last. A railroad car cannot house a large kitchen, and it was difficult to expand the menu. Seafood was added to the list, but the chain's popularity was heavily dependent on prime rib, which began to fall out of favor with the upwardly mobile crowd. Eventually, burdened with too rapid expansion, it went bankrupt.

Still, the successful IPO helped boost RCSW's visibility. It got the attention of the Denny's restaurant chain, which then started giving RCSW some of its underwriting business. When a company offers public stock, there is generally one lead investment bank with main responsibility for arranging and selling the offering, and one or more others that help out by selling shares to their institutional clients. The lead bank controls "the book"— the list of people allowed to buy the stock at the issuing price. When a company issues stock, the prospectus lists the names of the different underwriters involved, with the lead banker on the left and the secondary bank or banks on the right. It was a big event at the firm when a Denny's prospectus listed Robertson, Colman, Siebel & Weisel on its cover.

When a new company's executives became familiar with this West Coast investment bank, they also discovered the other advantage of working with a specialty firm: personal attention from top management and long-lasting relationships. Weisel is almost fanatical on the latter point, and has developed some very loyal customers as a result.

A good example is Jamie Coulter, founder and CEO of Lone Star Steakhouse & Saloon. He first ran into RCSW in 1972, long before he ever became an entrepreneur himself. Coulter was a large franchisee of Pizza Hut restaurants, and he started getting to know Karl Matthies and (later) John Weiss because the restaurant analysts made a point of speaking to franchisees themselves when doing research. "They always seemed to have an eye out for interesting people with big plans," says Coulter.

Coulter eventually decided to move out on his own, bought the Steak & Ale restaurant from Pillsbury, and changed the name to Lone Star Steakhouse. Two decades after he first met the RCSW analysts, as his company was getting into shape for a public offering, Weisel said he wanted to meet Coulter. "We had an instant liking for each other," says Coulter. "Thom understood the strategy, gave me advice, and told me, 'If you can run it, I can finance it.' There are a lot of people with dreams, but Thom can pick out the people who can actually do it." Coulter chose Weisel's company (by then called Montgomery Securities) over Alex.Brown and Oppenheimer to have sole management of his IPO in 1992.

The technology sector also provided ample opportunities for the young company. ROLM was a computer company that got its name from the initials of its four founders, Richeson, Oshman, Loewenstern, and Maxfield, engineers from Rice University and Stanford. In 1969, after being rejected by Art Rock, the foursome had managed to get some money from Palo Alto Investments, a brand new VC firm started by two engineers named Burton J. McMurty and Jack Melchor. Melchor had started the fund with a few million dollars contributed by Saudi Arabian tycoon Adnan Kashoggi.

For the first few years, ROLM looked like a second-string computer company. It specialized in large computers for the military, and orders were sporadic. ROLM almost fell into bankruptcy in its first year. But it then switched its focus from military computers to another new market, digital telephone equipment known as private branch exchanges (PBXs), and skyrocketed. In 1975, ROLM had $18 million in revenues, $10 million of it from its two-year-old PBX business.

Even so, it was still tough to find both private investors to help get the company started and banks that would help take it public. "In 1975, it wasn't so much a matter of choosing which company to take us public as finding one that was willing to do it," recalls Ken Oshman, ROLM's former CEO. "There were almost no IPOs in those days, very little venture capital, and no public market for stocks. The average guy on the street didn't talk about stocks. It was almost unheard of." Not even taxi drivers were buying stocks yet.

Oshman managed to convince E.F. Hutton to lead the public offering. That meant figuring out the price of the stock and how many shares to issue and finding institutional investors who would buy the IPO shares. "The CEO at E.F. Hutton said they could do the whole deal out of their Philadelphia office," says Oshman. "But they barely got the damn thing sold!"

Fortunately, Sandy Robertson had gotten to know Jack Melchor, the ROLM investor, who was also on its board. Melchor introduced Oshman to Robertson, who brought in RCSW to play second fiddle on the offering. RCSW helped push the offering over the top by tapping its own investing clients. The stock went public at $12, but rose only to $12.05 on its first trading day and stayed there for almost two years. ROLM still failed to generate much excitement among investors, despite the fact that PBX sales rose to about $50 million the year after the IPO and continued their meteoric rise.

Since RCSW seemed to do a much better job finding investors, Oshman dropped E.F. Hutton and took on RCSW as ROLM's main banker for subsequent stock offerings. Finally, as more companies started installing their own PBX systems, ROLM's PBX business and stock got noticed. As ROLM's primary banker, RCSW got more notice as well. In 1984, ROLM reached revenues of $600 million. In November of that year, IBM came in and scooped it up for $1.3 billion.

(Although that was a big valuation for a tech company at the time, it's interesting to note the contrast with the dot-com boom. After ROLM, Oshman went on to start a new company, Echelon, which creates home networks for electronic devices. It managed to go public in the late 1990s when its revenues were in the range of $10 million and profits were nowhere in sight. In the height of the dot-com bubble, with its revenues reaching just a $40 million annual run rate, the market value of Echelon peaked at about $4 billion. Fifteen years earlier, ROLM's revenues had reached an annual run rate of about $1 billion and were growing 50 percent a year when IBM valued it at just $1.3 billion.)

By dabbling in the newfangled technology business, RCSW kept hitting an occasional home run. Sometimes it took a while. In 1972, for example, RCSW took Applied Materials public. It's now the world's preeminent company making the esoteric equipment that chip makers use to etch circuit lines on their ever shrinking semiconductors. Not many investors had faith in that kind of company, because its market was highly cyclical and the company's revenues rode that cycle up and down every couple years. Again, Sandy Robertson's VC connections brought the equipment maker to RCSW. Its IPO was lukewarm, but it eventually became a powerhouse.

The same thing happened with Tandem Computer, a company specializing in large, "fault-tolerant" computers designed for reliability, with redundant backup systems. Tandem was incubated at Kleiner Perkins, and the VC firm brought RCSW in to help with its IPO in 1977. The offering raised $8 million, although RCSW was not the lead investment banker. Tandem ended up becoming a huge mainframe company, and was eventually sold to Compaq Computer in 1997 for about $2.5 billion.

Although these companies were relatively unknown when RCSW took them public, and in many cases none of the large banks would touch them, their later successes helped bring the investment bank more business. Once the public companies became giant, successful tech businesses, the investment bank could boast that it took them public. The message was, "Hey, if we're good enough for Applied Materials . . . ".

However, tensions also started building at RCSW by the mid-1970s. Business associates say that the personalities of Robertson and Weisel were too stubbornly similar. They're at opposite ends of the political spectrum (Weisel is a big supporter of the GOP, Robertson is a Democrat who contributed heavily to Bill Clinton's campaign), but both are strong-willed, determined, and opinionated. Both believed in their own ability to lead and build a new industry. And both can be intimidating to people who disagree or fail to deliver on promises. Weisel, in particular, is known for his temper, and can lash out at associates if he disagrees with them.

Weisel is also known as a strong leader, a team coach who can really inspire the players. In part, he does that by rolling up his sleeves and getting right out there with them, helping to close deals, meeting with clients, and working incredibly long hours (he has generally put in about eight hours by 1 P.M., and may keep going until anywhere from 3 P.M. to late in the evening). The people who work for him follow his lead.

But as a young executive, he was brash, not always as diplomatic as he might have been. He was an excellent salesman, and his institutional brokerage business brought in a lot of revenue for the firm. He also had strong opinions on the strategies needed to move the firm forward and was not afraid to express them. Consider the fact that the company was started by three other partners, with Weisel coming in as the fourth. Now he was bringing in the most business, and as a result his partners' percentage ownership in the company declined while his own held steady. He was also clearly ambitious, obviously interested in becoming the boss himself. A clash with the other partners was probably inevitable.

It began to show among the other partners. "Sandy never said a bad thing about Thom," says Oshman, "but I always sensed there was tension there." The tension was exacerbated by a difference in management styles. Weisel was devoted to no-nonsense, straight business practicality. He would eventually become known for his team-building skills and ability to generate strong camaraderie among employees. But this was not yet his team or his company. He concedes that he probably affected some of his colleagues like static electricity on the back of your neck. "Twenty-five years ago I was volatile, young, and immature," he says. "I didn't have the patience I should have had with people. I was Darth Vader as far as they were concerned."

Siebel notes that "The only friction was over ownership of the company." Weisel felt that the partners who brought in the most revenue deserved the most equity. "I asked Thom, 'Are you happy with what you're making?'" says Siebel. "He said yes, but he was more concerned with what everyone was making."

Ruthless practicality and honesty, however, are almost Weisel trademarks. Just as he was later to tell Lance Armstrong that he wasn't a strong enough team player to join the U.S. Postal Service cycling team after Lance recovered from cancer, he was straightforward with his opinions about the firm and the other partners. It simply made sense to him to award more equity to the most productive partners. Dick Barker, a principal at Capital Group, which manages a family of mutual funds for company retirement plans, IRAs, and pension funds, notes that both men are very aggressive businesspeople. Barker's firm, which now manages $275 billion in investments, first started working with RCSW in its early days. "I was always impressed by Thom's energy, focus, and determination in whatever he did," says Barker. "But there's a dark side of aggressiveness, too. His strength is also his weakness. I've never had any doubt about what Thom's opinion was on any matter. He stated it whether I liked it or not."

RCSW continued to grow and generate profits, although its growth was modest. The high commissions from the institutional brokerage business provided the funding to do the research reports and still leave substantial profits for the firm.

However, just as ERISA opened the door for more stock investing, the Securities and Exchange Commission erected a big screen that restricted the amount of money that could flow through that door to the brokers. In 1975, the SEC ordered that brokers cease their industry-wide fixed fee of 35 cents per share, and instead required them to bid against other brokerages for their fees. In a competitive environment, the fees dropped to as little as eight cents per share. That was a windfall for stock investors and may have helped contribute to more stock investments, but it was a big pain in the wallet for the brokers. The change took place in May, and brokers despised it so much they started referring to it as "May Day." Weisel believes it also took its toll on the quality of research in the industry, since the banks could no longer afford the really in-depth reports.

Weisel realized that once the industry shifted to competitive brokerage fees, the company's main revenue stream—the business that he ran—would drop dramatically unless he could significantly increase the volume of trades his firm brokered. The solution was to enter the world of big-block trading.

Block traders are institutional brokers who specialize in buying and selling huge chunks of stock, negotiating the price separately from the market exchange. If one pension fund, for example, has a block of 100,000 shares of Hewlett-Packard it wants to sell, it can accomplish this in one of two ways. First, it could simply put the shares up for sale on the NYSE and sell to the highest bidders. But a large block suddenly going up for sale generally causes a hit on the company's stock price. It's a simple matter of supply and demand: Increase the supply of stock for sale without increasing the number of buyers, and prices drop.

In order to prevent that, and to get a higher price for the shares, the pension fund might turn to a block trader to sell the stock for it. The trader gets on the phone with other institutional investors that may be interested in buying the stock and tries to find the highest price possible. The stock is sold in a private transaction to one or more buyers. If it's a public stock, the sale is then reported to the stock exchange. If the block trader manages to get a price close to that listed on the Nasdaq, the transaction will not affect the price. If it is substantially lower, however, the stock price may drop on the exchange as buyers reevaluate how much the stock may be worth. Block traders can also help institutional investors interested in private stocks to buy large blocks of stock in pre-IPO companies.

Since the block traders are essentially running a separate market, one in which only big investors can play, and since they often have to provide capital to successfully complete a specific block trade, they are also known as *market makers*. Says Weisel, "To draw an institutional order, you have to be able to create a market in a stock. Most of the boutique firms that did not do that went out of business."

Tim Heekin, who is the head of the trading desk at Weisel's new company, Thomas Weisel Partners, refers to institutional block trading as the "cash register" of the firm, the business that pays for cost centers such as research reports. "Montgomery was one of the first companies to bring block trading to the West Coast," says Heekin. That move was to prove a great one, and has helped keep Montgomery ahead of the pack. Recalls Fredericks: "We were way more prepared for May Day than our competitors."

In 1974 Weisel began looking for some expertise in block trading, before negotiated commissions took place. His network, of course, started with friends from Stanford and Harvard, many of whom were now working on Wall Street. But it's astounding how many of his business connections over the years have come from his sports activities. Skiing, in particular, seems to be the sport of investment bankers. Hang around Thom Weisel long enough and it will begin to seem as though everyone on Wall Street is a ski fanatic who spends most of his or her free time in Sun Valley, Idaho.

Will Weinstein was one such person. He was an extraordinarily successful trader at Oppenheimer who loved skiing in Sun Valley. By 1975 he decided he'd had enough of Wall Street, moved to Sun Valley, and opened a private investment business. It's not a big enough town for two senior investment bankers to avoid meeting.

One of Weisel's classmates from Harvard, Brock Stokes, introduced Weisel to Weinstein. They started spending time together on the slopes. Weinstein, in turn, introduced Weisel to many of the other block traders on Wall Street. On skiing or business trips, the traders began to fill Weisel in on the intricacies of block trading. "In those days, Goldman, Salomon, and Oppenheimer were the three big block trading firms," says Weisel, "and I had pipelines into all three of them. Every one of these guys turned out to be incredibly helpful and supportive when we got started."

Weisel launched his block trading business by hiring away the head of block trading at Lehman Brothers, a man named John Tozzi. Another new partner Weisel brought in was Dick Fredericks, a prominent banking analyst at Dean Witter until 1974, when he joined Sherman Agnew. That bank was then bought by Morgan Stanley in 1977, and Fredericks decided to escape the New York conglomerate scene and try the entrepreneurial firm where he already had friends. (Fredericks, who went to school with Bill Clinton, became the U.S. ambassador to Switzerland toward the end of Clinton's final term.) The firm was now up to about 25 employees. Siebel, meanwhile, left in 1976 to start his own money management firm.

In order to hire top people to start new businesses, Weisel had to do something fairly unusual for the 1970s: offer them stock in the firm. That really exacerbated the disagreements among the partners, because in order to award equity to newcomers, some of the existing partners had to keep giving up some of their equity. To Weisel's thinking, most of that equity should come from the least productive partners.

The investment banking and VC business still wasn't paying off well, and that meant further reducing the equity of the original partners. "We changed our partnership every year," says Fredericks. "And Thom was creating all the profits."

Robertson wasn't exactly a slacker. His connections in the venture community were growing, and the number of company IPOs he had managed to help underwrite was impressive for a company that finished its fiscal year on September 30, 1978 with $10 million in revenues.

Another VC Robertson had met was Kip Hagopian. Hagopian's firm, Brentwood Associates, was in Los Angeles rather than Silicon Valley, but it was keeping an eye on the start-ups to the north. RCS helped Brentwood do several private placements, then helped Hagopian raise money for Brentwood's second venture capital fund. Robertson traveled the country with Hagopian to visit institutional investors that might put money into the fund, while Weisel worked the phones to find other investors and set up meetings. Together, they managed to bring in the $23 million Brentwood wanted to raise and, in fact, had to turn away some people who had wanted in on the deal.

Hagopian noticed that, during the tour, Robertson was spending an inordinate amount of time on the phone to Weisel back in San Francisco. "We joked that if we were to see a phone booth 100 yards ahead it would probably ring and be Thom calling for

Sandy," says Hagopian. It turned out to be the last deal Weisel and Robertson would do together as partners. One reason Robertson spent so much time talking to the home office during the trip was to negotiate his exit from the firm.

Karl Matthies had other things on his mind. He planned to get married on October 1, the day after the close of the company's fiscal year. (Executives at financial service firms often wait until the end of the quarter or fiscal year for important personal business, because the pressure and demands from the company are much reduced once the books are closed.)

On September 30, Matthies spent the day playing golf with his father and his best man, then started preparing for the rehearsal dinner. At that point, Weisel showed up at the dinner and dropped the news: Sandy Robertson and Bob Colman had quit.

Everyone at the firm had been invited to the wedding reception at the prestigious San Francisco Golf Club. The firm's employees ended up spending a lot of time in the locker room of the club during the reception, discussing where they would be working on Monday morning. Sandy Robertson didn't attend the wedding.

Matthies was curious about what would happen on Monday as well, and decided to forgo his honeymoon. It was probably a good idea, because he ended up with the job as head of research. In fact, most of the senior employees decided to stay with Weisel, in part because they all got promotions to replace the defectors. "For almost all of us it was one of the best things that ever happened to us, because it jumped everybody up to higher level," says Matthies. "It rejuvenated us."

Robertson took Colman with him and added two new principals, Paul Stephens and Dean Woodman. The firm was named Robertson Colman Stephens & Woodman, coincidentally a name that was very similar to that of the company he left behind, Robertson Colman Siebel & Weisel. Some people believe it wasn't so coincidental, but was designed to make clients and partners believe that Robertson's group was the real successor to the original, especially since both firms were often referred to as Robertson, Colman, or by their initials, RCSW. "There was real confusion on Wall Street as to which company was which," says Dick Fredericks.

Weisel decided not to name his company after himself and other partners. For one thing, with the game of musical partners in full swing, it was safer not to name a company after the current partners. Robertson Colman Stephens & Woodman, for example, soon became Robertson Colman & Stephens, then later just Robertson Stephens.

Weisel's headquarters were on Montgomery street, which was named after Captain J.B. Montgomery, who sailed into San Francisco (then called Yerba Buena) in 1846 and declared it to be part of the United States, taking it away from Mexico. Weisel had been reading about Montgomery, thought he was interesting, and decided *Montgomery* would be a good name for his firm. Besides, he liked the idea of trying to make Montgomery Street "the Other Street"—the West Coast version of Wall Street.

The split created a celebrated rivalry. It made good copy for the press and kept both firms aggressive in seeking out business. Several of the partners believed—and still believe—that Robertson felt Weisel stole from him the firm he had created.

The news certainly came as a surprise to some of the company's clients. Byron Wien, an institutional investor who is now chief U.S. investment strategist at Morgan Stanley, recalls when the split happened. Before one of the RCSW conferences in late 1978, several clients were invited to a weekend retreat at the tony Silverado Resort north of San Francisco. Weisel got up and read a prepared statement about Robertson's departure. "It was kind of a shock," says Wien. "We were stunned because Tommy was always viewed as the marketing guy, the conceptualizer, but not as the business manager." But Weisel managed to prove himself. "I don't think anybody expected Montgomery to become the investment powerhouse it eventually became. Most of us watched with admiration and a little astonishment. He's a real leader."

As Weisel had predicted, the precipitous drop in brokerage fees had driven a lot of brokerage firms out of business. The underwriting business was still weak, but the block trading business, led by John Tozzi, kept Montgomery afloat. A *Business Week* article on November 2, 1978, noted that, due to the change from fixed fees to negotiated fees for brokers, Montgomery had survived while most of the small investment banks and brokers had gone out of business or had been bought out by larger banks.[2] William Hutchinson itself lasted only a few years past Weisel's departure, and was bought out by another company.

The *Business Week* article described Montgomery as a firm that "dabbled occasionally in corporate financing," which was the side of the business that Robertson had run. *Business Week* mentioned that Montgomery had brought "two small high-technology companies" public—Tandem and ROLM—and had managed to raise a total of $70 million for Victoria's Station in 10 financings. The article quoted John Kissick, first vice president at Drexel Burnham, saying that Montgomery was going after "a market niche that a national firm would not go after." Of course, that was before Wall Street discovered that technology was going to become a niche like the Grand Canyon. "We made decent money," says Matthies. "It wasn't spectacular, but we were all happy. These were pretty fun times."

The article also noted that Montgomery's institutional trading had grown large enough to now account for nearly 1 percent of the daily trading volume on the New York Stock Exchange. This was an impressive number for such a small firm, with 13 analysts and just $10 million in revenues. (At that time, Goldman Sachs handled about 5 percent of the NYSE volume and Merrill Lynch 10 percent.) *Business Week* noted that the firm's real success was acting as an institutional research and trading house and that it had 120 institutional investors on its client roster. That was the business that Weisel ran.

If Robertson's efforts in underwriting were considered "dabbling" by *Business Week*, Weisel's efforts in that part of the business must have been considered negligible. When Robertson left, Weisel lost his main contact with the venture capital community and the Silicon Valley entrepreneurs who were working toward public offerings. It took him years to get that business flowing again. "If there was any bad thing about the split-up, it was the loss of those relationships," says Matthies.

But Weisel had what he wanted. He was the senior partner and the biggest shareholder and was now clearly in charge of his own company. Now it was time to lead.

The slopes of Sun Valley seem to provide Thom Weisel with more executive candidates for his investment bank than a four-star headhunter firm. But it wasn't the only reason he hung out there. He's never lost his passion for skiing.

In 1974 he bought a condo in Sun Valley and spent as many weekends there as possible. He's the kind of guy who likes to be first on the slopes at 8:30 in the morning, before the snow is ruined by the shredders.

That same year Weisel was offered the opportunity to do something for the sport of skiing other than supporting ski resorts by buying more lift tickets than Picabo Street. Warren Hellman, who was at that time president of the investment bank Lehman Brothers (he's now a venture capitalist and a member of the board of the Nasdaq), called to ask a favor. Hellman was also chairman of the board of the governing body of the U.S. Ski

Team, and he needed some help. There were often great skiers on the American team who won gold medals, but the quality of the skiers was never consistent. "Historically, the U.S. alpine team generally had one or two top skiers. We won some Olympic medals," says Hellman, "but the team had no depth. It still had an obsolete, amateur orientation."

Hellman needed a new board member, someone who could add more professionalism to the organization. Weisel decided he could spare the time to help out. Says Hellman, "Thom Weisel became one of our most important trustees."

The problem was that so many other countries took the sport much more seriously than did the United States. Many governments or corporate sponsors provided a livelihood and training for athletes in their countries so they wouldn't have to go work for the local Home Depot—or, worse, turn professional and disqualify themselves from the Olympics in order to make money. (It would be several years before the Olympics was opened up to professional athletes.)

The American ski organization was run by skiers, ski shop owners, and volunteers who believed in amateur sports. "The U.S. team was run by old Olympic types who still believed in the purity of the sport," says Hellman. "It was a world that no longer existed."

Hellman found something of a soul mate in Weisel. Weisel was not interested in the "purity" of amateur competition; he wanted the United States to *win*, damn it. That required organization, training, and money so that Olympic skiers could afford to stay with the sport for years and mature to winning stature before leaving the Olympics for professional sports and Chap Stick commercials. While European teams routinely brought in funding at least in the hundreds of thousands of dollars at a time, a donation of $10,000 was big for the U.S. team.

Hellman argues that the dichotomy was unfair and dangerous to American athletes. Downhill racers can reach speeds of 90 mph on packed snow sprayed with water to make it icier, wearing no more padding than a skin-tight ski suit. "We'd take an American kid, 19 years old, from a country where ski racing is not a major sport, and put him heads up against an Austrian or Swiss athlete in their mid- to late 20s who looked like a running back for a pro football team and was trained by professional coaches," says Hellman. "Not only can you not compete effectively, you're putting your athlete in serious danger."

Hellman had already had some successes in finding more money. One of his biggest fights was with the executives at ABC's *Wide World of Sports*, which had for years held the exclusive rights to broadcast the U.S. Ski Team when it competed. The annual fee ABC paid the team was $75,000. Hellman argued that the rights were worth about $1 million a year. ABC executives responded that they thought $75,000 was already too much.

So, in the early 1970s, Hellman put the television rights for the U.S. Ski Team up for competitive bid. CBS won with a bid of over $1 million. ABC tried an end run by buying the television rights to the major ski events themselves from the people that put them on. Fine, said Hellman, just make sure the U.S. team didn't appear in the broadcast. ABC executives thought that was a ridiculous idea. Hellman filed suit to stop them.

The network probably thought it would be easy to roll over an amateur sports team run by volunteers. But some of these volunteers were also powerful corporate executives. One trustee was John McMillan, the chairman and CEO of Northwest Energy. He hired a huge New York law firm to defend the ski team's claim. ABC lost the battle and the broadcast rights. Hellman's favorite part of the whole incident: "Howard Cosell was just furious."

When Weisel joined the board, he helped turn skiing into a big-money event. He donated his own time and money and helped with "Ski Balls," black-tie fundraisers for the kind of people who own their own tuxedos. The San Francisco Ski Ball became one of the biggest contributors, along with a version held in New York. Weisel tapped his connections to bring in corporate sponsors who could donate hundreds of thousands, and later millions, of dollars.

"Thom has been one of the most generous donors I have ever seen," says Jim McCarthy, another board member. "There are people in skiing you can always count on, even if they think you're going in the wrong direction. Thom doesn't just write the check, he puts in time and effort. Skiing was damn lucky to have people like Thom involved."

Weisel also recruited more corporate executives for the governing board, including top people from Sprint, Eckerd Drug, and partners in the venture firms of Kleiner Perkins and TA Associates. "Thom brought a whole new group of people into the foundation," says Chuck Ferries, who has been involved for years with the ski organization and replaced McCarthy as chairman in 2002. "He strengthened the organization every year."

Finally, Weisel improved the quality of the sports medicine team, and eventually became the key player in a complete reorganization of the organization. Fortunately, he has an uncanny ability to manage his time. He seems to be able to do three full-time jobs at once.

But it wasn't all work. He got involved on the slopes as well as in the boardroom. He got to know the young athletes, like Phil and Steve Mahre and Picabo Street (just starting her Olympic career), as well as Tommy Moe, Hilary Lindh, and Diane Roffe, all of whom became stars at Albertville in 1992 or Lillehammer in 1994. He skied with them and watched them compete in the Olympics, an opportunity he had passed up himself when he was their age. "These kids really inspired me," he says.

He had already had a taste of what it was like to return to competitive sports with the San Francisco bankers' SROG and then training and competing as a runner. It's like rediscovering a sweet taste from childhood that you'd almost forgotten, and, as time went on, Weisel seemed more and more interested in savoring it again.

So in 1976, at 35 years old, he decided to become a downhill racer. He had never been a downhill skier, but was always more of a powder skier, which entails a different technique. But he figured he could learn a few new tricks.

He recalls vividly what it was like to put himself up against real competitors again, this time in a brand-new type of race for him. "I just got dusted," he says. "It really pissed me off."

In order to go anywhere in this sport, he needed thorough training and a fantastic instructor. The first place to look, of course, was Sun Valley. It has always been a popular training spot for Olympic and professional skiers, and there were plenty of instructors around to help them, so Weisel figured he could hire one for some private lessons. A Sun Valley bar called the Oar House (actually owned by one of Weisel's fraternity brothers from Stanford) was a popular hangout for the ski instructors. One of the best of them was a guy named Boone Lennon. Weisel sought him out at the Oar House one day. He walked up to Lennon, introduced himself, and said, "I really need you to teach me how to ski race."

But Lennon didn't know Weisel from Abraham. "When I approached Boone Lennon for help in skiing, my company was a little $10 million drinkwater investment bank," Weisel says. It wasn't enough to impress Lennon. Nor, apparently, was Weisel's position on the U.S. Ski Team board.

"Look me up next year," Lennon replied.

"There's still another month of skiing left this year," Weisel pointed out.

Lennon's response: "Look, I'm busy, and I'm not too sure I want to do it, anyway."

Wiesel wasn't happy with this dismissal. But he couldn't change Lennon's mind—at least not that season. So he held Lennon to his first offer and approached him again the following year, at the start of the season. This time he convinced Lennon to become his personal trainer.

For his first lesson, Weisel showed up in the latest, hottest gear: Scott boots and Bobby Burns' "The Ski." Lennon took one look at him and said, "The first thing you have to do is get rid of those boots and skis."

Weisel switched to Lang boots and Rossignol skis, more favored by downhill racers. He put them on, headed down his first slope, and discovered how much difference there was between sport and racing skis. "I couldn't turn the damn things!" He says it was like learning to ski all over again.

Eventually, of course, Weisel and Lennon became friends. As Weisel became more involved with the U.S. Ski Team, he also became friends with the head coach for the team, Harald Schoenhaar, and got more guidance from him. Later, Weisel paired the two up by making Boone the head technical coach for the U.S. Ski Team.

Things were busy enough at work, since this was about the time that Robertson left the company and Weisel had to build up the organization. Nevertheless, he managed to keep running as well as skiing. In 1980, competing in the Corporate Challenge for track, he came in third in the Nationals. He completed the Pacific Sun 10K in Marin in 37:58 minutes, and the Dipsea race in Mill Valley in under an hour. In 1981 he ran the Oakland half-marathon in 1 hour, 19 minutes.

In 1982, at 41, he competed in the National Championships in Masters Skiing (over age 40) in Anchorage, placing third in the slalom, third in the giant slalom, and third overall.

In 1983 he was elected president of the U.S. Ski Team. That's when he really started shaking up the organization.

That year was significant to the future of Weisel's sports career in another way as well: He bought a new bicycle and started riding again.

Thoughts for the Entrepreneur

Thom W. Weisel

As an entrepreneur myself, and someone who has spent a lifetime working with entrepreneurs, I've picked up a few thoughts that might prove to be useful to any future entrepreneurs and leaders who may read this book.

1. **Choose your leadership style.** Building a distinctive culture and operating philosophy will define your organization, help you attract and retain talent, and get you through the toughest of times.

2. **Chose your management team wisely.** It can be very difficult to disengage once people are in place. I will always err on the side of bringing in the most talented people I can find, even if it's somebody I don't necessarily get along with. That will come later.

3. **Set the standard for your entire organization.** You can only earn the trust and respect of your employees through your actions, not your words. Set the bar high, and you'll build great teams.

4. **Establish optimistic but attainable goals.** Building expectations that consistently are not met can be destructive when it comes to attracting additional capital and retaining customers and personnel.

5. **Encourage your people to take risks.** Encourage them to take responsibility for their actions, and reward results. I personally have had great success in picking solid managers and then getting out of their way. I've also had great success at picking young, untested professionals who have risen to the occasion. I judge them by their results. In our business, it's important to have risk management tools in place because of the capital risks we take. That may not be as essential for your business.

6. **Be prepared for problems.** Most CEOs don't think that storm clouds will come, but they will. Have a disaster plan in place just in case.

7. **Lead by example.** Be the first person to arrive in the morning and the last to leave at night. Be on top of all aspects of your business. You should spend the majority of your time out selling with your people. Listen to your

customers. You'll learn what the market thinks of you. Be the most effective communicator and advocate for your firm, both internally and externally, and do it on a regular basis.

8. **Pay particular attention to the franchise, building accounts early.** Work with your customers to make them successful, not to make yourself successful. Your own success will follow.

9. **Be straight with people.** Your employees want to know the truth. You're not running a popularity contest; you're running a company. Don't fall into the trap of telling your employees what they want to hear. Tell them what they need to hear to improve, to advance, or to look for another profession if necessary.

10. **Be humble.** Luck is a huge part of any successful venture. You might be the brightest, most talented person around, but if you're a real jerk to work with, no one will care. The best, most enduring leaders have a healthy dose of humility and a deep respect for the dignity of others.

11. **Be the catalyst of change.** A company that isn't growing and constantly trying to reinvent itself is a company that will end up uncompetitive. Change and new challenges are what keep a company competitive. While it's important to set goals, I've come to see that the road is more important than the destination. You have to come off the mountain you just climbed and find another one.

6

Passion Is Good

I create nothing. I own.

— *Gordon Gecko*

Do not overwork to be rich; because of your own understanding, cease! Will you set your eyes on that which is not? For riches certainly make themselves wings; they fly away like an eagle toward heaven.

— *Proverbs 23:4–5*

Wall Street in the 1980s will probably be remembered by the famous guiding principle uttered by Gordon Gecko (played by Michael Douglas) in the 1987 film *Wall Street:* "Greed is good." The phrase was reportedly lifted from a speech by Ivan F. Boesky, who told graduating UC Berkeley students: "Greed is all right, by the way . . . I think greed is healthy. You can be greedy and still feel good about yourself."[1] It was a time of speculative finance, the proliferation of junk bonds, and arbitrageurs who became wealthy buying and selling companies, often in hostile takeovers. Eventually, the go-go business environment got out of hand. It turned into an era of Savings and Loan scandals, investment banking scandals, and bankruptcies.

Boesky and Michael Milken, the man who learned to use high-risk, high-yield junk bonds as a lucrative financing tool, were convicted of securities fraud and spent time in prison.

The New York investment banks seemed preoccupied with handling mergers and acquisitions and financing large corporations rather than taking new companies public. Corporate mergers and acquisitions soared during the decade. In 1986 alone, there were nearly 3,000 mergers and buyouts worth more than $130 billion.[2] The capstone of the decade came in 1989, when the New York leveraged buyout firm of Kohlberg Kravis Roberts & Co. (KKR) paid $24.7 billion for RJR-Nabisco, a firm with annual revenues of $17 billion. At the time, it was the most money ever paid for a corporate acquisition.

In Silicon Valley, however, money was made the old-fashioned way: by inventing and building things. A sense of idealism still permeated the culture of the Valley. Executives like Andy Grove, Steve Jobs, Bill Gates, and others knew they were changing the world and treated their efforts not merely as the creation of a new company but the creation of a whole new industry and way of life. They were right.

The personal computer industry, which consisted of a scattered group of companies with different software and incompatible systems in the 1970s, was set on the path of standardization when IBM introduced its first PC in 1981. Anxious to get its admittedly late product out quickly, IBM bought chips and software from Intel and Microsoft rather than developing them itself, its usual approach.

That inadvertently christened Intel and Microsoft as the PC standard-bearers for the rest of the millennium and changed the very nature of the computer business. One company no longer controlled an entire market; rather, other companies could come in and make competing products based on industry standards by licensing chips from Intel and software from Microsoft. Compaq started the trend by coming up with two new ideas: building portable computers rather than those bound to the desktop, and making them from the same chips and software as IBM's PC.

That standardization created an extraordinary boom in the personal computer business, which pulled the business of semiconductors, disk drives, and other components along with it. Technology entrepreneurs were transformed from largely ignored geeks into famous and wealthy executives who put the acronym IPO into the vocabulary of the general public.

As the 1980s began, the growing technology scene was rapidly transforming Silicon Valley from a spattering of open fields, quiet neighborhoods, and 1950s-era office buildings into a circuit board landscape of modern, low-rise offices and manufacturing plants. Sometime during that decade, business in Silicon Valley grew so large that the commute between San Francisco and Silicon Valley actually reversed: More people were living in the city and commuting to work in the suburbs of Silicon Valley than the other way around. (Weisel moved north to Marin and commuted into the city.)

Some of these world-changing executives had mixed feelings about both the VCs and the investment banks. On one hand, they were a vital part of the virtuous cycle, a yin and yang relationship between financiers and entrepreneurs, feeding each other in a widening spiral. On the other hand, they were the money people who kept stealing away some of the best management talent in order to start new companies, often didn't really understand the companies' technology, took equity away from the people doing the work, sometimes held too much power, and made unreasonable demands.

Even some of the VCs, while they acknowledge that investment banks were necessary to help with an IPO, maintain an attitude that there is not a huge amount of difference between the different underwriters. When a company and its investors are ready to seek an underwriter for their stocks, sales teams from the different investment banks will visit them in a ritual known as the "beauty pageant." All the firms argue that they have the best research analysts and the best salespeople and will do the best job finding stock buyers after the IPO. They all come up with statistics proving that their IPOs have the best track record and that the bank does the most IPOs in the company's space. The statistics are generally carefully selected in order to make the investment bank look like a leader in the category (for example: "We did the most IPOs for service companies younger than three years old in this industry over the last 18 months.").

Reality is not as clean-cut. "In fact, they don't want to admit it, but there are half a dozen major firms that will do the same job for you," says Warren Hellman, a VC who used to be a top executive at Lehman Brothers. "These guys are experts at covering up their own warts and uncovering other people's warts. They're really in the business of selling a fungible product, so parts of their claims will be real and parts will be a charade. You've got to think through the part that isn't charade."

Hellman adds that there are certain questions a company can ask the prospective underwriters: Who is actually going to work on the underwriting? How good are the analysts in our field, and what role will the senior analysts play in my IPO? How well regarded are the junior people who might do a lot of the work? If I'm the CEO, am I going to be able to get your CEO on the phone? Are any of my competitors already in the pipeline for IPOs with your firm?

Hellman likes working with Weisel. "Weisel is an example of doing things the right way. He doesn't try to be everything to every company. He's got the best research analysts, many of whom may know your company better than your board does. They can give advice on competitors and possible mergers, or suggest alternatives like selling convertible stocks.

"The great thing about Weisel is that he'll be at the table and will get involved himself. He's a good judge of what he should and shouldn't do, and when he decides to do something he has a great single-mindedness to get it done. He thinks about things so differently than anybody else, he's truly a unique individual."

Despite his exuberant flattery, Hellman has had his own disagreements with Weisel. Hellman was an early investor in a restaurant chain called Il Fornaio, and in the 1990s felt it was ready to go public. He chose Montgomery to handle the IPO. But as the date approached, the company had an unexpectedly bad quarter—not down, but earnings weren't up as much as expected. Weisel called and told Il Fornaio's management they would have to delay the IPO until finances were straightened out.

That left a bad taste in the restaurateurs' mouths. So the company's projections were a little too aggressive in the pre-IPO glow. The bank had been through the process 500 times; why didn't it recognize and flag that earlier? "I was annoyed, the management was annoyed, and after that they felt like using anybody but Montgomery," says Hellman.

Still, Weisel stayed in touch and managed to talk his way into the beauty pageant when the company was ready for its IPO again, about two years later. "They came in and made a presentation, and we said, 'Let's not kid ourselves, it's the best company for the job,'" says Hellman. "It was like a jilted lover coming back to an old flame." Montgomery did the IPO after all, and Hellman adds that it did a "great job."

Montgomery's biggest difficulty was not usually in being too reticent to take a company public, however. If anything, its aggressiveness was what drew criticism. Competitors have claimed that Montgomery had developed a reputation as the firm to call when other banks turned you down. The implication is that many of those firms deserved to be turned down. "I don't think Montgomery had a very big quality screen," says one.

On the other hand, some of those companies that others wouldn't touch, such as ROLM and Micron Technology, proved to be extraordinarily successful. "Montgomery, on any scale, would have been the most aggressive company around," agrees Dick Barker, principal at Capital Group, one of the biggest institutional investors in the country.

In the late 1970s and the very early 1980s, there were allegations that some of Montgomery's institutional traders or analysts were buying stocks before recommending them to institutional clients. "Maybe they weren't as careful in the early days at making sure the (institutional) clients got the first crack at new ideas," suggests Barker. "The sales and research people shouldn't be buying in front of the clients."

Weisel insists such allegations are groundless. His people were aggressive, but he says he has always operated under the philosophy that the only way to succeed is to put customers first. Indeed, Barker considers Weisel to be a highly respected and "principled individual," an assertion echoed by many of his clients and business associates. Many of Weisel's friends and business associates believe that most complaints directed at the firm were aimed by competitors. "If you're hugely aggressive and successful, you generate a certain amount of envy," says Barker. "It generates some suspicion that you cut corners to get there."

It could be a situation analogous to the constant allegations that Lance Armstrong must use performance-enhancing drugs, because he just seems too good to be true. That's despite the fact that Armstrong has never tested positive in any drug test, either those conducted during the Tour de France or surprise, unannounced tests performed when racing officials showed up at his door at dawn during training season. Armstrong may be the most tested athlete in any sport. And yet, many of his competitors have been caught with drugs, and have been suspended from racing for periods of time.

Montgomery's strength was still the institutional trading business that Weisel had built up over the previous decade. It was a good bet. In the early 1980s, institutional trading began its inexorable rise, a trend that has never really ceased. The popularity of mutual funds was a big part of the reason for that. Even average Americans with retirement plans could now participate in institutional trades through their mutual funds. Most people first learned about mutual funds through their company 401(k) plans, and started putting more and more of their investments into the funds in order to take advantage of the deals and connections of these institutional traders. While institutional trading accounted for just 17 percent of the trades on the New York Stock Exchange in 1975, by 1985 it had risen to 52 percent.

Montgomery's revenues went along for the ride. In 1982, it reached nearly $20 million in sales. While Montgomery's San Francisco rivals—Robertson Colman Stephens and Hambrecht & Quist—focused mostly on technology, Weisel kept his firm more broadly positioned. He not only had the institutional trading, he also maintained research groups that followed restaurants, hotels, and financial services. In the early 1980s, Montgomery helped underwrite stocks for Alaska Pacific Bancorporation, Brock Hotel Corp., Chart House Enterprises, Denny's, Maxicare Health Plans, Ponderosa Inc., and Saga Corp., plus others. "We really did kick butt in those areas," says Karl Matthies, who by now had been promoted to director of research.

But there was also a problem with the diversified strategy. As the decade progressed, money available from venture capitalists increased, technology companies flowed onto the public markets, and the demand for investment banking services for tech stocks began to expand dramatically.

For example, in 1975, the year E.F. Hutton and RCSW took ROLM public, there were only five IPOs in the United States that raised $5 million or more, according to Securities Data Corp., a division of Thompson Financial. In 1977 that number increased to 13. But in 1980, the IPO business began to look really interesting, as 81 companies went public, raising a total of $1.2 billion.

Montgomery was still not well connected to the venture capital community that backed the new entrepreneurs. Although it did strong analysis of tech companies, most entrepreneurs bypassed it for their IPOs. And IPOs were becoming a business with cachet. When it came to the prestigious area of underwriting technology IPOs, Montgomery was a little like a sailboat without a spinnaker trying to catch a huge tailwind.

A successful IPO is as dependent on prestige as anything else— or so most entrepreneurs believe. Many Wall Street investment banks, in fact, did look up from their takeover portfolios and notice the rise of the new technology business. Silicon Valley start-ups found they could now get the big names behind their stock offerings.

Just as start-up companies discovered that their credibility surged if they got funding from the most prestigious venture capitalists, such as Kleiner Perkins or New Enterprise Associates, they also found that getting a large investment bank, such as Morgan Stanley or Goldman Sachs, to take the lead in an IPO helped get more investors excited about their stock. They could not only tap the broad network of investors these banks served but could also more easily gain the attention of the press and increase the interest in the IPO.

But public offerings are often handled by more than one investment bank. In many cases there is a lead bank and a secondary bank that helps get the offering going by bringing in its own list of stock buyers. In a particularly large offering, several banks may co-manage the deal. This increases the number of institutional investors that might come in on the IPO, keeping the price as high as possible. Many of the new technology entrepreneurs started choosing a major bank to take the lead on their offerings, with a technology-focused bank and its list of specialized buyers to help out as secondary.

RCS and H&Q had squarely positioned themselves to take advantage of a surge in technology IPOs. Both companies had nurtured strong relationships with venture capitalists, which would bring them deals. H&Q in particular, founded in 1969 and specializing in computer technology and biotechnology, had an extraordinary start. It was the lead manager for 21 equity underwriting transactions in the 1970s, compared to RCSW's 4. This was in part because cofounder Bill Hambrecht had developed very good ties to Morgan Stanley.

Two other companies, CE Unterberg Towbin in New York and Alex.Brown in Baltimore, also put a strong focus on emerging growth companies, especially those in technology. That gave entrepreneurs the chance to go with some specialists that were a little older than the San Francisco banks. Although they were more diversified like Montgomery, their size gave them an advantage. Both firms dramatically outperformed Montgomery in stock underwritings: Unterberg Towbin was the lead in 44 transactions in the 1970s, while Alex.Brown led 22 transactions that decade.

RCS, H&Q, Unterberg, and Alex.Brown became known to the technology community in the early 1980s as the "Four Horsemen," the ones to ride to the IPO party. These banks caught fire like hot coals that were just waiting for a good breeze. As Robertson had predicted, the combustion came from the venture capitalists who fanned start-ups with cash and then tossed them to the investment banks like so much dry tinder. From 1980 to the end of 1984, newly merged LF Rothschild Unterberg Towbin led 123 underwriting transactions, Alex.Brown led 64, H&Q 40, and Montgomery 28. Despite its reputation in technology, RCS actually led only 18 transactions in that period.

Montgomery did get some technology business. It led the IPO of biotech firm Lyphomed and participated in the IPO of Amgen.

But it was the biotech firm Genentech that set the precedent for wild technology stocks with its October 1980 IPO. The company had no profits yet, or indeed any substantial revenues. Underwritten by a syndicate of investment banks, including Hambrecht & Quist, the stock opened at $35 a share and soared as high as $89 on the first day of trading. The phenomenon of outrageous IPO runups was born—although it would be another 15 years before the technique was perfected, helping to inflate the enormous dot-com bubble.

In 1980, Apple Computer selected Morgan Stanley to take the lead on its IPO, with H&Q as comanager. Compaq, which grew to $111 million in revenues its first year, becoming the fastest-growing new company in history, went public in 1983, tapping E.F. Hutton and L.F. Rothschild to handle the deal. Morgan Stanley and Robertson took 3Com Corp. public in 1984. Microsoft picked Goldman Sachs and Alex.Brown in 1986, while Silicon Graphics went with Morgan Stanley and Alex.Brown for its offering that same year.

Montgomery seemed to be missing out on the technology revolution, at least as far as IPOs were concerned. Although Montgomery's revenues were probably as high as or higher than those of its San Francisco rivals (all the companies were private and did not have to report their finances), the IPO business became the investment bankers' field of dreams and captured the attention of the press. In terms of visibility, Robertson and H&Q began to overshadow Montgomery.

It really bugged Weisel.

Montgomery worked hard to break through to the big-time underwriting business, but progress was slow. The firm tried to focus on quality research and developing its customer base one by one, building on the start that Sandy Robertson had given the firm a few years earlier. The company worked on getting relatively small deals—anywhere from $6 million to $80 million. To

Karl Matthies, deals like the work for Victoria's Station and then Denny's were important, if tiny by the standards of the big firms. "That's how the whole firm grew, taking baby steps for a long, long time," says Matthies. "From the 1970s to the 1990s, it was a series of little victories like this."

In the 1980s, Weisel started tapping some of his own contacts for investment banking deals. One was his old pal and skiing buddy Steve Wynn. The firm's first attempt to raise money for Wynn was actually in 1978, one of the first deals Montgomery got involved in after Robertson and Colman left. It was one of the deals that got away.

Originally, the hotel and gambling tycoon wanted to add a tower to his Golden Nugget casino (now the Mirage) in Vegas. Wynn called Weisel to see if he could help raise the money. Karl Matthies, the analyst who covered hotels, restaurants, and gaming, recalls going to meet Wynn at one of his hotel restaurants on a Friday night to discuss the deal.

As they all gathered around, Wynn got a phone call. "It was from Resorts International in Atlantic City," says Matthies. "Suddenly, [Wynn's] face gets white, and he says, 'Gentlemen, this meeting is adjourned.'" Wynn had just been told the first day's returns on the slots at the Resorts casino in Atlantic City, which was then in the process of converting into a gambling mecca. Wynn decided it was time to get into Atlantic City.

He tapped Montogmery to raise about $150 million for the venture, a large amount for a small firm. They went on the road show to find investors, but couldn't quite put it over the top. Many institutional investors were not allowed to invest in either gambling or tobacco stocks. Montgomery didn't have the resources to provide any debt financing that would allow Wynn to borrow the money for his project. Wynn ended up going to Mike Milken at Drexel, and became one of the first clients to use junk bonds to finance a large project.

Still, Wynn remained friends with Weisel and used the firm for later financings that didn't depend on debt, raising some $500 million in several deals as the gambling empire grew, according to Wynn. "Even though every major firm wanted to represent us, we ended up picking Montgomery," says Wynn. "Weisel's own energy made his firm competitive with anybody's."

In 1982, Weisel put some of that energy into moving the company up a notch on the scale of stature and power in order to catch up to the Four Horsemen. He started with the area he knew best: institutional brokerage. John Tozzi had helped build up the block trading business, but it was now time to go to the source— Will Weinstein, the former head of block trading at Oppenheimer and the man who had recommended Tozzi in the first place.

Weisel was still spending a lot of time skiing with Weinstein in Sun Valley. In 1982, he talked Weinstein into coming out of retirement and joining Montgomery Securities as managing partner and chief operating officer. In the summer of 1982 they hired Bobby Kahan, who knew Weinstein from covering him at Goldman Sachs, to run the institutional trading department.

Weisel offered partnerships and equity in Montgomery to Wall Street hotshots willing to take a chance on a smaller but more interesting company. They brought in John Weiss, the food and restaurant analyst from Dean Witter, described by *Forbes* magazine at the time as a "Wall Street star," and hired Manny Goldman from Sanford Bernstein, who *Forbes* described as "the industry's top beverage analyst," and a few other stars.

This wasn't Weisel's first fling with star analysts. Karl Matthies, who had skipped from Hutchinson to follow Weisel to RCSW, was a very highly respected restaurant, hotel, and gaming analyst, largely responsible for Montgomery's reputation in those fields. And Dick Fredericks, who Weisel had hired in 1974 as part of his strategy to diversify RCSW, was an enormously highly regarded financial services analyst.

In 1988, *U.S. Banker*, a trade magazine, wrote an extraordinarily glowing profile on Fredericks and his team, which, it said, had "turned Montgomery Securities into a power in the banking world."[3] Fredericks had developed a reputation for a paper he wrote a few years earlier titled "Darwinian Banking," in which he predicted market forces were about to bring huge turmoil and consolidation in the banking industry. He outlined the cash and balance sheet strengths necessary to survive and warned about the vulnerability of bank loans to Third World countries and a business environment that would decrease corporate borrowing. It all came true. The *U.S. Banker* article noted that he took a strong stance on which banks would succeed or fail, and even those on his list of losers acknowledged his influence on the industry. The article quoted a senior officer of a New York bank, panned by Fredericks, who said he was surprised to find that one of his biggest shareholders always read Fredericks' reports. The shareholder explained that whenever he visited a bank, he noticed that Fredericks' reports were invariably on the CEO's desk.

In 1984, an article in *The Wall Street Journal* noted the quality and bold stance of all Montgomery's research. From June 1982 to the end of 1984, Montgomery's 35 favorite stock picks increased in value by 124 percent, according to the *Journal,* while the Standard & Poor's 500 was up just 60 percent in that time. In 1984, 5 of Montgomery's 21 analysts were named to *Institutional Investor* magazine's All-America research team.

Clients like Steve Wynn were not surprised. "Thommy has been a terrific picker of people," says the blunt-speaking Vegas tycoon. "He has the rare ability to spot others who are good at what they do, and convincing them to join him. If you think that's coincidence, you have to get your eyes checked."

Investors were impressed. Peter Lynch, the famed one-time head of the Magellan Funds, now vice chairman of Fidelity Management & Research, has also known Weisel and his team for decades, starting with some of the original Hutchinson analysts such as Karl Matthies and John Gruber. "You deal with people at a firm," says Lynch, "and the people I dealt with at Montgomery were always first-class."

In order to fill the role that Robertson once played—underwriting the issuance of new stocks—Weisel hired Alan Stein, a partner at Goldman Sachs (and also California's secretary of business and transportation under Governor Jerry Brown), to handle the company's corporate finance business. Stein played an enormous role in beefing up Montgomery's investment banking business, including underwriting stocks and advising companies on mergers and acquisitions.

And finally, Weisel entered the venture capital business. Montgomery managed VC funds that totaled nearly $100 million on behalf of investors such as Prudential, CIGNA, Westinghouse, and General Electric.

In April 1982, Montgomery had 18 partners out of an overall staff of about 130 people. By the end of 1983, there were 25 partners and a staff of about 260. The salaries and bonuses rivaled those of the largest Wall Street firms. In late 1983, the average institutional salesman at Montgomery was earning an astounding $200,000, while the top partners were taking in over $1 million apiece every year. In 1983, Weisel moved the company to lush new offices in the Transamerica Pyramid.

They earned their pay. In 1983, the company's revenues had risen to $61 million, a sixfold increase in five years. The firm underwrote just 4 to 6 IPOs per year until 1983, when, under the guidance of Stein, the number jumped to 12. But more importantly, the amount of money it raised for companies doubled twice in that period: from $76 million in 1980, to $141 million in 1982, to $296 million in 1983. The mid-1980s were tough for all firms as the technology industry went into recession, but by the end of the decade, Montgomery's own revenues had grown to nearly $100 million.

It still took Montgomery a while to make a strong name for

itself in underwriting stocks. The 1984 *Wall Street Journal* article said that the Four Horsemen had a reputation for bringing higher-quality companies public than Montgomery did. *Fortune* magazine ranked Montgomery last in performance for companies brought public on the New York Stock Exchange in 1983.

That may have been due to the fact that, as a latecomer, Montgomery still had trouble getting the best deals. Its benefit was that it was more aggressive and willing to help put through the tough deals that others shied away from. To be fair, Montgomery's major technology and biotech IPOs in the first half of the 1980s—including Amgen, Integrated Device Technology, Lyphomed, Micron, and a network equipment company called Timeplex—didn't seem like blockbusters at the time Montgomery took them public, but they became so later. Amgen became one of the largest biotechnology companies, while IDT and Micron are two of the largest chip companies in the United States. Today, Micron is the second-largest memory chip company in the world, which Weisel attributes to his analysts' abilities to find the jewels hidden among the coal.

Either way, the expansion was a turning point for Montgomery. The quality of the people Weisel brought in helped to boost the firm's standing and eventually helped turn it into one of the most influential investment banks outside of Wall Street. Alan Stein, the talented banker from Goldman—one of the largest investment banks in the world and one of the biggest underwriters of technology stocks—started putting Montgomery on the Silicon Valley map. In 1985, Montgomery raised $1.5 billion for companies by underwriting their stock offerings, up 200 percent from 1984.

Weisel also worked on increasing the firm's ability to lure IPO clients by making his own connections with the venture capital community. One of the first was Dick Kramlich, the founder of New Enterprise Associates. Kramlich had grown up in Milwaukee and had known Weisel when they were young. They ran into each other one day in the early 1970s, standing in line for a movie. Weisel struck up a conversation and renewed the relationship.

After Robertson left to start his own firm, he asked Kramlich to join a consortium of venture capitalists acting as an advisory committee for his firm, and Kramlich agreed. But he called up Weisel to let him know it was happening, so he wouldn't be taken by surprise. "He told me exactly how he felt about that!" says Kramlich. Still, he says, "I kept a lot of integrity with Thom, because I always told him the truth."

New Enterprise Associates eventually went on to do business with Montgomery as the firm built up its technology practice, especially after Robertson's advisory committee disbanded a few years later. Eventually, Kramlich's daughter even worked at Montgomery as the company's liaison to the venture community. And much later, when Weisel was starting Thomas Weisel Partners, he asked Kramlich and other VCs to invest. The VC firms and partners had always been reluctant to invest in any of the young San Francisco bucks who played such a key role in the money cycle of Silicon Valley, not wishing to appear to play favorites. This time, with the other local banks swallowed up by the bigger fish, there was no conflict, and Kramlich became an investor. Besides, he adds: "My wife said, 'Dick, if you're going to invest in anybody, invest in Thom.'"

Weisel also worked on improving his relationship with some of the venture capitalists that Robertson had introduced to the firm. One was Kip Hagopian at Brentwood Associates, the VC firm that raised a new fund in 1978 with the help of Weisel and Robertson. "At that time I didn't know Thom very well at all," says Hagopian. "But I developed enormous respect for Thom after working with him and talking to others." One money manager at J.P. Morgan told Hagopian he thought Thom was "the best institutional sales guy in the country. I was very impressed by that. This guy doesn't give out compliments very easily."

By the mid-1980s, IPOs accounted for 25 percent of Montgomery's investment banking revenues. The firm still wasn't as strong in tech IPOs (or other stock underwritings) as the competition. But its diversified strategy and strong institutional brokerage business suddenly became an advantage as the market shifted. With the Japanese onslaught hurting some tech companies, tech stocks became depressed and the number of IPOs bottomed out. While Hambrecht and Robertson suffered from their focus on technology, Montgomery's other businesses lessened the impact of the tech recession.

A 1985 article in the *San Francisco Chronicle*[4] said that the Four Horsemen had lost share to Morgan Stanley and Goldman Sachs, as both increased their technology business, and that the prestige specialty firms in San Francisco were now the "Big Two"—Montgomery and H&Q. In November 1985, *Time* magazine described Montgomery as "among the top 20 U.S. investment companies" and noted that it did more business than any other firm outside Wall Street.

Of course, the press sometimes has a bad memory about these things. Soon, papers and magazines were describing Montgomery as one of the original Four Horsemen, apparently forgetting that L.F. Rothschild ever played a significant role in technology start-ups. And if Robertson was weaker in 1985, as the *Chronicle* reported, it recovered quickly along with a revitalized tech market.

Soon, the new acronym was HARM, for Hambrecht, Alex.Brown, Robertson, and Montgomery. In the first half of the 1980s, the HARM companies led slightly more than 5 percent of the nation's stock underwritings, accounting for more than 3 percent of the money raised ($2.7 billion out of $81.6 billion total). Hambrecht and Alex.Brown were by far the HARM leaders, involved in a total of 147 and 140 offerings, respectively (including deals they did not lead), compared to Montgomery's 77 and Robertson's 72. The fame of the HARM companies lasted to the end of the century.

Certainly, bringing in a higher caliber of executive made a huge difference in Montgomery's rise. Still, aside from hiring the most prestigious people he could find, Weisel also continued his unusual strategy of hiring some of the world's best athletes and turning them into bankers. And some of them were surprisingly successful.

The story of Otto Tschudi is a classic example of Weisel's unusual hiring practices and willingness to take chances where others might not. Born in Norway to Swiss parents, Tschudi was a very highly ranked skier and had skied all over Europe. He skied for Norway in the World Cup as well as in two Olympics, in 1968 and 1972. After the 1972 Olympics he turned pro and made a pretty good living. He was rated as one of the top 15 slalom skiers in the world, and one of the top five in World Class Skiing.

During the Christmas holiday in 1974, Tschudi stayed, as usual, at his condo in Sun Valley, Idaho. One morning, as he was sitting outside his condo filing his skis, he noticed, out of the corner of his eye, someone watching him. The guy seemed very interested in what Otto was doing.

In a few minutes, the man walked up to Tschudi and introduced himself as Thom Weisel. He had a question for Tschudi: "Why are you holding the file that way?"

That's typical for Weisel. When he's interested in something, he wants to know as much about the topic as possible. If he sees something new, even as simple as a different method of filing skis, he has to find out about it.

With that introduction, the two became friends. Weisel told Tschudi to call him when he had the opportunity to come to San Francisco, which he did. They would go out to lunch at

Sam's, a popular San Francisco restaurant in the financial district, or run track together. Tschudi had absolutely no clue at that time what it was that Weisel did for a living.

But the elite group of world-class skiers is a small one, and Thom Weisel was becoming part of that circle. The amount of time he spent at his own condo in Sun Valley helped. It turned out that Tschudi also knew Will Weinstein, as well as Boone Lennon, the ski instructor Weisel had first hired to teach him to ski race.

When Tschudi finally retired from professional skiing in 1980, he had to search to find a new career. He got a real estate license, then tried marketing for a while, but was not satisfied. In 1983 he decided to call his friend Will Weinstein, who had now gone to work at Weisel's company, for advice. Weinstein returned his call the next day and invited him to come check out Montgomery. Several days later, Tschudi was on a plane for San Francisco.

Tschudi didn't seem the banker type. He had long hair and a goatee (ski friends had dubbed him "the fastest goatee in the West"). But he met with some of the Montgomery people and talked with Weinstein and Weisel. They decided to hire him, even though Tschudi himself was not sure why or what they wanted him to do. "They just said, 'Why don't you just try and figure it out?'" recalls Tschudi. He was employee number 131 at Montgomery, representing the start of Montgomery's massive buildup.

Tschudi still knew nothing about the brokerage or investment banking business. He went through training, took the Series 7 exam, and wandered around from department to department at Montgomery in order to find a place for himself.

What Tschudi found was that Montgomery as yet had no real presence or contacts in Europe, while its San Francisco competitors, Hambrecht & Quist and Robertson Stephens, already had offices there. Weisel's strategy was to keep everyone in a single building in order to foster good communication from his experts in different fields. Being European himself, Tschudi came upon the idea of helping the company start making contacts in Europe. His main qualification: He spoke Norwegian, Swedish, Danish, French, German, Italian, and English.

For the next 17 years, Tschudi would get up at his San Francisco home at 3:30 in the morning in order to compensate for the nine-hour time difference in Europe, arrive at Montgomery's offices, turn on the lights, and start making calls. In the beginning, he just made cold calls to potential institutional investors in Europe, trying to drum up some buyers and sellers. It took more than a year for him to start getting any significant business for the firm. Today, Tschudi runs the European operations for Thomas Weisel Partners from London.

Can an Olympic athlete really learn the business? Surprisingly, yes. In fact, one of Montgomery's most interesting successes in the early 1980s, when the company was still struggling to bring in the underwriting business, was brought in by Montgomery jocks.

Micron Technology was a Boise, Idaho, manufacturer of memory chips. With all these Montgomery bankers passing through Boise on their way to and from Sun Valley, it may have been inevitable that one of them would discover Micron.

Clark Gerhardt ended up being that person. Some of Weisel's friends had gone mountain climbing with Gerhardt in Nepal, and were so impressed with his personality and stamina they introduced him to Weisel. "They liked him so much they told me, 'You've got to interview this guy,'" says Weisel. "I hired him on the spot, and he was a partner for 15 years."

Gerhardt traveled through Boise frequently in order to visit his girlfriend, who lived in Sun Valley and produced her own brand of ski clothes. He started noticing, as he flew over Boise, a new office building rising out of the soil that was more famous for producing potatoes than high-tech firms. So one day he rented a car, drove into the parking lot, and asked to speak to the boss.

The boss was Joe Parkinson. Before helping to build Micron Technology, Parkinson had been a tax lawyer. But his brother, Ward Parkinson, was a superb chip designer who worked for other chip firms and probably held more patents than any other chip engineer. The brothers decided to team up and start their own firm. They managed to get an investment from Idaho's wealthiest businessman, J.R. Simplot, who had made his fortune by convincing McDonald's to use him as the exclusive supplier of potatoes for the burger chain's French fries.

Intel had pioneered the memory chips known as DRAMs (for dynamic random access memories), one of the first major semiconductor markets, which has become a huge international market. The chips are used in virtually every electronic device that has a memory, especially in the fast-growing personal computer business.

The problem was that Japan, and later Korea, decided to build their own high-tech industries on the backs of DRAM chips. This was the time of the great fear of the Far East, when American companies were concerned that Japan and other Asian countries would steal the entire semiconductor business from the United States. Aggressive pricing, often subsidized by the governments of the Asian countries, eventually drove virtually all American chip makers—including Intel—out of the DRAM business faster than Taliban soldiers retreating from U.S. ground troops.

Micron, almost alone, was convinced it could compete with Japan Inc. and the other Asian nations known as the "Seven Tigers." Ward Parkinson had come up with designs that were half the size of competing chips from overseas, and therefore cheaper to build and faster (since the electrical signals had less distance to travel across the chip).

Despite the superior design of the chips and the dedicated backing of Simplot, the Parkinsons had trouble raising enough capital to grow their company. Since the best chip companies in the United States couldn't handle the business, few investors had faith in this unusual company started with French fry money. "In general, potential investors didn't just say no," recalls Joe Parkinson. "They said, 'Hell, no!'"

Eventually, though, Parkinson managed to secure a $7.5 million loan and the company began building its own headquarters, enabling it to move out of its first office in the basement of a dental center and attracting the attention of Gerhardt.

Joe Parkinson (who is a pretty good skier himself) hit it off with Gerhardt and started showing him the design and capabilities of the chips they were just starting to build. Gerhardt liked what he saw. He called Weisel and told him, "You've got to come to Boise and see this company!"

When Weisel arrived in 1983 to check out Micron, it was too young for any investment banking business, which usually only gets involved in companies when they're close to going public. In those days, institutional investors preferred to buy equity in companies with a track record and at least a plan to generate profits in the foreseeable future.

Weisel got the pitch from Joe Parkinson and was impressed with the technology and amazed to see that the company had actually started making chips already. He decided on the spot to invest $1 million in Micron.

It was the start of a friendship and business relationship that would last decades. Montgomery later started finding institutional investors to take a chance on the upstart. Says Parkinson, "Thom Weisel has raised just about every dime for me that I've ever raised for my companies, in any incarnation."

The chips turned out to be a huge hit—at times. With demand fluctuating in the PC business like a sine wave, and with foreign chip makers dropping prices dramatically every time demand waned, Micron went through periods of prosperity and near bankruptcy. Every time Micron produced a new generation of chips, the performance was so superior to anything else on the market that sales boomed. But eventually, Japan Inc. would manage to produce a new generation of chips so inexpensively that Micron had trouble making money. In the mid-1980s, the U.S. government decided that foreign companies were dumping chips on the U.S. market, selling them below cost with government subsidies in order to drive American companies out of business. It levied heavy fines on Japanese chip makers, eventually helping U.S. companies to become more competitive, although the strategy ticked off some of the PC and software makers.

In July 1984, Micron was ready to go public. Joe Parkinson wanted Montgomery to help manage the deal. But Montgomery was still a small West Coast "boutique," and Weisel felt Micron needed a major firm to help it float its IPO. Recalls

Parkinson: "He told me, 'Joe, you've got to get a big-name underwriter.'"

Parkinson responded, "I want you in on the deal. How about if you co-manage the offering with a big New York firm?"

But Weisel knew that the East Coast banks still regarded Montgomery as a second-string player. He told Parkinson, "Joe, they won't have us. They won't even let us be on the paper with them."

Parkinson insisted: "Either you're in on the deal or we don't do it."

Parkinson began talking to the large investment banks, such as Goldman Sachs, Merrill Lynch, Lehman Brothers, and Morgan Stanley. They were interested in Micron's business, but, as Weisel predicted, not in letting Montgomery in on the deal. For some reason, they seemed to think Montgomery was full of hip-shooters, hot dogs, and unreliable opportunists. The big East Coast firms, however, promised professionalism and pledged that they would stick with Micron through thick and thin, recalls Parkinson.

Finally, Morgan Stanley called Montgomery and broke the ice with Weisel, and agreed to let Montgomery in on the IPO. Possibly it was because Jack Wadsworth was the Morgan Stanley banker who would handle the Micron IPO, and he was more down to earth and practical. The company went public in the summer of 1984, raising $29 million.

Within two more years, however, DRAM pricing was again so tough that Micron was in danger of running out of cash. It needed to raise more money fast. The company had a $40 million line of credit with a bank, but had already tapped about $30 million of it. So Montgomery raised enough money for Micron to pay off the loan with a convertible offering, essentially a loan that could be converted into stock later at a predetermined price. The plan was to pay off the bank loan so that Micron would have its full line of credit back, available to tap as needed.

Then disaster struck. The bank decided that it could no longer risk a loan of that size with a company that had a questionable future, and it called the loan. Micron had to pay it off, and the line of credit was canceled. It had no line of credit to tap into and no cash. "It put us in a deep hole," says Parkinson.

It was the Christmas holiday, and Weisel had one of his usual holiday dinner parties at his condo in Sun Valley. Parkinson and Wadsworth were both there, and they began discussing ways to raise more money. They came up with the idea of going to Europe in order to find new investors. They could do a convertible offering that wouldn't have to be registered on the U.S. exchanges until exercised. Weisel wasn't sure he could contribute much, since the company still had very little presence in Europe, so Morgan was to handle the offering.

But Morgan Stanley was next to get cold feet. After the holidays, Wadsworth called Parkinson and sheepishly said that this had never happened to him before, but the executive committee had rejected the plan. Not only did it refuse to handle the European offering, but it was dropping Micron as a client altogether. So much for thick and thin. When Wadsworth told Weisel, he was incredulous.

And then Weisel decided. "Well then, we'll just have to do it ourselves." Recalls Parkinson: "Thom said, 'I've got this guy working for me who speaks a lot of languages.'" It turned out to be a former Olympic skier named Otto Tschudi.

So Gerhardt, Tschudi, and Parkinson headed for Europe and began knocking on the doors of institutional investors in

England, France, and Switzerland. "We had hundreds of documents, and were lugging this stuff from door to door," says Parkinson. Gerhardt would make the argument for the company, with Tschudi acting as translator. Parkinson, a Vietnam vet, would offer encouragement every time they approached a new potential investor with the peppy phrase, "Let's tag 'em and bag 'em!"

They showed charts demonstrating that, while DRAM prices were at rock bottom now, it was a cyclical business that always rebounded. They argued for Micron's technical superiority. At the time they made the trip, the stock was trading at around $6 1/2. In order to raise the desperately needed money quickly, they offered notes that could be converted into stock at $4 3/8. Within a few days, they raised about $15 million. Three months later, aided by a weakening dollar that made Micron's chips a cheaper alternative to foreign imports, Micron's stock was back up to about $27.

For years after that, Parkinson was very fond of telling people how Otto Tschudi saved Micron from bankruptcy. In 1988, Weisel promoted Tschudi to partner in the firm.

The Basics of IPOs

Thom W. Weisel

The CEO of any entrepreneurial company is going to be heavily involved in raising financing, both public and private, for many years. There are several issues that a wise entrepreneur should consider before going through this process. By preparing yourself adequately, you'll find the process easier, and you will minimize mistakes and manage the process more smoothly in an uncertain world. Here are some of the important factors you should consider, along with the best advice I can offer.

Before the IPO

- **Raise money before you need it, and raise more than you need.** The cliché is true: Timing is everything. Obviously, it's great when you can raise capital while the market is going up and when the market happens to be valuing your company very highly. But you don't always know when those opportunities are going to come along or how long they will last. Therefore, it is of the utmost importance that you have enough capital to sustain yourself for the downturns in the market. These downturns may be due to real economic factors, or they may be simply due to the psychology of the market, completely beyond your control. Either way, you don't want to have to raise money in a down market.

- **Choose your venture backers wisely.** Your initial investors speak volumes about your quality and the quality of the company you want to have.

- **Get your management team in place.** Before you can even consider a public offering, you need a complete management team that's competent and working well together. Can we believe management when it says profit margins are going to be 85 percent—as they may be for a software company? If the CEO has 25 years' experience in the industry, then investors have a reason to believe that projection.

- **Build a sustainable business model.** Build a broad customer base and recurring revenue stream with sustainable profit margins.

- **Prove you're competitive.** Clearly, the best position to be in is to stake out a large and growing unserved market and demonstrate that your technology or other factors make you the category killer in that market. Also make sure you are well on your way to developing your next generation of product so investors can see continued revenues into the future and an ability to endure a competitive threat. But don't go overboard. You want to grow, but you want to do it in a sustainable way. Do you have the resources to pursue all your products under development, or should you focus on a few now and come back to the rest later? An R&D budget varies a lot by industry and by company. It can be 3 percent of revenues or 15 percent. But 50 percent is generally not sustainable.

- **Think your sales channels through carefully.** You have to show that you can distribute your product on a cost-effective basis. Are there alternative channels to consider? What will be the impact on the bottom line? For example, many software companies are switching from selling a product up front to licensing it over many years. That creates a great backlog, but it can move much of the revenues out several years. If that's going to be the strategy, it's best to do it before the IPO. If you change after that, your revenues—and your stock price—will take a hit.

- **Choose your investment banker early and carefully.** Some executives think that investment banks are only interested in pushing through transactions and charging exorbitant fees with little or no redeeming value. And sometimes they're right. But if an investment banker has the right skill sets, and the trust of the CEO and the board, the banker can be very helpful leading up to the IPO. The better investment bankers are in touch with potential buyers on a daily basis and are a fountain of knowledge about the marketplace that can prove to be invaluable.

What to Look for in an Investment Banker

- **Track record.** Has the bank had success in dealing with your kind of company in the past? How well did it perform for those companies, especially in difficult markets? Do the analysts have credibility in your market space? Do they understand your company, your competition, and your market in general?
- **People.** Who will be responsible for actually dealing with your company during the process? How senior is that person? How is the chemistry between the key people within the organization and between the firm and your company? Will the CEO call you back?
- **Trading and capital market support.** You want to pick a company that will trade your stock on a consistent basis, so that even if you fall on bad times the company will be there backing your company. The capital markets desk needs to provide you a consistent flow of ideas about how you can raise capital as well as what your competition and similar companies are doing.
- **Institutional ownership.** You want a good feeling that the entire firm you are choosing is enthusiastic about your company and your industry.
- **Strategic advisory services.** Down the road you might want to acquire or be acquired. Check out the M&A transactions done in your space by each investment banker you look at.

During the IPO

- **Listen to your banker about timing.** If you've chosen carefully, the investment bank should know what its buy-side clients are thinking. It might suggest considering delaying the IPO until a better time.

- **Consider alternatives.** An acquisition may be better than an IPO, especially if there's a good strategic partner. In some cases, a partner may be willing to pay more than the public market will logically pay over the next couple of years. That was true in the case of Baja Fresh, a company that filed for an IPO with TWP as a co-manager. The IPO would have given the company a market valuation of about $200 million, but Wendy's was willing to pay $275 million for the franchise. The board decided to go for the strategic sale.

- **Listen to your banker about pricing.** Pricing an IPO is a difficult task. All company CEOs think their stock is undervalued and their fundamentals are underappreciated, whether seeking public or private financing. But you have to be reasonable. We dealt with a company recently that was seeking private financing, but the CEO got greedy and wanted a ridiculous valuation—$2 billion for a company that didn't even have a full beta product yet. He never got the transaction done and the company shut down, and now we'll never know if the product worked. Your banker should understand the psychology of the market as well as comparable valuations.

- **Think long term.** The market will set the price, so don't be overly concerned about getting the last nickel. This will be a long game. You want your new shareholders to make money and stay shareholders for a long time.

- **Consider the exit strategy of your private investors.** After 180 days, the private equity owners can sell their stock. That can account for half to two-thirds of the company's ownership, and that can be a crushing event. Some investors are going to be pretty cagey about what they're going to do. They're trying to maximize the value for themselves and their limited partners. It's best to have a coordinated distribution event to minimize this impact. The banker can help straighten this out. It has a direct pipeline into institutional growth buyers and knows when private company investors are looking to place stock coming off a lockup. It can place insiders' stock, minimizing the disruption to the public market.

- **Take the road show seriously.** You have to sell yourself to the people and organizations that will be your first public stock buyers. Afterward, maintain a regular and consistent calling effort with your current and prospective shareholder base. Establishing trust between your company and your investors will prove to be invaluable over time. The IPO is not the end of the journey; it's just the beginning.

- **Look at the overall reputation of the firm.** If you are an emerging growth company with less than a $2 billion market cap, be sure to find out what the institutional investors think about the investment bank you're going to use. Do they rate it highly, and if so, for what reason? Do they like the firm's ideas, analysts, portfolio advisors? Do their references check out?

After the IPO (and Sometimes Before)

- **Be conservative in managing expectations.** Embrace conservative revenue recognition policies. Investors need to know that your revenues are real. They want to be comfortable with your current revenues and projections. Smart managers never overestimate their earnings. The quickest way to kill a company is to put overly aggressive estimates out in the marketplace and then not meet them. Once that happens, it's difficult to reestablish your credibility. Trust and relationships are built over years, not quarters. Microsoft, for example, goes out of its way to be conservative in its projections, because it's better to beat the Street's expectations than to fall short. Tell it like it is, but be conservative.

A company doesn't necessarily have to have all these attributes or do all these things in order to be successful, but a majority of them must be present. A good investment bank can help a company develop these attributes. Choosing an investment bank early and using it as a resource will help ensure your success.

Skiing, Cycling, Selling Stocks

It's not the size of the dog in the fight, it's the size of the fight in the dog.

—*Mark Twain*

As the 1980s advanced, Weisel's expansion of the firm, with the help of Will Weinstein and Alan Stein, began to pay off, although still at a moderate pace. Technology stocks grew in number and price. American companies managed to gain an overpowering lead in biotechnology, software, communications technology, microprocessors, and personal computers, although the threat from Japan in memory chips intensified and industry executives and politicians worried that Japan might be slowly taking over the technology scene.

Montgomery started getting the hang of this stock underwriting thing. Weisel's aggressiveness and personal involvement finally started edging the company deeper into the technology business and established strong relationships with many of Silicon Valley's venture capitalists.

Because of the recession, especially in technology, in the latter half of the 1980s, the number of companies issuing new stock actually declined a little compared with the first half. But

Montgomery was moving up the underwriting scale, although Alex.Brown charged prominently to the front. From 1985 through 1989, Alex.Brown handled 204 underwritings, with Montgomery in second place among the HARMs with 83. Hambrecht dropped to third place with 71, and Robertson followed with 69. Together, the HARM companies increased their market share of all transactions to nearly 17 percent, accounting for almost 12 percent of the money raised ($111 billion). Among all investment banks, Alex.Brown had become a powerhouse, now fifth-largest in the country in terms of number of transactions. The other three were bunched together, with Montgomery at 17, Hambrecht at 18, and Robertson tied for 19th place with Shearson Lehman Hutton.

In the latter half of the 1980s, Montgomery helped raise capital for biotechnology companies such as Chiron, Genzyme, Gensia Pharmaceuticals, Liposome Technology, and IKOS Systems. Underwritings for technology companies included Chips & Technologies, Pyramid Technology, Teradata, Maxim Integrated Products, and Conner Peripherals. It's an impressive group of companies.

Of course, there are always a few mistakes. In May 1989, Montgomery joined Morgan Stanley in a $70 million convertible offering for a computer networking company called Network Equipment Technologies. In November, venture capitalist Don Valentine approached Weisel to see if he wanted to help out on an IPO of another network company. But Weisel likes to stay loyal to existing customers and not take on competitors at the same time. He said no and missed out on the IPO of Cisco Systems.

Montgomery managed to get involved in several nontechnology company stock offerings in the latter eighties as well. It managed offerings for Chart House Enterprises, Coca-Cola, Good Guys, Ross Stores, Sierra Spring Water, Sizzler Restaurants International, and Staples. Many were sole or Montgomery-led offerings; some were with big banks like Goldman Sachs, Merrill Lynch, Morgan Stanley, and Paine-Weber.

The company also started developing clout in the financial services business as a stock trader, underwriter, and advisor. It helped underwrite offerings for BANC ONE, the Student Loan Marketing Association (Sallie Mae), and Chemical Bank. Its institutional trading arm pulled off a real coup, though. Investors at a large mutual fund called up Bobby Kahan, who ran Montgomery's trading floor, and asked if Montgomery could buy 3 million shares of BankAmerica stock at close to the market price. Kahan said he would call right back. He scrambled his traders to hit the phones as a seller of BofA. In 11 minutes, they found buyers willing to pay $42 apiece for the 3 million shares. The stock was publicly trading at $42 1/4 at that moment. The transaction was made—the largest block of BofA stock ever sold.

Montgomery's financial advisory business took a bold step or two. In 1987, Montgomery stunned the banking industry with its audacity by convincing, and then helping, First Interstate Bank to launch a $3.1 billion hostile takeover bid for BankAmerica. Normally, First Interstate would have used Goldman Sachs as adviser on such a big trade, but Montgomery had come up with the idea, and Goldman reportedly didn't like doing hostile deals. BofA managed to fend off the attack, but just the fact that Montgomery, which had revenues of about $80 million, could orchestrate and lead such an ambitious plan indicated, in the words of one New York investment banker, that Montgomery's "corporate finance arm has come of age."[1] The irony of Montgomery helping with an attempted takeover of BofA would not be realized for another decade.

The 1980s were not a smooth ride to the top, however, either for Montgomery or the technology industries. Chip makers and manufacturers of related products went through boom and bust cycles of alternating shortages and gluts of chips. Computer makers had their own ups and downs. Steve Jobs was kicked out of Apple Computer in 1985 after trying to stage a coup against the CEO he had personally brought in, John Sculley. The stock market crash in October 1987 didn't help much either.

Montgomery was playing in the big pond now, with enough diversification to smooth out the wakes to some degree, but it wasn't one of the big fish yet. It still couldn't participate in some of the really big, highly leveraged deals that were making Wall Street executives rich. It didn't have the capital or debt products to offer—the same problem it had run into when trying to help Steve Wynn finance his casino in Atlantic City back in 1978.

And, finally, the adolescent firm started showing a few growing pains. Hiring star players for a small and intimate team also has its consequences. Sometimes stars are also temperamental, and Weisel has always had a penchant for particularly forceful personalities. Already an aggressive, competitive jock-filled environment, after a new top tier of Wall Street megabucks superstars were added, Montgomery could get as heated as a fast-food deep fryer. Will Weinstein, himself very vocal and confrontational, was one of them. But, says Weisel: "This guy was scary smart, as good as it gets in the business. He's one of the great talents, the geniuses of the business." And, adds Weisel, "He and I never had any problem" getting along together.

Weinstein's style was part of the reason he finally left Montgomery in 1986. He went off to manage investments for the Pritzker family, one of America's wealthiest families and owners of the Hyatt hotel chain.

But Weisel found a new player, just as brilliant and just as mercurial as Weinstein: Jerry Markowitz, from L.F. Rothschild (which went out of business in 1988). Markowitz, who happened to be one of Weinstein's oldest and dearest friends, took charge of the over-the-counter (or the Nasdaq) trading desk and worked closely with Bobby Kahan at Montgomery. A Harvard Business School case study described the tough environment on the trading floor at Montgomery Securities in the 1980s:

> On bad days chief trader Jerry Markowitz, who was described as charming out of the office, had been known to "take a phone and slam it down so hard it shatters. That kind of thing happens all over Wall Street," recalled a trader, "but it seems to happen a lot more at Montgomery."[2]

Markowitz acknowledges his aggressive approach, but feels it was necessary in order to get the trading desk to compete on a par with the New York banks. "All good traders are intense and aggressive," says Markowitz. "This is a very manic-depressive business, and it takes a lot of energy to do it. Bobby Kahan and I introduced that culture at Montgomery. We're talking, yelling, joking; it's the same in any New York firm."

Besides, Weisel notes, they "introduced a level of customer ser vice that we didn't have before they got here." Kahan and Mar-kowitz made sure every salesperson was constantly in touch with clients, ensuring that when they wanted to buy or sell stocks within Montgomery's target markets, the salespeople were ready, even if it meant putting some of Montgomery's cash on the line. Kahan and Markowitz "went absolutely berserk if another firm put up a big-block trade in a firm in which we were the dominant player," says Weisel. And they got the job done.

Weisel knew that some of his stars also caused problems. "Mar-kowitz was an 'in your face' manager when he was running the OTC trading desk. But the minute he moved into another role at the firm he totally changed his approach. He turned out to be a phenomenal leader."

As the bank got bigger, Markowitz took on new duties, including overseeing capital markets and Montgomery Asset Management, as well as starting new businesses, including a prime brokerage business. Eventually, in the mid-1990s, he gave up his duties on the trading desk altogether to run the day-to-day operations of the firm. "Thom was the boss, the leader," says Markowitz. "He set the strategy, but I took some of the burden off his back."

Weisel, who has been known to raise his own voice on occasion, does not appear to have any hiring filter against difficult personalities. He's interested in talent, aggressiveness, and professional honesty, and that's about it. He even hired one executive from a giant Wall Street firm who was fired after admitting to having a drug problem. Weisel gave him the chance to clean up his act.

That attitude continues today. After Weisel started TWP, he found that an extraordinarily talented, powerful, and well-paid executive at a large New York firm had become available. This man had stepped down from the firm after his temper and some issues regarding his personal life had become widely publicized. Just as movie studios may avoid using a star who is known to be temperamental and gets caught in a scandal, many investment firms would be reluctant to hire someone in that situation.

Weisel made the executive a partner. "He had some personal problems, which came out in the workplace," says Weisel. "I'm a big believer that people can make mistakes, as long as they correct the problems. You take a risk, and sometimes you win. People change. I brought quite a cast of characters into Montgomery, and I'm sure people outside the firm thought I was crazy. But not only did they work out, they did phenomenally well. I've been nothing but surprised at the results when quality people are given another chance."

Weinstein's departure even had one benefit: The Pritzker family became the first outside investors in Montgomery, buying a 12 percent stake of the firm in 1986 for around $12 million, giving the firm roughly a $100 million valuation. Montgomery also set

up a convertible arbitrage fund for the family, making investments on behalf of the Pritzkers.

Convertible arbitrage is a fairly sophisticated hedging technique: The arbitrageur buys bonds or preferred stock in a company that can be converted into common stock at a later date
(with luck, at a higher price). But just in case, the trader also buys
a short position in that company's stock. If the stock goes up, the
convertible stock makes a profit while the short position takes a
loss. If the stock goes down, the opposite is true. Successful convertible arbitrage requires the investor to buy the right balance of
each type of investment, so that the losses are more than offset by
the gains—or, at least, if there is a net loss, it's minimized by the
profitable part of the transaction.

However, the deal ended up being a mistake for everyone. The
trader Weisel hired to make the investments turned out to talk a
good game but to lack the necessary skills to handle the deals. It
was one of the times when Weisel's people judgment failed him.
Says Weisel: "We made a mistake on that guy. Several months
later, the guy had lost an incredible amount of money."

In the spring of 1987, Weisel decided to shut down the fund
and return the Pritzkers' money. But Montgomery only had about
$20 million in total available capital, and paying back the Pritz-
kers would take half of it. Weisel called Tom Pritzker and told him
he would make the family whole again, but he needed a little time.

"Talk about crisis periods!" says Weisel. "Who knows what the
Pritzkers could have done to us? But they were really quality people. They just said, 'Sure, we'll work with you.'"

It took nearly three years to pay them back. The Pritzkers
remained an investor in Montgomery for a decade.

The screwy economy in the 1980s was tough on small investment banks, but Montgomery dealt with it by being just as tough.
Brentwood Partner Kip Hagopian used Montgomery to handle

the IPOs of about a dozen of his firm's portfolio companies. "I was always impressed with how competitive and tenacious Thom is," says Hagopian. "If he committed to something, you could pretty much put it in the bank. Almost anybody can get a deal done in a good market. But when the market turns on you, you want somebody you can count on."

An example of that was the public offering of Maxim Integrated Products, a Brentwood-funded semiconductor company that was ready to go public in October 1987, just as the stock market crashed. Virtually all IPOs were then called off for several months. Goldman was supposed to be the lead bank, with Montgomery in the number two position. By January 1988, Maxim's CEO, Jack Gifford, decided the market had recovered enough to do the offering, although at about half the original price. Goldman said it couldn't get the deal done in the current environment.

Hagopian recalls Gifford and Weisel, two men of very like minds, sitting down in a meeting to figure out what to do. "It was so funny to listen to Jack and Thom. They just said, 'Forget it, let's go without them.'" The offering succeeded, and Maxim never had to raise money again. Although Maxim hasn't become a household name like Intel (analog circuits just aren't as sexy as microprocessors), in 2001 *Forbes* magazine called Maxim, which now has a market cap of about $10 billion, "the most successful semiconductor company you've never heard of."[3] It has been one of the best-performing technology stocks since its founding. Hagopian now considers Weisel to be one of his closest friends.

Weisel is also famous for working right alongside his sales team to make sure deals are done, and he personally made sure his VC friends were happy. Hagopian recalls one time that his firm had picked Montgomery as the lead bank to take a biotech firm public. They were having trouble getting enough commitments from institutional investors, so Hagopian called Weisel to see what the problem was. Weisel gathered his entire team together and told them to assume they had to find all the investors themselves, as though there were no secondary firm to help out. Then Weisel started calling investors himself in order to help put the deal over the top.

"All the partners in our firm were enormously impressed with that," says Hagopian. "He didn't just direct his sales team; he jumped into the fray personally. I don't know how he gets everything done. There must be three of him. Thom Weisel is a guy who really doesn't understand why they put doorknobs on doors. He just kicks them in."

Another Brentwood company that Montgomery helped take public was Teradata, which was creating an extremely powerful database system. The company originally thought it would take $10 million to get its system built. It took around $40 million. Weisel decided the company was promising enough to stick with it, got personally involved in helping Teradata raise its private funding, and then helped take it public in 1987 as the co-lead manager along with Salomon Brothers. "Salomon did a good job," says Hagopian, "but I really looked more to Montgomery to get the job done."

Four years later, NCR bought Teradata for $520 million in stock and began transforming itself from a hardware company to software. Today, Teradata is considered the fastest database on the market, outperforming both Oracle and IBM's DB2.

Montgomery's conference business, which was started back in 1971, also became a powerful force in the 1980s, with influence way beyond what would be expected of a company its size. There were other popular conferences; H&Q held a famed life sciences conference every January, and Robertson had its own tech conferences that drew elite audiences. But two things set Montgomery's investment conferences apart. "All three conferences were terrific," says New Enterprise Associates partner Dick Kramlich. "Montgomery's conference was notable because it attracted a lot more institutional investors, and it had fantastic entertainment."

The conferences are designed to show off impressive growth companies that the investment bank either does business with or would like to, under the wandering eyes of money managers looking for new companies to get in bed with. Most conferences start by first gathering the best group of entrepreneurs they can, often through their VC contacts. If it looks like an impressive roster and is at a convenient time of year, it can attract many of the country's top money managers.

Montgomery worked the other way around. Since its big asset has always been its tight relations with the money managers, Weisel did everything he could to first bring in an impressive array of investors. With investors representing billions of dollars, entrepreneurs flocked to get into the invitation-only conference. In general, about half the companies that showed up were not yet Montgomery clients.

Weisel also took some of the more select individuals to special dinners and other events in the Napa Valley, in order to both flatter them and keep them away from other investment bankers. "All our competitors saw how many money managers and companies were coming into town for our conference, and they started pecking away at them," he says.

Since money managers tend to be very wealthy themselves, Weisel made sure to spend freely and entertain lavishly. These were always high-class events, held at San Francisco's fanciest hotels such as the Fairmont, the Mark Hopkins, and the St. Francis. Then in the late 1980s the Ritz-Carlton underwent a major renovation, and the conference settled there. Plush venues, the best food and booze, and red carpet treatment kept the money managers coming back. And while there, they even paid attention to some of the companies making presentations.

Joe Parkinson, the former CEO of Micron Technology, a chip

company that Weisel took public, thought Weisel did a brilliant job on the conferences. "What impressed me after we went public were those annual conferences," Parkinson says. "At every conference I went to, Thom always hosted me in a private room to meet new [investors]. And they really wanted to understand the business."

Fidelity's Peter Lynch was also impressed with the Montgomery conferences. "You don't have to do any homework," says Lynch, who has a reputation as one of the most well-prepared investors in the world. "The research is excellent. You could see 10 or 12 companies a day. There was always something there to chew on."

The entertainment had two purposes: It gave the money managers a reason to attend this conference rather than someone else's as the field became overly crowded, and it gave the money folks a reason to stay at the conference rather than allowing Montgomery's competitors to draw them off to dinner or other events. By the late 1980s and into the 1990s it was attracting talent such as Kenny Loggins, Earth, Wind & Fire, Bill Cosby, Bruce Hornsby, and Huey Lewis and the News. One year Chuck Berry headlined a group of performers for a 1950s revival.

An article in *Forbes* magazine in December 1983 described the scene at one of the conferences. Art Buchwald was the dinner speaker (collecting his usual $15,000 fee). He got up to the dais and said, "Who the hell is Montgomery Securities?" The article went on to say that although Montgomery was "just about unknown to the general public," it was "almost a household name on Wall Street." The conference drew 400 of the country's top money managers, who together controlled half a trillion dollars in assets. *Forbes* said that the Montgomery conference was the "place to see and be seen."

Press reports kept track of the growing size and influence of the Montgomery conference. In 1993, the conference drew 1,500 attendees, 400 of them institutional investors controlling over $1 trillion, plus Bruce Hornsby for entertainment and a stack of Saks

Fifth Avenue beauticians providing services for the women attendees. This time, a 1994 *Forbes* article described the conferences as "successor in many ways to the late Drexel Burnham's once famous Predators' Ball."[4] In 1997, *Institutional Investor* magazine called it "arguably the world's premier growth stock conference."[5]

With that kind of clout, company presentations at the conference could move the stock price of the presenting companies. The 1994 *Forbes* article noted that after Texas Instruments Chairman Mark Shepherd Jr. spoke at a Montgomery conference, TI's stock dropped 8 percent in the following week. His presentation was apparently not as encouraging as he had hoped, possibly because he refused to answer some questions the investors thought important. But two years later, a *Wall Street Journal* article asserted that a good presentation at a Montgomery conference could make a company's stock jump by 10 percent. And *Institutional Investor's* 1997 article noted that three days after a presentation by one company, that company's stock jumped 19 percent. It also noted that by the end of the conference, the total market value of the 233 companies presenting collectively increased by about $5 billion.

Weisel continues his tradition of having conferences at his new company, although he has fewer, partly because Wall Street firms created a conference glut during the 1990s. He describes the success of his conferences this way: "Everybody's got conferences now. You go to any one of a dozen conferences and you'll find the same companies are there with the same slide show presentation. How do you bring clients in and give them a very rich experience? We've tried to create conferences that have topical investment issues. We bring in executives to discuss the issues challenging their industries, and challenges investors will face with those stocks. And we've tried to keep this small. If over a couple thousand people attend, the interaction between corporations and money managers isn't as rich. You also end up with too many people who don't belong there.

"These days, we also try to make our conferences family-oriented. People don't get to see their families enough, so they can bring their kids with them and find things there for them to do. We're constantly trying to reinvent ourselves."

Reinvention is the mother of success in any business. By 1989 Montgomery ranked 19th in equity underwriting among investment banks in the United States. Its revenues grew about an order of magnitude in that decade, to about $100 million. But the company's best—and final—decade was about to begin.

Considering all that was happening in the eighties—as technology companies seemed to alternate between taking over the U.S. economy and falling into recession, as giant Wall Street firms began increasing their competitive threat in the West, and as Weisel struggled to expand his firm and shift it to a high-growth track—one might think he would slow down on some of his extracurricular activities. One would be wrong.

As far as the U.S. Ski Team was concerned, Weisel was just getting started. Warren Hellman retired as chairman of the team in 1982 and was replaced for a very short time by Ed Hamerlie, a man Weisel describes as a spendthrift who lacked leadership skills. After Hamerlie had been on the job for just a year, ski team board member John McMillan invited Weisel to visit him at his office in Salt Lake City.

"Thom," he said, "we want to kick out Hamerlie. You're the board's choice to take over as chairman."

"I'm busy running my own company," said Weisel. "Why would I want to do this?"

But McMillan talked him into it. "I had to think long and hard about it, but John is an outstanding individual, and he leaned on me pretty hard," says Weisel. The next step was a board meeting in New York, in which Hamerlie was told he was being fired and replaced with Weisel. "It was an unbelievably rancorous meeting," says Weisel. "It was one of the most difficult sessions I've ever been in."

The ski team did well in the 1984 Olympics, with five medals, its best performance ever. But Weisel took over just as things got really tough. After 1984, several of the team's best athletes retired, and there were few rising stars to replace them. In 1986, both the head coach and executive director resigned. As a result, funding also dried up. Nobody likes donating money to a mediocre team.

"We were in a crisis management mode," says Chuck Ferries, who took over as executive director through the summer. "It came down to, 'How are we going to keep this thing afloat?'"

Ferries, a former Olympic skier and businessman who founded Pre Skis and was president of Scott USA (which bought and revitalized Schwinn Bicycles, among other things), joined with Weisel in bailing out the ski team budget by guaranteeing some loans.

But that wasn't enough for a man who treats all his ventures as he does a ski trip down a remote mountain in fresh powder—jumping in with both feet and powering ahead as fast as possible. "Thom always saw the bigger picture," says Ferries. "He wasn't content with the Ski Balls the way they were, and was never content with the organization the way it was."

Weisel decided it was time to completely reorganize the whole business. The problem was that the U.S. Ski Team only competed in international events, such as the World Cup and the Olympics, with no involvement with up-and-coming skiers competing in domestic programs. Domestic ski competitions were handled by the national governing body of an organization called U.S. Ski Association, or USSA. That split fundraising efforts and meant that the U.S. Ski Team had no influence or responsibility for training domestic competitors who would go on to become Olympic athletes.

Weisel was certain that a merger was called for. Many people agreed with him. "The organization needed to be professionally managed from top to bottom," says Ferries. "Thom was one of the first to see that, and made it happen."

But there was a slight problem with the idea. The USSA and the U.S. Ski Team had been battling for control and money for decades. The USSA was a volunteer organization, with about 125 board members and the philosophy that everything should be run democratically—which meant getting the board to vote on everything. The U.S. Ski Team, by contrast, had an 8- to 10-member board, most of the members now business executives with a penchant for moving quickly. If the organizations were to merge, the vast majority of the USSA board would have to go. "The operation was awkward and unproductive," admits Jim McCarthy, who was a board member with USSA at the time. "Thom was absolutely, steadfastly opposed to this inefficiency and bureaucracy."

Most of the USSA board members seemed to think this was a bad idea and rejected the whole plan. "There was a huge cultural conflict between the two organizations," says McCarthy. "The USSA side said, 'If we relinquish control to the business guys, they'll run away with the whole thing.'"

In fact, they were right. But that didn't prevent it from happening. Notes Hellman: "When Thom is willing to do something, it happens. You either go with it or you get run over."

To prove his point, Weisel hired Bob Waterman, a McKinsey & Co. consultant and the coauthor of *In Search of Excellence*, to come and analyze the situation. After studying the organization of the U.S. Ski Team and its overseas competition, he recommended just what Weisel predicted: Merge the organizations.

Weisel not only argued the business sense of a merger, highlighting the conclusions of his hired gun, he just plain argued. One particularly rancorous meeting in Colorado Springs ended up with a shouting match in the parking lot at 3 A.M., with Weisel screaming at the USSA members: "You're going to blow up the whole sport!" He didn't make a lot of friends in the process. "Those folks will tell you how painful and despicable I am," he says with a laugh.

The arguments went on for several years. Finally, toward the end of the 1980s, Weisel called a meeting in Chicago, inviting sympathetic members of both organizations, ostensibly to discuss plans for cross-country skiing. McCarthy was one of the members of USSA who attended. "It turned out it was a ruse to bring people together to see how we get out of this dilemma we're in," recalls McCarthy. In that meeting, Weisel devised a plan for a "super-board," with members coming from both organizations, about 15 people in all.

This board would be an overseeing body for both groups. It was effectively an interim merger for the two organizations. It put both the domestic and international competitions under one governing body and combined some fund-raising efforts, although the two separate boards would still continue to exist for each organization. To make it more palatable to the USSA folks, Weisel put Howard Peterson, who was running the USSA at the time, in charge of the super-board.

It still took several months and several more meetings for enough people to agree to the plan, but it was finally approved in late 1988. A lot of the people from the USSA side were still not happy with these aggressive businesspeople. "Thom doesn't lack for taking initiative for speaking his side," chuckles McCarthy. "That can be overwhelming and intimidating to some people. One board member always accused him of treating the USSA board members like they were shoe salesman. I told him, 'That's your problem, not Thom's. Thom speaks his mind.'"

Weisel stepped down as chairman in 1994, but remained a member of the super-board. His goal of fully merging the two organizations was finally completed a few years later. The USSA was now involved in Olympic competition, and after the 1994 Olympics, the U.S. Olympic Committee informed the organization that the USSA's huge, complex board was not in compliance with U.S. Olympic Committee rules. That finally forced the organizations' members to complete the merger and drop about 100 people from the USSA board. The merged organization took the name USSA, the name that persists today, although it now stands for the U.S. Ski and Snowboard Association.

Even as he became deeply involved with the ski team, Weisel himself had to give up competitive skiing. By the mid-1980s, his bad knee gave him too much trouble to allow him to continue. His pal Boone Lennon, however, was also fond of a summer sport that Weisel was familiar with, although he hadn't done it competitively since before his failed Olympic bid: cycling. This is the sport that still consumes Weisel today, the one he'll probably remain dedicated to for the rest of his life.

Weisel and Lennon had another friend who liked to both ski and cycle: Steve Johnson, an associate professor of exercise physiology at the University of Utah. In 1983, the trio started the Montgomery cycling team and began racing together.

One of Weisel's first official races on a road bike was sponsored by the Elephant's Perch sports retail store in Sun Valley. It was a figure-eight course, and Lennon would sit at the apex of the course and yell out to Thom which gears to use and when to change them. He wasn't surprised to get dusted this time.

In 1985, the Elephant's Perch sponsored a three-day stage race. Endurance was key, and wind resistance was a killer. Lennon, watching the cyclists sitting atop their seats, hunched over into the wind, thought there must be more they could do to improve aerodynamics. Experienced with the enormous speeds of downhill skiing, Boone knew a lot about wind resistance. He'd seen many wind tunnel tests. He came up with an idea for improving aerodynamics: attaching wooden slats to the handlebars.

Weisel, Boone, and Johnson competed in the race as a team, and Boone offered his wooden slat approach to them. Says Weisel, "I wasn't about to try the damn things. I was sure you'd crash." But Lennon used them, and he won the race. That was the origin of the Aerobar, which gained fame when American Greg LeMond used them to win the 1989 Tour de France by eight seconds. Armstrong uses aerobars, and Boone still collects royalties off the invention. These days his main occupation is running a snowboarding school, using innovative training techniques he invented, which he claims can teach people to snowboard in record time.

But Weisel found, just as he did in 1958, that a speed skater also had the right build for cycling. He decided to get serious this time. His cycling career was also given a boost by the recession of the late 1980s. The investment banking business slowed, and Weisel decided to take the opportunity to put some real effort into his training. "I decided I would try to find out what I missed in 1960," he says.

Of course, that meant he would need another top coach. The

trainer for the U.S. Olympic Cycling Team seemed like a good choice. Ed Burke, the trainer for the U.S. Olympic Cycling Team, was introduced to Thom by Tauger Hagerman, the trainer of the U.S. Olympic Ski Team. Ed Burke in turn introduced Thom to Eddie Borysewicz (known as "Eddie B"), who was the coach for the American cycling team in the 1980 and 1984 Olympics. Ed helped Weisel for several years and continued to be one of the major thought leaders in cycling, writing books on training and sports physiology. Unfortunately, Burke died recently at age 53 while on a training ride in Colorado Springs. "Ed will be sorely missed," says Weisel. "He's the kind of individual who was self-less in his desire to help the sport and individuals."

In 1984, the American cyclists won nine medals, the best the United States had ever done in the sport. So in 1985, Weisel called Borysewicz and offered to hire him as a personal coach. He went to the National Training Camp that Borysewicz ran in Fresno, California, and spent many weekends for three years training with Borysewicz at his different training camps—in addition to working out on his bike every day after work during the week.

The added perk was that he once again got to hang out with Olympic athletes at the peak of their abilities. He even joined in Borysewicz's Olympic training sessions, the old man among a group of hot athletes. There, Weisel met people like gold medalists Mike Gorski and Steve Hegg, and world champion Mike McCarthy (who later went to work for Weisel's investment bank, where he remains today).

The young cyclists warmed to him and helped out with tips and advice, and Weisel listened and learned. Unlike Armstrong, who is a distance road rider, Weisel is a sprinter, and did best in one-day criterium races. In 1987 Weisel competed in his first National Cycling Championship in Houston, Texas, placing third in the kilo for men over 45. Then he really started racking up some impressive wins. In 1989 he was part of a team that won the AT&T Four Man National Championship. That year he also placed fourth in the Master Criterium Nationals in Long Island and won a silver medal in the 1K Nationals in Portland, Oregon, and a gold medal in the World Masters Games in the match sprint and kilo in Finland. He set a national record in the 1K in 1989.

Steve Johnson wasn't doing badly either. In 1989, he was named Masters Athlete of the Year by the U.S. Cycling Federation. In all, Johnson has won two Masters road cycling World Cup championships, eight national road championships, and 16 district road titles.

In 1990 and 1991 Weisel won five gold and two silver medals in national championships, and added another world title in 1991. That year, it was Weisel's turn to be named National Masters Athlete of the Year. It may not be the Olympics, but it was pretty satisfying for a 50-year-old investment banker.

In 1991, Weisel also installed Dr. Johnson as director of sports science for the USSA. Maybe it was to get him off his bike so Weisel wouldn't have so much competition in Masters cycling.

Eight Attributes of a Great Professional Services Organization

Thom W. Weisel

As I have participated within the financial services industry for over three decades, I have crystallized my thoughts, through trial and error, on what it takes to be a success as a professional services organization. I've ended up with a list of eight important attributes. As you'll see, there is quite a bit of overlap. Some of the approaches we take benefit us in several of the categories.

1. Vision

Any successful professional services company has to start with a unique vision and the strategy to make that vision a reality. You have to know where you want to go and how you plan to get there. Without that, you can't attract great talent or clients.

A vision starts with the mission statement. Both my companies, Montgomery Securities and more recently Thomas Weisel Partners, have had the same mission: to be the premiere growth-focused investment bank. We want to be the best firm researching, trading, advising, financing, and investing in the stocks of companies in the growth categories we have targeted. But at Thomas Weisel Partners, we've added a large and important private equity business that we never had at Montgomery.

Your vision should target a large and growing marketplace, but it should be carefully defined. Our marketplace, for example, is roughly $40 billion. We want to do business with small- to mid-sized companies with leadership positions in markets that are growing rapidly. These companies have a large need for capital in order to dominate their market and grow, and often they need excellent strategic advisory services.

We choose our targeted categories by attempting to identify the significant growth drivers in the economy. For example, right now the Baby Boom generation is approaching retirement age, which acts as a driver for companies that can cater to this population with products and services. That includes such things as leisure activities, educational opportunities, and health care products and services (more about that in Chapter 14).

Our model also includes being a fully integrated merchant bank. We can employ our intellectual property from one line of business to help us with the others. Our research team, for example, helps us identify the best companies in the growth categories. Our brokers can then work on selling those stocks to our clients. Our private equity professionals can use the intelligence to identify promising investment opportunities.

To facilitate these integrations, we use a form of knowledge management. We create "tiger teams"—structured units consisting of representatives from various business units, focused on an industry from a collective approach. These teams get together weekly to map out the spaces we want to be in and identify who the winners or losers will be in those categories, both private and public companies.

2. Sustainable Business Model

You need a sound business model, particularly one that can deal with cyclical downturns in business. Investment banking tends to be a very cyclical business. To deal with that in our case, we have diversified the company.

First we diversified our lines of business. As I mentioned, we have a private equity business. We also have an institutional brokerage business, which sells research, gives portfolio advice, and trades for institutional investors. The brokerage business is very steady. We have the investment banking business, raising capital for public and private companies and offering these companies strategic advice. We lead with our advisory services so that we have already established a relationship with companies before they decide to do an IPO or secondary offering.

We are also diversified by industry. Currently, at Thomas Weisel Partners, technology is about 40 percent of our business. Consumer is 30 percent, health care is 20 percent, and financial services, media and telecom services, defense, and industrial growth add up to the remaining 10 percent. It's a fairly heavy reliance on technology, but we had alternatives when the latest downturn hit.

The business model should also include a philosophy on how the firm should be organized. Our business is run as a partnership. We have 66 partners at the firm, all owners. The partnership makes money based on the bottom-line results. If we're more profitable in one area one year, we'll be more profitable in another later. No matter what line of business each partner is in, though, they get paid on the basis of the firm's overall profitability. It keeps everybody rolling in the same direction.

This also gives us a variable cost structure. If we're not profitable, then the top 67 people don't make any money. We don't have top people just sitting around collecting paychecks. Throughout the rest of the company, people get bonuses driven more or less by their performance.

And finally, we have an important network of outside investors and advisers. At Montgomery, we had very few outside investors. But at TWP we thought it was important not only to secure adequate financing for the next five years, but also to use our outside financing as a way of building a supportive system around us. Our initial capitalization came from 22 private equity investors and a few large institutions like GE and Sun America. Collectively, they put in $35 million for 7 percent of the firm. The original partners also put up $30 million, so our original capitalization at the start was $65 million.

We put together an advisory board made up of key executives in the areas we are focused on, as well as executives in business law or politics who can provide very helpful advice.

Next we gathered 120 CEOs together in a CEO Founder's Circle. This group invested over $100 million into our largest private equity fund, Thomas Weisel Capital Partners (TWCP). Many of the executives are from companies that I've dealt with for a decade or two. These people are extremely helpful in securing deals, doing due diligence, and just giving us a backboard to bounce ideas off. In 1999 we received a $100 million investment from CalPERS, one of the largest institutional investors, for a 10 percent stake in the firm. In addition, CalPERS committed to $1 billion of additional private equity in the future. To date we have drawn down approximately $350 million of that commitment. This relationship has been extremely beneficial and helpful to us, thanks to Barry Gonder, Rick Hayes, and the entire board of CalPERS.

3. Financing

A company must be well financed in order to have sustainability. As you can see from the previous two sections, our financial investors are not just passive investors but partners. This shows the value of developing long-term relationships. We have the balance sheet to survive any economic environment. We've used the capital to continue to diversify and grow our business. Some of the new areas of growth for us are convertible arbitrage, money management, and program trading. We continue to actively look at other areas for possible expansion.

4. Leadership and Management

Obviously you have to have strong leadership. It starts with articulating the vision I mentioned earlier. In my opinion, the CEO should be both a player and a coach. I personally get involved directly in the business, whether it's having direct responsibility for corporate clients, handling a transaction, helping our institutional people with accounts, or writing investment positioning pieces for our overviews in research. Active participation keeps the executive on top of the business and builds loyalty. Everyone knows that I would never ask anyone to do anything I wouldn't do myself.

Another aspect of management is identifying, attracting, and motivating people. Talent is a rare resource. It just doesn't grow on trees. It needs to be cared for and nurtured. Regular and consistent communication internally and externally is also management's job.

5. Value Proposition

You should be able to demonstrate clearly to your clients what unique value you offer, especially if those clients have many larger and better-capitalized firms to choose from.

With our institutional brokerage businesses, that value is first and foremost to bring money-making ideas to the portfolio managers. We have an entire process that leads up to our recommendations, which also requires us to constantly come back to these recommendations. The process also mandates that we constantly reexamine these recommendations. Follow-through is important.

Second, our analysts are responsible for developing their own independent models for a company's profit and loss. The research isn't just a rehash of the statements from management at the companies we follow. We want to be the thought leader in our markets, so we come up with our own models and triangulate our information by talking extensively to customers and suppliers. We communicate these thoughts to our institutional accounts, which in turn pay us a commission for our work. We also write white papers, which are industry overview pieces that outline what we believe to be the next growth areas. Since starting the firm four years ago, we have published over 70 white papers.

Third, we have a portfolio product called the Green Book, published every month, that outlines our views on the economy, the stock market, portfolio asset allocation, and stock recommendations by sector.

Fourth, we provide a liquidity function in trading that was virtually nonexistent before in the emerging growth space. For small-cap companies, the trading volume at times can be minimal, and it can be difficult to buy or sell stocks of a particular company. We are willing to put our own capital on the line—either to help our money management clients get a position started, or to buy a position that our clients want to sell.

In the investment banking business, we have a compelling value proposition by virtue of being tightly focused on growth companies. We have deep industry knowledge, which is very different from the approach used by the large investment banks. They employ a "relationship manager," who brings in "product specialists" when appropriate. We don't just sell a transaction to clients, we work as a team to build long-term relationships, with senior-level attention in all aspects of our business with them, including strategic advisory and capital raising functions.

6. Operating Philosophy

A great company has a distinctive operating philosophy. In our business, putting clients first is of extreme importance. We maintain a team approach in order to avoid having individual stars develop a "my client" philosophy and a need to protect their own "territory." That enhances the entire firm's capability to serve a client as a cohesive, synergistic unit. It also helps to attract, keep, and motivate the best talent. Part of this philosophy is a fair, honest, transparent style for advancement of our employees, with a regular review system.

7. Strong Culture

Does culture really matter? It does. It matters more when times are tough. A strong culture is what holds people together. They need to believe in the company, in the people, and in what they're doing even when times are tough. Look at the companies that have been able to get through tough times, like Microsoft and Intel. They all have strong cultures.

Our culture includes a strong sense of entrepreneurship: We encourage appropriate, well-thought-out risk-taking, assuming responsibility for and running with an idea—and giving rewards if the idea works.

We also like to win. We have real passion in what we do. Even over the last two-plus years of this bear market, coming to work is easier because of the passion that we bring to the business. We like our clients and it shows.

Last, we are having fun. Life is not all about making money and being efficient. We feel there needs to be a lighter side to business and one that encourages individualism, dignity, respect, and fun.

8. Unique Brand

You should have a strong brand. What does your company really stand for? What unique experience do you offer a client?

Our brand is made up of several of the factors discussed in the previous sections. We go the extra mile for our clients. We put them first and develop long-term relationships.

We hope we're smart money makers and thought leaders, that we understand the growth spaces better than our competition.

We also have a better understanding of entrepreneurial companies, because we're an entrepreneurial company ourselves, and we're a strong advocate for emerging growth companies.

Postal Services

The great thing in this world is not so much where we
stand, but in what direction we are moving.
                                    —*Oliver Wendell Holmes*

I f Lance Armstrong has proved anything (aside from the fact that he may be the most extraordinary athlete in the world), it's that there's really no reason American athletes can't become winning cyclists. Norwegians may outperform American skiers in the Olympics because they grow up on skis in the midst of snowy mountains, but there's no lack of ground in the United States to ride on. Cycling has just never caught on in the United States as it has in Europe, and there have been few role models to inspire young athletes.

When the Tour de France is held every year, *The New York Times* usually has a small daily article on the event buried in the middle of the sports section, even if an American happens to be winning for the fourth year in a row. At the end of the 2002 Tour, the *Times* finally put a picture of Armstrong on the front page. French newspapers, by contrast, cover the event like it was the coronation of a king. It's the French equivalent of the World Series, although you don't need season tickets to go to the game. You can park yourself anywhere along the 2,000-mile road race at the right time and cheer on your team, and it seems as though most of the country is doing just that.

As Weisel was training and becoming a cycling champion himself, he decided to also test his entrepreneurial skills in the sport of cycling. He was still on the board of the U.S. Ski Team, running his own company, and racing bicycles himself, so in 1987 he decided that it was a good time to create a world-class cycling team. With the help of Eddie B, Montgomery Sports was born. Soon after its inception, Dan Osipow joined Montgomery Sports to help run marketing and business operations. Dan continues to help guide the cycling operation to this day.

Montgomery sponsored an amateur cycling team and brought in Avenir, a company that makes cycling accessories, as cosponsor. The team attracted a few top riders, such as Leonard Harvey Nitz, who raced in four Olympics, winning a silver and a bronze medal in 1984. Weisel would ride with the Masters side of the team, appearing in amateur competitions for older riders, segregated by age groups.

Nitz would sometimes train with Weisel, and likes to tell the story of when he went to Weisel's house for a ride. Weisel called and said he'd be a half hour late, so Nitz went downstairs to check out Weisel's private gym. He noticed that the squat rack, used to strengthen the legs, had a lot of weight on it. So he sat down to give it a try, and couldn't budge it. At the time, Nitz was one of the two or three fastest road sprinters in the United States. So he braced himself, concentrated, and tried again. "I couldn't move it an inch!" he says.

As they started their ride, Nitz told Weisel he had seen the squat machine and asked if that was really the maximum weight Weisel could lift. Weisel replied, "No, it's where I start my workout."

Many people on Weisel's new team thought he was crazy. He made it clear that his long-term goal was to have a team that could

win the Tour de France. The riders would mutter among themselves, "Thom just doesn't know how hard that is." Riders who
have stayed with the team have been amazed to see how it came
together over the years. "I've never seen anybody who thinks in
such a big picture as Thom," says Nitz, who still rides part-time
with the USPS Masters team. "He knows his goals and how to get
there step by step."

In 1990, Weisel talked Subaru into becoming a sponsor for his
first professional team, the Subaru-Montgomery team, again with
Borysewicz in charge. Borysewicz started recruiting a few more
impressive riders, including former Olympian Steve Hegg and an
extraordinary young triathlete named Lance Armstrong. In 1991,
while Weisel was winning gold medals in Masters cycling, Armstrong won the U.S. Amateur Road Championship for Subaru-
Montgomery. Weisel also set two national records, for the kilo and
200 meters, in Colorado Springs that year.

Mark Gorski is a top American cyclist, a gold medalist in the
1984 Olympics. Gorski first met Weisel at Eddie Borysewicz's
Olympic training camp in Dallas, in 1987, when the investment
banker showed up for lessons and practice with the young athletes.
Gorski didn't know much about the old guy, but had heard something about him flying to camp with Borysewicz in a private jet.

Weisel was pretty rusty, and Gorski gave him some tips along the
way: where to sit on the saddle, how to position the handlebars,
when to peddle hard and when to keep it soft. "I could see that he
was very intense, very motivated and anxious to improve," says
Gorski, and Weisel seemed to appreciate the advice.

Gorski next saw Weisel a year later. Gorski was living in Indianapolis, and Weisel showed up to compete in the Masters Track
Nationals (45 and over). Weisel came in second, and Gorski was
impressed with the businessman's ability to improve so much in a
year, even while running his own company. Most of the competitors have raced their whole lives, not taken up the sport at 47.

In 1989, at 29 years old, Gorski decided to retire from racing. He had no idea what to do next with his life. But he had studied economics at the University of Michigan and was interested in stock investments, so the first thing he did was call Weisel's office and leave a message asking to speak to him.

He was surprised at how quickly Weisel called back, and more surprised at how receptive Weisel was to the idea of giving a cyclist an opportunity to join the investment banking business. "I know how competitive you are," Weisel said, "and you're a bright guy. Why don't you come up and spend a day at Montgomery Securities and see if this is the right business for you?"

Gorski interviewed with Weisel and some key executives, and in a few weeks was offered a job in institutional sales—the position that really launched Weisel's own career. But he declined the offer. He had just moved with his wife to Newport Beach and was reluctant to pack up and move again. Wells Fargo offered him a vice president position in Los Angeles.

But Gorski watched Weisel's attempts to get a strong cycling team going from a distance. After a decent start, the team started sliding. Although Armstrong was clearly extremely talented, Eddie B wouldn't let him ride all the races because he was so young. It was the usual training approach, because trainers felt that a body that young couldn't handle the physical demands.

But Borysewicz wasn't the only one who noticed Armstrong's potential. So did Chris Carmichael, the director of the U.S. National Cycling Team. So in addition to racing for Subaru-Montgomery in the U.S., he started racing with the U.S. National Cycling Team overseas.

Things got complicated when in 1991 both the U.S. national team and Subaru-Montgomery entered a race in Italy, the Settimana Bergamasca. In his autobiography, Armstrong describes how Borysewicz (who used to coach the U.S. national team himself) told him he should show team spirit and purposely let one of the Subaru-Montgomery riders win the race. Armstrong didn't like that plan, and became the first U.S. cyclist to ever win the Italian race. He never got along with Borysewicz.

In 1992, Armstrong left Subaru-Montgomery to join the Motorola team, the legendary team that was run by the equally legendary Jim Ochowicz. Team members were amazed that Weisel let Armstrong out of his contract in order to pursue a better opportunity. Nitz says that attitude wasn't unusual for Weisel. When Nitz burned out in 1991 and decided to retire, Weisel offered to keep paying his salary for the last five months of his contract, even though he wouldn't be racing. He even let Centurion Bikes out of its second year of a two-year contract as sponsor because it was having financial troubles.

After Armstrong left, Subaru-Montgomery still had some strong showings, but struggled through several upheavals as Borysewicz kept bringing in different riders.

Gorski, meanwhile, lasted four years as a banker. Although he was one of the top salespeople at Wells Fargo, he had concluded that he "just didn't have a burning passion about business." He missed cycling too much. So he dropped out of the banking world in 1993 and secured a job as director of corporate sponsorships for USA Cycling, the domestic governing body for the sport.

In 1993, in his new position with USA Cycling, Gorski ran into Weisel again at a cycling competition in North Carolina. Weisel had come with the Subaru-Montgomery team, which was competing in the event. That evening, Weisel and Gorski went out for some beers along with several people from Montgomery that Gorski had met when he had interviewed there four years earlier. Gorski asked them about other people he had met at the firm, people who were also new to Montgomery at the time and would have been his colleagues if he had also joined. He got responses like, "Oh, his career is just taking off. He'll make a million this year."

"I had a lot of sleepless nights after that," Gorski says. The success of Weisel's company almost made banking sound good again. Had he made a mistake turning down the job offer? Probably. On the other hand, there was still that passion thing. He kept his job with USA Cycling.

Weisel's cycling team was not doing as well. Two years later, on a spring day in 1995, Gorski crossed paths with Weisel again, this time at a bike race in Santa Rosa, California. Weisel told Gorski his lament: Subaru had pulled its sponsorship of the team in 1993, and Weisel could not find another major sponsor after a year's effort. He finally provided most of the financing himself, and cajoled Terry Lee at Bell Sports (a company Montgomery helped take public) to put in a little money, creating the Montgomery-Bell team, but was having a difficult time getting things really rolling. The team's paltry budget—about $800,000—was not going to take it into the top tier in a sport where a single top rider can earn more than that in a year.

It was extremely difficult to find sponsors for an American team. The Subaru-Montgomery team, with Subaru contributing $500,000 a year, had a budget of about $2.5 million at its peak. Even then, Weisel and Montgomery had actually provided the bulk of the budget. Overall, Weisel had poured about $5 million of his own money into the team since its inception, with little to show for it. Investing in an American cycling team was kind of like tossing millions of dollars into creating a Jamaican bobsled team.

They parted ways again and Gorski boarded a plane for Colorado Springs. On the flight, he kept thinking about what Weisel had said. Then, "a lightning bolt kind of hit me," he recalls. "A concept just crystallized in my mind."

Gorski was in charge of finding sponsors for the USA Cycling organization; why couldn't he do it for Weisel? Sitting on the plane for two hours, he wrote up a detailed proposal in the form of a handwritten letter to Weisel. Creating a team that could win the Tour de France, he said, would require a budget of at least $3.5 million, and more likely around $5 million. Gorski would develop a new marketing campaign, help find new sponsors over the next few years, and recruit some top riders to the team. It might leave Weisel a little more time to run his other company.

On a Monday morning Gorski overnighted the letter to Weisel, then followed up with a phone call a few days later. Weisel's assistant said he would call back.

Then two weeks went by with no word. In the business world, two weeks of silence means "No." Well, thought Gorski, it was a good try. But the next day, Gorski came home to find a message on this answering machine, saying Weisel was trying to reach him. Weisel told him he had gone through the plan in detail, he really liked it, and they should do it. Gorski was shocked. He had figured that if Weisel had any interest, they would get together, go through the plan, and discuss the options before making a final decision. But Weisel had already decided.

"I never anticipated that I would get that kind of response," says Gorski. "But it epitomizes Thom. He's incredibly bright, can process a lot of information, and then make a decision immediately."

On May 15, 1995, Gorski went to work for Montgomery Sports, joining Dan Osipow to lead the team to new heights. In 1996, the team won its second U.S. Pro Championship. Soon Gorski was pounding the road in search of sponsors, explaining their goal. For several months he was traveling five days a week. He figures he talked to over 100 companies over three or four months.

At the end of it, the two best prospects were the U.S. Postal Service and United Parcel Service. They liked the idea of being associated with speed, especially in these days of overnight deliveries and instantaneous e-mail. Gorski spent another couple of months going over the benefits: advertising opportunities, promotional events, even employee morale. A big part of the plan was to help the Postal Service get the attention of Europeans, with the hope that more could be enticed into using its international services. They signed an agreement with the U.S. Postal Service in September 1996.

Loren Smith, who was chief marketing officer at the USPS at the time, was a strong champion for the sponsorship. He began an ad campaign for Priority Mail that included the cycling team. But in the process of trying to get real traction out of it, he overspent his budget significantly, and had to resign just a year after the contract was signed.

Gorski had gotten a three-year contract, but it was reviewed once a year. As soon as he heard that Smith had resigned, he figured that the USPS cycling team was toast. He sat down with the marketing staff at the USPS and discussed ways of salvaging the situation. They decided that the international focus was not going to be successful. But, the USPS agreed, if the team sponsorship could demonstrate significant success in raising sales of its services domestically, the Postal Service would stick to the contract.

Gorski hit the road again to find more sponsors. He even visited as many Montgomery clients as possible, not only to solicit money but to try and convince them to use USPS services rather than Federal Express or UPS.

Sometimes Weisel even helped out. He personally called up Tom Stemberg, the cofounder and chairman of Staples (a company Montgomery helped take public in 1989), and convinced him to switch his delivery business from Federal Express to the U.S. Postal Service.

This plan, working in conjunction with the Postal Service's sales team, was a success. Every year, Gorski had to justify the sponsorship again by itemizing the business that came in because of their efforts. Gorski estimates that the cycling team brought the USPS new business worth about four times the amount it was spending on the sponsorship.

The team's budget increased each year. In 1997, Trek and Yahoo! (another Montgomery client) came in as sponsors and the team budget reached about $3.5 million. Visa joined the following year. Aided by a decent budget, Eddie B was able to recruit some top talent. In 1996 he brought in Viatcheslav Ekimov, an extraordinary Russian cyclist and Olympic gold medalist.

Eddie B then stepped back, handing the team over to the assistant coach from the Motorola team, Johnny Weltz. In 1997 Weltz signed George Hincapie, another American, who is still one of the team's star riders, and the French rider Jean-Cyril Robin.

But they failed to lure one top rider: Lance Armstrong. In 1996, Gorski talked to Bill Stapleton, Armstrong's agent, about possibly joining the USPS team. Armstrong chose to stay with Motorola. Then, on October 2, 1996, Armstrong was diagnosed with testicular cancer. Not many people expected him to survive.

The USPS team had performed well enough to consider the Tour de France. In order to qualify for the Tour, the team's cyclists have to earn a sufficient number of International Cycling Union points from their performance the previous year, or else get in as one of two wild card teams selected by the Société Tour de France. Gorski began lobbying in 1996, meeting with Société officials, taking them to dinner, and getting to know them.

Gorski had to overcome a little bad blood between Weisel and the organization's French director, Jean-Marie le Blanc. In 1993, le Blanc had offered Weisel's Subaru-Montgomery team a chance to send at least some of its riders to the Tour. The proposal was to send a split wild card team, with half the members coming from Subaru-Montgomery and the other half from a French team, Chazal, which had an unexceptional record. Weisel had refused the offer, saying, "If we don't get a full invitation, we're not going."

The USPS team was ultimately chosen as one of the wild card

teams for the Tour in July, 1997. The lead rider, Jean-Cyril Robin, came in 15th. But the entire team of nine riders also managed to finish the race, which was a good showing in itself. "We didn't embarrass ourselves," says Gorski. His plan called for winning a Tour de France within 5 or 10 years.

They also ran into Lance Armstrong at the 1997 Tour. Armstrong had finished his chemotherapy; he wasn't racing, but was there as a commentator on the race. A huge drug scandal tainted the race that year, and several riders were suspended. None were from the USPS team.

Later that year, Armstrong announced that he was attempting a comeback. Before his cancer, Armstrong was riding for the French team Cofidis, but the team decided a comeback was unlikely and dropped him.

Among others, he and his agent approached Gorski to see if there was still an opportunity on the USPS team. Gorski made it clear that it would be tough, and that the team had already frozen its 1998 budget, while Weisel expressed his own reservations about Armstrong's ability to be a team player. But Gorski did approach the team's sponsors to see if they would be willing to come up with some extra money in order to support Lance's comeback. All of them said yes, providing $200,000 dollars to pay his salary. But Stapleton also wanted bonus payments that would depend on Lance's performance. Despite Lance's recent illness and chemotherapy, Gorski thought that accepting these terms could break the team's budget if Lance proved to be successful (an assumption that turned out to be correct).

Finally, at a critical meeting between Gorski, Stapleton, and Weisel in San Francisco, Weisel ended his resistance and announced that he would cover the bonus payments himself. Armstrong was on the team. That also happened to be the year that Weisel sold Montgomery Securities to NationsBank.

It took Armstrong a little while to get his confidence back. He dropped out of the first stage of the Paris-Nice race in 1998. After a difficult start, he just didn't have the heart to continue the grueling race in a bitter rainstorm. In retrospect, Gorski realized that Armstrong had simply not yet conquered the psychological pain from the cancer and was fighting with huge self-doubt. Gorski gave him time, and told him there was no pressure to make the comeback quickly, or at all if he decided not to. But at the same time, he says, "I knew it wasn't the end of the story."

Weisel was going through his own ordeals at the time. On September 18, 1998, he resigned from NationsBank Montgomery Securities, angry at the way NationsBank had treated his firm and whittled away at his responsibilities.

Lance did get his cycling legs back, of course. And then he came back with a vengeance. He performed well in Atlanta, his first race after Paris-Nice, in May 1998. "You could tell he was back," says Gorski. "He made people hurt by taking long pulls at the front. It gave him confidence."

Part of the strategy in cycling is to have some team members act as *domestiques,* who help to "pull" the teammate chosen to win the race by acting as a windbreak, leaving the chosen winner enough energy to sprint at the end. After surviving cancer, Armstrong became a better team player, working to win some races and to help teammates to win others. In May 1998 Armstrong won a race in Austin, Texas, and then helped pull Hincapie to a win in Philadelphia, the biggest race in the United States. Armstrong then went on to win races in Europe, and placed fourth in the Tour of Spain world championships. Gorski knew he was a champion again. Not only that, but he was a better rider: thinner, better at powering up hills, as tenacious as ever, and training so hard that at times even his coach thought he was crazy. "People were seeing a new Lance Armstrong," says Gorski.

In 1998, Armstrong did so well that he ended up costing Weisel over $1 million in bonus payments. Gorski is still amazed that the USPS team was the only one to offer Armstrong a contract after his cancer. He was a star cyclist before the cancer, and knew he could do it again once he was cured. But the bias against severe illness is strong, and it was hard for people to get over the idea that Armstrong was sick. "It's incredibly mind-boggling when you think about the fact that all these other managers, some of the best minds in cycling, missed the opportunity to sign Lance Armstrong," says Gorski.

The performance in 1997 automatically qualified the team for the 1998 Tour de France. Just before the 1998 Tour, Gorski asked Armstrong if he wanted to take on the race. At that point, so soon after dropping out of Paris-Nice, Armstrong hadn't even considered the possibility. Gorski told him he might not be team leader, but he could contribute to the team's efforts. Armstrong decided to sit it out. Still, the team made an impressive showing, with Hincapie, Hamilton, and Robin all staying with the lead groups on different days. Robin finished sixth overall.

But Armstrong's increasing success started creating problems on the team. "Nobody knew where Lance would fit in," says Gorski. "He was one of the great champions of the sport, then went through illness and was making a comeback. Where would he fit on the team? Could we rely on him?" But after his great showing at the Tour of Spain, it was clear that Armstrong was leadership material again.

Not everyone was ecstatic. Robin saw Armstrong's star rising the way, say, a founding partner of a firm might watch the newest partner outperform the others and gradually take over. "There was definitely some friction developing," after the 1998 Tour, admits Gorski. There was only one solution. Gorski did not renew Robin's contract. Ekimov also left the team that year after getting a richer offer on another team. At Armstrong's insistence, coach Weltz was replaced with Johan Bruyneel, who had just retired from racing himself.

Considering everything, 1999 turned out to be a pretty good year for Weisel. He launched his new company, Thomas Weisel Partners, just as the Internet went boom, and, with Armstrong as captain, the USPS cycling team won its first Tour de France. Weisel was behind Lance in the follow car as he climbed the mountain called Sestriére, the point at which Armstrong knew he had won the race. Weisel was probably as ecstatic as Armstrong, who shouted as he crossed the summit, "How do you like them apples?" At the celebration dinner in Paris after the end of the race, Weisel had an arrangement of apples placed at every table.

Ekimov also returned to the USPS team that year. The team he was riding for ran into financial difficulties and couldn't pay him anymore. Weisel picked him up and paid his salary himself the first year, although at a much lower rate than Ekimov had been getting, since there was no allocation for it in the budget. But at the end of the season, at a team banquet, Weisel announced that he was giving Ekimov a $100,000 bonus for his hard work.

Armstrong and the USPS team repeated their Tour de France wins in 2000, 2001, and 2002. These days, you can see Armstrong's picture in television ads and on the side of postal service trucks across the country.

The team dominated the race so powerfully in 2002 that most observers knew it was the winner more than a week before Armstrong actually crossed the finish line. Weisel knew Armstrong would be the winner months before the race began. Not only was Armstrong as spectacular as ever, but the USPS team showed such teamwork and discipline, with nearly flawless execution, that there seems little doubt that it is now the best cycling team in the world—at least as far as the Tour de France is concerned. Weisel and Gorski built the team specifically for this race, the only one that most Americans even know about. Weisel sought out and hired riders with all the different skills necessary to support Armstrong and help him win the Tour. The rest of the year, other riders get their chance to dominate other races. But it's the Tour de France that brings in the sponsors.

Riders confirm that the team's morale and teamwork is awesome. "When teams don't ride well, it's generally because the players don't get along," says Nitz. "You always hear stories about how half a team belongs to one clique or another. Weisel demands and rewards excellence. He's a great motivator. He gets you to do more than you otherwise would."

After the U.S. Postal Service team won its first Tour de France, Weisel started thinking about what else he could do for cycling in the U.S. He created a foundation, called USA Cycling Development Foundation, to fund a development program aimed at helping young people (under 23) in the sport. The Foundation has contributed several million dollars to the sport in the United States, financing several elite cycling programs, including those for young riders.

Weisel also decided that the US Cycling Federation (USCF), the governing body for the sport in the United States, had some serious issues to deal with. Having already spent over a decade reorganizing and rebuilding USSA, he now saw the same problems at USCF: poor funding, lack of vision, and no consistent development program. At the time Weisel got involved in 1999, USA Cycling, the parent organization of USCF, had a $1.4 million deficit. With the help of Mike Plant, who was then president of USA Cycling's board, Weisel got the board to make some changes, including adding three Foundation members—venture capitalist Jeff Garvey, Mick Hellman (Warren Hellman's son), and Weisel himself.

Of course, some of the existing members didn't like the intrusion by the suits and wanted to continue making major decisions through a vote of the membership even though the major elections rarely brought in even the 10 percent quorum required. Les

Earnest, a cycling fan and Stanford lawyer, sued because the board didn't have the authority to make the changes without a vote. He won in court.

That required a new election in order to try to implement the changes once again. Weisel's team put a proposition on a ballot, while Earnest put up a competing proposition maintaining the approach of keeping decision making decentralized.

Weisel also had the help of Steve Johnson, his old cycling buddy, who was elected chief operating officer at USA Cycling (in addition to being executive director of Weisel's federation). With the endorsement of Weisel, Johnson, and Lance Armstrong, the reform measure beat Earnest's proposal 6,007 to 432 in October 2001. Earnest vowed to keep fighting in the courts, claiming the measures were improperly listed and promoted to members, backed by the federation's money. The second suit was settled in January 2002. In July, 2002, USA Cycling named a new CEO and appointed Johnson head of athletic financing. Weisel has now spent over three years reorganizing USA Cycling, and his team is largely in charge. Expect changes in American cycling.

Does Weisel want to make cycling a major sport in America, as it is in Europe? After all, cycling has had a resurgence in the United States—especially mountain biking, although the percentage of Americans who take mountain bikes off-road is probably roughly equivalent to the number of people who do the same with their SUVs. (Maybe they're the same people.) Weisel was instrumental in bringing a new annual street race to San Francisco, the SF Grand Prix, which draws an audience of about 400,000 people lining the route. The course was designed by Dan Osipow to showcase the magnificence of San Francisco. Armstrong and the USPS team competed in the race. George Hincapie won the first year, 2001.

Weisel would like to see American cycling increase in popularity, but it's unlikely. "Both cycling and skiing are minor sports in this country," he says. "It's not like watching the Redskins on TV every week. We'll always be struggling to put together a consistent, competitive, world-class effort in these sports."

Still, you can expect him to try.

Thom W. Weisel

There are a lot of similarities between running a sports team and running a successful business. I've already outlined the eight points of a successful professional services firm in Chapter 7. Now I'd like to elaborate on how I've also applied these points to the creation of a great sports team.

We started Montgomery Sports—now Tailwind Sports—with a single, simple vision: to create the finest professional cycling team in the world. It took over 10 years to do it, but we're there.

We have a sustainable business model. We needed an anchor sponsor so that we could have a consistent revenue source from year to year. In the beginning of our relationship with the Postal Service, we put together a strong marketing effort. We worked with the inside tactical marketing people at the USPS to deliver clients to them. Our sponsors sign long-term contracts. The Postal Service contract has three more years to run. With luck, we'll even be able to make a profit some day. We're not there yet.

In order to make sure we have adequate financing, we have to work diligently to keep new sponsors coming in. Besides the lead sponsor, the USPS, our other current sponsors include Visa, Yahoo!, Nike, Trek Bicycles, Volkswagen of America, and TWP. This business goes up and down depending on our ability to market the team and get sponsorships. We work hard to add synergy for our sponsor-partners. We encourage our sponsors to get together in order to cross-promote each other's products.

We have strong leadership and management. We have strong management in Mark Gorski, a gold medalist himself, and Johan Bruyneel, our *direction sportif* (team coach), who was also an exceptional cyclist. Bruyneel has incredible knowledge of our riders and their capability, and he knows how to prepare and motivate them for the world's biggest cycling race. He knows every course we race on. He goes out and walks them every year to see what might have changed from the year before.

Our value proposition is easy. No other U.S. team has ever won the Tour de France before, let alone four times. Sponsors and riders want to be with a team as outstanding as this one.

The culture of our team is to get everyone to work together, not to just have individual stars who may or may not succeed on their own. Cycling is a team sport. It would be impossible for Lance to win the Tour without a strong team. Our entire organization works incredibly long hours to reach our goals, including the mechanics, *soigneurs,* and administrative and support staff.

Sure, it's an enormous advantage to get a Michael Jordan or a Lance Armstrong, but you have to deliver a solid team as well, a value proposition that goes beyond your star players. Most great organizations have to transcend any individual star. It's the team that wins.

Our team is run as a meritocracy. That means being supportive of the other team members in their down periods. When you reward players for performance, you don't just reward them based on how well they competed, but you reward those that are also good team players. We try to make those people an example for the others.

We try to support Lance with a broad-based, world-class group of people. We have attracted a lot of great athletes on our team besides Lance. Lance's success is dependent on how well others do their job. The team has to surround him. They have to act as a windbreak for him. They need to provide Lance with a wheel if he has a flat and food or water when needed.

Several years ago when Lance was climbing a mountain, we found that the rest of the team couldn't keep up with him, putting him at risk if anything went wrong. So two years ago, we added Roberto Heras and José Luis Rubiera, two Spaniards who can keep up with Lance in the high mountains and offer support. It was gratifying to see that plan work out so well in the 2002 Tour de France. When Armstrong started blowing past others in the mountains, where he gains most of his lead, Heras and Rubiera were right up there with him.

But there are more races than the Tour de France. In the Tour, the other team members support Lance. But in the spring and fall classics, Lance plays the supporting role for others. In the San Francisco Grand Prix in 2001, Lance supported George Hincapie, who won the race. When Hincapie crossed the finish line with his hands in the air, everybody went crazy. Lance did the same thing for Tyler Hamilton, who won the Dauphiné Libéré earlier that year.

Our culture is also distinctly American. In Europe, a lot of companies are trying to develop their brands by sponsoring cycling teams. They want the teams on TV a lot. And that means they can run their teams into the ground. We focus and pick our races. We're not in the Tour of Italy, and we're not in three races every weekend. We give our riders enough opportunity to shine in other races, but don't burn them out.

Our operating philosophy is simple: to win.the Super Bowl of cycling—the Tour de France. We get great value out of the Tour de France by not racing all the time and saving our riders by allowing them to rest.

Every sports team has limited funds, so you have to use them wisely. You can pay a lot of money for the stars, but you also have to have a culture that gives a chance for the younger athletes. We are very proud of our heritage as a sports program. Tyler Hamilton, now the lead rider on the CSC Danish team, was with us from 1995 to 2001. Levi Leipheimer was one of our great young riders and finished third in the Tour of Spain last year. This year he is the team leader for Rabobank. Kevin Livingston was with us for a number of years, then became one of Jan Ullrich's key lieutenants on the Deutsche Telekom team and just recently retired. We have two young riders, Floyd Landis and Christian Vande Velde, who could be the next champions in a few years, and there are several others behind them. Developing a deep bench is a major part of institutionalizing a great organization.

The ability to dominate the Tour de France, and Lance Armstrong himself, make up our brand. A sports team's audience is also its clientele. The product you're offering is content in the form of entertainment. That's really what sports are. People come to watch Lance Armstrong.

You want to look at the long-term picture. The leaders, the smart athletes and professionals, figure out that if you want sustainable wealth creation, you don't accomplish your goals by getting the last nickel out of a yearly contract. A lot of players fall into the trap of free agency. But with that approach, they can end up on a lousy team, and their career is over. They made a few more dollars for a couple years, and then they're out. Free agency can be the death of a sport and the death of a business.

The Buildup

*Obstacles are those frightful things you see when you
take your eyes off the goal.*

—Henry Ford

In June of 1990, Robert N. Noyce, cofounder of Intel, co-inventor
of the semiconductor chip, and one of the most highly respected
executives ever to live in Silicon Valley, died of a heart attack. It
was an inauspicious start to the decade for technology companies.
Fortunately for Intel and the rest of the technology world, a new
CEO had already taken over: Andrew S. Grove, who, by the end of
the decade, managed to build Intel into one of the greatest companies in the world.

Silicon Valley seemed to follow the same kind of path through
the decade. The 1990s started with a whimper and mixed financial signals and ended with a bang that reverberated through the
financial centers of the world like a cannon blast echoing through
the Grand Canyon.

In 1990, Silicon Valley was still recovering from the Loma Pri-
eta earthquake that had rocked Northern California the previous
October. Some Silicon Valley and San Francisco companies were
still fixing or tearing down damaged buildings, while collapsed

bridges and overpasses created a traffic nightmare from which the region has never fully recovered.

At the start of the decade, Microsoft was trying to convince the world to switch from its DOS operating system to OS/2, jointly developed with IBM. In the meantime, Microsoft was taking over control of the computer industry while almost every other software company in the world was being battered like a racquetball in a finals tournament. Adobe Systems, one of the few exceptions, was working on a software program to transmit images efficiently over networks, a program later named Acrobat. The Federal Trade Commission was pursuing a fruitless antitrust case against Microsoft, but would finally hand it over to the Department of Justice in 1993.

U.S. semiconductor companies were still losing ground to the Japanese, and had entered the downside of their perpetually cyclical market, which followed the also perpetually cyclical PC market. The only really promising development was Intel, which had started working on its first Pentium chip. Apple Computer, under the control of CEO John Sculley, was beginning a downward spiral that would not end until ousted founder Steve Jobs was returned to power in 1997.

Most of the cutting-edge biotech companies had been dulled, and Genentech was sold to the Swiss drug giant Roche Holdings Ltd. However, a new star had hit the biotech stage—Amgen, the company Montgomery had taken public in 1983. EPO, a genetically engineered compound used to help fight anemia and stimulate white blood cell production, had made it to market in the late 1980s, and by 1991 Amgen's stock had soared to over $100 a share. That gave it a market capitalization at least 50 percent larger than that of its closest rival, Genentech.

Montgomery Securities was involved in only three IPOs in 1990, none of them as the lead manager. Digital Sound's IPO was led by Goldman Sachs, while Alex.Brown controlled the books for the IPOs of Gensia Pharmaceuticals and IKOS Systems.

Within a year, however, the economy and Montgomery started to soar. The stock market recovered relatively quickly from the 1987 minicrash. Baby Boomers, reaching their forties and fifties, had started saving more rather than spending. That fueled strong growth in mutual funds, which invested the money in the stock market. Job growth moved to the small- and mid-cap sector, while the Fortune 500 companies dropped jobs.

These factors, combined with the rapid improvement of technology in the electronics sector, pushed tech companies into their decade-long boom that culminated in a mountain of wealth towering like a magma dome ready to burst. In 1991, Montgomery took 29 companies public, half of them as book manager. It was mostly up from there.

In the 1990s, technology companies, especially in Silicon Valley, became a major force in the U.S. economy, and the HARM companies became a major force in investment banking. And now Alex.Brown and Montgomery were the clear leaders.

Look at the statistics from the start of 1990 through the third quarter of 1998 (Weisel's last at Montgomery): There were about 7,300 new issues of stock in that period. Montgomery was involved in 838 of them, placing it fourth in the nation (behind Smith Barney, Merrill Lynch, and Goldman Sachs). Alex.Brown was 5th, with 837, Robertson 10th, with 544, and Hambrecht 11th with 518.

In terms of the amount of money raised, Montgomery finally made it into the top 10, raising $59 billion. The rankings of the HARM companies in that period were: Alex.Brown at number 8, Montgomery at 10, Robertson at 13, and Hambrecht at 15. And this was the decade when stock underwritings exploded. Companies raised $560 billion in stock offerings from January 1990 through the third quarter of 1998, compared to a total of $193 billion in the previous decade.

And that was just the underwriting business. Montgomery's substantial capability in institutional brokerage also continued to grow. By 1994 it was trading 12 million shares of stock a day on what was often described by the press as the largest and most sophisticated trading floor outside of Manhattan. The firm could promise emerging companies that it would not only take them public, but would be able to make a market in the companies' stock after the IPO. Montgomery also began to become a force in advising companies on mergers and acquisitions.

In fact, Weisel had developed enough influence on Wall Street by 1994 to get the New York Stock Exchange to abandon plans to start trading half an hour earlier each day. He argued that West Coast brokers already had to start their day at 4 A.M. in order to be prepared for the opening bell on the East Coast, and refused to go along with the plan. The NYSE gave in.

Small-cap companies had started experiencing what was called "IPO pops," an immediate run up in the price after their stock hit the market. In Montgomery's case, said *Forbes*, the pops averaged about 20 percent.

In 1995, Markowitz was promoted to help Weisel run the firm, effectively becoming chief operating officer. They added some new businesses to Montgomery that created more synergy: its own mutual fund and private client business. They formed Montgomery Asset Management in 1990 to help institutional and wealthy private investors decide where to put their money. Under that umbrella was a group of mutual funds called the Montgomery Funds, designed to invest directly on behalf of the wealthiest Baby Boomers it could find. Its best source of clients: executives who had become rich when Montgomery took them public. Montgomery was also able to recommend promising new investments to these clients and let them in on some of the IPOs it was underwriting.

Growth investing was in style, and in 1994 Montgomery Asset Management had the highest returns among growth funds. With

$5.5 billion under management, this business accounted for 20 percent of the company's revenues by 1994.

But Montgomery still did not narrow its focus to technology, the field that the other San Francisco firms were known for. Montgomery also focused on such industries as restaurants, retail chains, and gambling. In the 1990s, Montgomery was the leading trader in the consumer space. The research capability it had built up in the 1980s now really began to pay off, getting the company noticed by corporate executives in these categories.

One of Montgomery's best markets was the restaurant business, backed by the research of Karl Matthies and John Weiss. It was involved in the IPOs of Au Bon Pain Co., Bertucci's Brick Oven Pizzeria, Cheesecake Factory, and Papa John's pizza restaurants.

Montgomery handled the IPO of Lone Star Steak House & Saloon without a secondary underwriter. CEO Jamie Coulter, who first came across Montgomery two decades earlier, had since developed a close and long-term relationship with the firm. Hugely ambitious, Coulter had wanted to go public when he had just two restaurants operating and two more under construction. Weisel had told him to come back when he had eight, which he did, in 1992. The company was still small, but Coulter told Weisel that if he was willing to work on the IPO, Montgomery would be allowed to handle it alone. "There are not many investment bankers who would have done that," says Coulter.

Lone Star went public in March at $13.50; the business and the stock took off, split two-for-one in July, and by September had hit $24 post-split. But Coulter was upset when a *USA Today* reporter asked Matthies to pick his top 10 growth stocks and Lone Star was not on the list. In a private meeting at the Montgomery conference in September, Coulter stood up and complained, and Weisel told him his complaints were bullshit. "Thom speaks directly to you and you have to talk right back," says Coulter. The frank exchange actually strengthened their relationship, and Coulter called on Montgomery for a secondary offering the following month.

Montgomery was also involved in stock offerings for specialty retailers that dominated their field, including the IPOs of Eagle Hardware, Gymboree, PetSmart, and Sunglass Hut. It helped take Orchard Supply Hardware public, then advised it on its sale to Sears. Weisel feels he had some of the best retail analysts in the business at the time, whizzes at spotting new trends early.

Hotels and casinos proved to be a good bet for Montgomery as well. By the mid-1990s, Montgomery had raised $2.5 billion in equity underwritings for lodging and gaming companies (including a $45 million IPO for Doubletree in 1994), putting it first in the category among all investment banks.

Montgomery's standing in the financial services arena also grew into prominence. It co-managed over $1 billion in equity financings for BANC ONE over a decade, and did offerings for First Interstate, First Republic Bancorp, Fleet Financial Group, Washington Mutual, and others.

Acting as an advisor on bank mergers was almost a market unto itself. Apparently making amends with BankAmerica after helping First Interstate make a hostile bid for the San Francisco bank seven years earlier, Montgomery represented BankAmerica in its $2.4 billion acquisition of Continental Bank in 1994.

But the most lucrative deal Montgomery ended up doing in that industry came later in the decade, in July 1997, when it represented itself in a sale to NationsBank for $1.3 billion. (Weisel insists, however, that he had nothing to do with NationsBank's subsequent purchase of BankAmerica in April 1998.)

Along with its technology and biotech clients (such as Actel, Calgene, Chipcom, Chiron, Conner Peripherals, Cray Computer, Flextronics, FTP Software, Gensia, Integrated Device Technology, Macromedia, Micro Warehouse, Novellus, Sanmina, Stratacom, Ultratech Stepper, and on and on), Montgomery was able to pull substantially ahead of its local competitors. The firm's different businesses were starting to come together like a sports team with top players in all positions.

One of the best deals Montgomery did in the 1990s came from a long-standing relationship dating back to 1976. It was a relationship that Weisel describes as "a huge labor of love," and it turned out to be a very profitable affair.

Dick Moley was a British engineer who came to the United States in 1966 to join Hewlett-Packard. He then joined Ken Oshman's team at ROLM, which the old Robertson, Colman, Seibel & Weisel took public in 1976, the young investment bank's third IPO. ROLM was sold to IBM in 1984 for $1.3 billion.

In 1986, Moley decided to try his hand at creating his own company, and founded Stratacom. The company made specialized equipment to control very fast computer networks for corporations. Local area networks (LANs) were not as widely popular as they are today, and not many investors understood the technology. Wide area networks (WANs), which connect not just people in a single building but can link a company's offices worldwide on a single network, are Stratacom's current specialty.

Stratacom went through two rounds of venture funding, then got some funding from Motorola, and then from Digital Equipment. But it kept eating through the capital. A year after its founding, it was getting close to breaking even, but had used up most of its funding.

Moley was pretty confident that Motorola would invest again. But he didn't really want to sell more shares in the company if he didn't have to, since it would dilute the ownership of its earlier investors (including Moley). So he turned to Weisel and partner Stephen Doyle, both of whom he admired enormously, for help. "I was confident in Montgomery's ability to raise the cash," says Moley. "I knew Thom's reputation as a banker who gets things done. I liked his dynamism and aggressiveness. He would tackle the harder deals and work at them."

Montgomery worked out a deal with Motorola: Instead of buying equity, how about simply helping to fund the R&D efforts at Stratacom? In return, Motorola would get the right to distribute the new products that Stratacom developed, selling them under Motorola's brand name.

The deal went through, putting another $7 million into Stratacom's research coffers. That got it to profitability by 1992, which (in those quaint days of pre-Internet investment banking) meant it could go public.

Initially, Moley decided to use Goldman Sachs as the lead banker and Montgomery as the secondary. He wanted the two firms to split the commission evenly (which was the usual arrangement in such deals) and thought he had agreement from both sides that that would be the approach. But there was apparently a misunderstanding at Goldman. Either whoever had agreed to the split fee didn't get word up the channels or someone shifted the strategy. Before the offering, Goldman demanded a "jump ball" approach: After the stock was sold, the commission would be split among the two bankers based on the percentage of investors each company brought in.

Moley, being British, thought that wasn't quite fair cricket. He felt that Weisel and Montgomery had always been ethical and fair to him in the past, and he didn't want to go back on his word to the firm. Goldman was one of the biggest investment banks in the world and had probably the strongest technology business among the big banks. And, as the lead banker, it would control the book, deciding who got the stock at the offering price, and would unfairly benefit from the transaction. "So I surprised the hell out of Goldman and dropped them from the deal," he says. Montgomery was moved to the left side of the prospectus, and Salomon Brothers was listed to the right as the secondary banker.

But in 1992, although the market was warming up, not many investors were willing to go in on an IPO with a company in a new field they little understood. "The deal was on the knife edge of being done, but below the price we originally wanted," says Moley. Investors indicated they would be willing to buy at $6 7/8, but $7 was Moley's magic number. At that price he would raise $20 million in the IPO and place the company's total valuation at $100 million. It was close, but they managed to push the IPO through at $7 per share in July 1992.

Stratacom's profits grew, the company began to look more promising, and when it decided to do a secondary offering in December 1994, Goldman wanted to renew its relationship. So Moley decided to let it back in, this time with Montgomery in the lead and Goldman as secondary.

Weisel, never one to be shy to assert himself (especially against people who had asserted themselves against him), then told Moley that if that was the case, he wanted to make it a jump ball deal. "I told him, 'Nice try,'" Moley laughs. "This was a matter of principle for me." The deal was done on a 50-50 split.

In April 1996, Montgomery helped negotiate a deal to sell Stratacom to Cisco Systems for $4.7 billion in stock. At that time, it was the biggest technology acquisition in history, and 47 times Stratacom's valuation at its IPO less than four years earlier.

In a prime example of how one Silicon Valley success story spawns another, and another, it's interesting to note that the head of marketing at Stratacom, Scott Kriens, went on to start a network router company called Juniper Networks, one of the few networking companies that has not been acquired by Cisco. Juniper's IPO in the heady days of 1999 was priced at $34 per share, but opened at $100 and closed at almost $99 on its first trading day. Kriens, however, chose Goldman Sachs, Credit Suisse First Boston, Banc-Boston Robertson Stephens, and Dain Rauscher Wessels to co-manage his IPO.

Despite its growth, Weisel kept Montgomery packed into a single building in San Francisco's Transamerica Pyramid. He found it easier to manage the diverse operations under one roof and felt it helped the different groups to work together synergistically. The company started 1990 with 364 employees and had grown to over 2,000 by the time Weisel left in 1998, after being acquired. Montgomery adopted the marketing phrase "The Other Street" to describe its namesake location around 1994, and "Power of Growth" to describe itself in 1996.

Competitors still claimed that Montgomery was dangerously aggressive, and short sellers liked targeting some of the firm's riskier clients, according to some press reports, although the short sellers were not always successful. But risk is part of the business. The issue is simply how much risk you can stomach and how well the risk is balanced with more conservative choices.

Montgomery did end up with one affiliation that sullied its reputation. In November 1992, it raised $45 million as the lead manager for a technology company called Media Vision. Everything started out looking terrific. Early in its history, Media Vision appeared to be an extraordinarily promising company. It built plug-in circuit boards that added rich sound and multimedia capabilities to personal computers. The field had been pioneered by a company called Creative Technology (later Creative Labs), which dominated the market, but Media Vision seemed to be gaining quickly.

Media Vision beat Creative Technology in putting out a new-generation board that used 16-bit chips, rather than the 8-bit chips of the previous generation, and it had worked with Microsoft to make its products easier to set up and run on PCs. An April 1993 article in *Business Week* magazine (ironically, written by Weisel's co-author on this book) asserted that Media Vision was likely to pose a strong challenge to Creative Technology.[1] Media Vision's stock peaked at over $46 in January 1994. Six months later, it was bankrupt.

It turned out that when Media Vision ran into trouble getting its products built and meeting its ambitious earnings projections, it resorted to a few accounting tricks to inflate profits. It reported revenue from the supposed sale of products that it had not yet finished building. It shipped slow-selling products to friends who returned them, then tucked them away in warehouses.[2] One of the tactics the company used sounds familiar to those paying attention to the twenty-first-century accounting scandals: It capitalized the cost of developing software, spreading the expense over several years rather than recording it in the year the money was spent, much as WorldCom recently capitalized operating costs like basic network maintenance. Generally, a company is supposed to capitalize only long-lasting and very expensive items, such as buildings or heavy machinery, with the justification that they will be used for many years and so can be written off over many years.

The CEO, Paul Jain, apparently had run into trouble before. In legal documents filed in May 1996, one of Jain's former bosses from another company criticized Montgomery Securities—as well as Media Vision's law firm, Wilson, Sonsini, Goodrich & Rosati, one of Silicon Valley's most prestigious law firms—for failing to conduct sufficient due diligence on Jain before taking the company public. The former boss told the *San Francisco Chronicle* that if they had spoken to him, he would have warned them about Jain's record of allegedly falsifying financial statements in the past.[3] However, no charges were ever filed against Montgomery or Wilson, Sonsini.

It was not the worst scandal to hit Silicon Valley, and, to be fair, no one else (including the press!) had done enough due diligence on the company to catch the problems until its revenue shortfall could no longer be hidden. And no investment bank can claim a perfect record.

The wheels of justice spin much more slowly than those of modern business. Jain finally submitted a guilty plea to two counts of wire fraud in August 2000, weeks before he was to go to trial. The former CFO, Steve Allan, was convicted in a jury trial in August

2002. By this time, of course, there were much bigger scandals to keep the press busy, and the case of Media Vision barely made a footnote in the local papers.

Risk Analysis

Thom W. Weisel

The investment banks I've run have always focused on the stocks of emerging growth companies. That poses a certain amount of risk. How do you determine which companies really have promise when they have little operating history? How do you know when it's time to take them public? How do you know if the company really has sustainability?

There's always a tension between risk and failure. But it's a necessary one. If you don't take risks, you don't accomplish anything. That's why risk takers tend to win and people who can't think out of the box don't. Nevertheless, keeping in mind the inherent risks involved, we try to be as conservative as possible.

I've already gone through some of the methods we use to make those judgments, including a strong reliance on our research analysts to help us find good companies with staying power. But even then, this still involves a certain amount of crystal ball gazing, because so many things can go wrong—from mismanagement to changes in the market to the arrival of a powerful new competitor.

One of the biggest issues that investment banks have faced in the last several years is determining the appropriate time to take a company public. The standards for determining the acceptable level of risk change over time. Should the company have at least three years of operating history, profitability, a large customer base?

I've been through it all. Even the largest investment banks, the ones with the most to lose for their franchise, have changed their focal length on what they deem to be an appropriate level of risk over the years. There was a time when Goldman Sachs and Morgan Stanley only wanted to take companies public if they already had several quarters of profitability.

But the HARM firms all made our living trying to find the next-wave companies. We wanted to get to them a little ahead of the curve, before the Goldmans and Morgans were there. In the 1970s we looked for some profitability, and by the 1980s we were looking for companies that at least had products that worked. When we took ROLM public, it was viewed mainly as a rugged computer company. But it was the PBX business that became a home run for ROLM. It wasn't a big business yet, but the products worked and were selling.

In biotechnology, however, even the rule of working products didn't always apply. Genentech went public without having any products on the market yet. When we took Amgen public in 1982, it had some products, but didn't yet have EPO, the drug that really made the company.

One of the most difficult companies I ever tried to take public was Applied Materials. Spending on chip equipment was very volatile, all over the map from year to year. Investors often don't like companies in cyclical markets, because it can be hard to predict future earnings. The lack of visibility of Applied's future profits was a hard thing to sell to investors. It was a lot easier to sell Victoria's Station with its railroad car restaurants than to sell Applied Materials. Victoria's Station's revenues and profits had more visibility, and it was a much easier concept for people to understand. But Victoria's Station eventually went bankrupt, while Applied has become a $7 billion company with a $31 billion market cap, the biggest chip equipment supplier in the world.

During the 1990s, however, the big investment banks went

way down the risk curve in order to catch these waves themselves, increasing our competition dramatically. Just as Genentech demonstrated that a biotech company didn't have to be profitable to have a spectacular IPO in the 1980s, Netscape proved that an Internet company could do the same in the 1990s. During the height of the dot-com boom, companies might go public at just one year old, without even a clear path to profitability. People accepted more risk because the promise of biotechnology and the Internet looked so big.

Periodically, we're reminded of the need for visibility in a company's projected financials. Without visibility, capital will not flow and market liquidity dries up.

Obviously, the tried and true rules of the capital markets were forgotten in the Internet boom. The Internet bust, and, more recently, accusations of faulty bookkeeping, again remind us of the need for transparency.

In large part, the investment banks respond to the level of risk the investors are willing to take. In the late 1990s, the investing public was willing to take a risk on companies with unproven technology or business plans that made little sense. The greed factor was so great that people discarded any sensible thought process. Major principles of investing were violated during this boom.

When you sit here in retrospect, you can ask how you could not have known that a particular company was going to fail when it had only three customers and they all canceled their orders. But its failure may have been completely unrelated to that. Its technology may actually be too early for the market. Or another company might take over the business with better marketing or newer disruptive technology. Or the market itself may simply change directions.

We have now returned to more traditional standards. Today, in order to find companies ready for an IPO, we look for those with unique technology, large growing markets, quality management teams, and visibility in revenues and earnings.

Given the early nature of the companies we deal with, we do as much due diligence as we can. We're in a service business that puts buyers and sellers together, with a lot of opinion from us in between. We talk to suppliers and customers. Then we do research on the market size and the company's development cycle and compare them to those of other companies that are similar in nature. When you're right and a Yahoo! happens, you get high fives all around.

Investing in consumer growth markets, for example, is complicated by the fact that the spending habits of the consumer are not that obvious. Why did Starbucks become such a huge success? It wasn't because of the coffee. It became a part of people's lifestyle, like walking to the store, meeting neighbors, getting a newspaper.

As a service provider for capital and ideas, we live in a risky world. We try to be smarter and better than anybody else. Our clients have confidence that we've checked all the boxes. But there are many uncertainties, given the state of the companies we work with. That's why in a prospectus the first few pages are titled "Risk Factors" and say things like, "We have a history of operating losses and our future profitability is uncertain," or "Two wholesalers account for a high percentage of our revenues." The list goes on and on.

As careful as you try to be, though, you can still be fooled. When we took Media Vision public in 1992, it looked like a good company. Its strategy made sense. It was a venture-backed company with high-quality VCs behind it. The venture capitalists generally do thorough due diligence. We heard that the CEO had some problems in the past, but the company in its current form had a good track record and lots of customers, so going back to what a guy did 20 years ago wasn't as relevant.

It turned out to be fraud. The company lied to us. Other companies, past and present, have used similar tactics to fool their investors, research analysts, and, yes, even their auditors.

The point is that if someone really wants to commit fraud, that person can hide the truth—for a while. Eventually, though, it comes out. The only way to prepare for this sort of thing, or any of the risks of the stock market, is to make sure your investments are always diversified. Never put all your money into one stock, no matter who tells you otherwise.

And thank God there are really very few companies like that.

Politics and Art

Think it more satisfactory to live richly than die rich.
—*Sir Thomas Browne*

Thom Weisel actually has other interests besides sports and business. He manages to spend some of his excess leisure time—and money—on politics and art.

The San Francisco Bay area is an eclectic political domain. The city itself is about as left-wing as any city outside of the former Soviet Union. But there is also extraordinary wealth packed so tightly into Silicon Valley that it can't help but ooze out through the entire Bay Area. Even with the devastating recession in technology at the start of the twenty-first century, the wealth (and its attendant political attitudes) continues to spread.

The Bay Area has become one of the most expensive places to live, spearheading a flight of middle-income families who didn't manage to buy a home before dot-com inflation took hold. Median home prices are over half a million dollars. In August 2002, Coldwell Banker's annual Home Price Comparison Index listed Palo Alto, the spiritual heart of Silicon Valley, as the most expensive market in the country for a "typical home" (defined as "a 2,200-square-foot, single-family dwelling with four bedrooms,

2 1/2 baths, a family room, and a two-car garage in a typical middle management transferee neighborhood").

The average price for such a home in Palo Alto is $1.26 million, according to the real estate company (San Francisco comes in at just over $911,000). It is the only such market in the United States where the price of the average home exceeds $1 million. The most expensive similar market outside of California is Darien, Connecticut, at $812,000. It's tough not to be rich in Silicon Valley.

Home loan foreclosure filings, which have been traditionally very low in the Bay Area, jumped 38 percent in the first quarter of 2002, and another 13 percent in the second quarter, over the same periods a year earlier. In order to try to maintain some semblance of a middle class, the City of San Francisco offers first-time home-buying assistance to residents unlucky enough to have a household income under $95,000.

This kind of wealth means there is also a strong antitax coalition with a predilection for Reagan-style Republican politics (and that includes the moneyed class in San Francisco).

Corporate politics are mixed. Executives in Silicon Valley were notoriously apolitical until fairly recently. They preferred to ignore the federal government whenever possible, hoping it would prove irrelevant. But in the mid-1980s, the semiconductor industry lobbied hard for (and won) retaliation against Asian companies that were dumping chips on the U.S. market, selling them at a loss in order to capture control of the market.

In the mid-1990s, most of the high-tech community became highly politicized when Bill Clinton vetoed a new regulation making it harder to file shareholder class action suits every time a company's stock dropped. Most Silicon Valley executives, whether liberal or conservative, consider such lawsuits to be overwhelmingly unfounded, dishonest, costly, damaging to America, and immoral.

The technology community felt betrayed by Clinton, and managed to muster up the lobbying effort to get the veto overturned. Today, just about the only proregulatory stance in the Valley is a near universal desire to enforce antimonopoly laws against certain out-of-state software companies (the results on this one have so far been disappointing).

There are also strong Democrats in Silicon Valley. John Doerr, a partner at Kleiner Perkins Caufield & Byers and probably the world's most visible venture capitalist, was a big supporter of Al Gore's 2000 presidential campaign, leading to rumors (denied by Doerr) that the VC could become Gore's running mate on the Democratic ticket. Perhaps the refrain some Silicon Valley wag came up with during Gore's 2000 campaign, "Gore and Doerr in 2004!" will make a comeback in a couple years.

In Silicon Valley, at least, politics rarely seem to get in the way of business or friendships. While Doerr is a powerful Democrat, another partner at his firm, E. Floyd Kvamme, is currently chairman of the antitax, minimal-government organization Empower America and is now President Bush's Technology Czar. Weisel is on the board of Empower America, is an admirer of Ronald Reagan, and is good friends with Jack Kemp, Bill Bennett, and former Republican California Governor Pete Wilson, while another of Weisel's friends and former colleagues, Dick Fredericks, is a Friend of Bill Clinton. Such diverse partnerships are common in the tech community. Politics are still not relevant enough to affect relationships, business or otherwise.

The majority of Silicon Valley executives who feel like talking about their political beliefs these days describe themselves as libertarian. That is not to be interpreted as card-carrying members of the official Libertarian Party, but a philosophical agreement that the smallest government possible is best. These executives believe in the basic honesty, fairness, and self-regulatory nature of the capitalist system. The libertarian culture in Silicon Valley is so strong that personal ads in the newspapers have been known, on more than one occasion, to express the advertiser's sensitive literary attributes by professing a strong fondness for the novels of Ayn Rand.[1]

A few executives in the area have actually thought about political philosophy for many years. Thom Weisel is one of them. His father was a huge fan of Ayn Rand. Weisel never read her books, but knew all about them through his father. In general, he and his father never discussed politics, but were more likely to discuss the societies of the ancient Greeks and Romans. Weisel is a powerful libertarian.

In the first decade or two after college, he focused on building his business. A friend got him involved in supporting the Republican candidacy of California Governor Pete Wilson, a friend of President Reagan, who was voted into office in 1993. Ted Forstmann, founding partner of the investment firm Forstmann Little & Co. and founding chairman of Empower America, introduced Weisel to his organization. Through Empower America, Weisel met Jack Kemp—one of the organization's founders, Bob Dole's running mate in 1996, champion of capital gains tax relief, and former football star.

Weisel and Kemp hit it off immediately, of course. Says the former quarterback and 1965 American Football League MVP, "He's much more of an all-around athlete than I am. He would have been a great pro football quarterback, and that's the highest compliment I can pay to anyone." As for politics, "He's a bleeding heart capitalist," adds Kemp. "He's a populist free enterpriser. He wants capitalism to work for everyone."

Weisel joined the board of Empower America in 1993, and when Steve Forbes resigned as chairman of the organization in 1996 in order to make his own bid for the presidency, Kemp asked Weisel to take over. He did so for three years, beginning in 1996. Then he got involved in starting his new company and turned over the chairmanship to Silicon Valley venture capitalist E. Floyd Kvamme. Weisel is currently still on the board of Empower America.

One of Weisel's most significant contributions to the organization may have been to build up its finances. Empower America was launched with about $5 million in financing, mostly personal contributions by the founders. "They went off into the sunset thinking they would never have to raise more money," says Weisel.

They were wrong, and the organization was in financial straits by the time Weisel took over. Weisel began lobbying friends and business associates for donations, and raised many millions for the organization. He has always been pretty good at fund-raising.

But money was certainly not the only support he gave to the organization. "His financial contribution was significant, but a big part of his contribution was leadership," says Kemp. "He tightened our belt, brought in a lot of his friends, and focused our energy on major areas of public policy where we could make a difference—such as capital gains taxes, free trade, the regulatory burden in telecom. He loved the issues of educational choice, welfare reform, and maintaining a strong national defense."

Weisel, in fact, unwittingly helped to politicize Silicon Valley by taking on the issue that Silicon Valley executives had chafed under for years: reforming the process under which class action suits may be filed against corporations for alleged financial misdeeds. It is, of course, an enormously controversial issue, unless your viewpoint comes from Silicon Valley.

In reality, there are merits to the technology community's complaints. Over the decades, dozens of companies have been sued whenever their stock price took an unexpected dip, generally under accusations that management failed to give sufficient warning. But technology companies have always had volatile stock prices. These are very young industries and do not have the steady, predictable growth that characterizes more mature businesses. Markets change; new technologies replace old ones; some technologies never catch on; market shortages and gluts come and go.

And, to be fair, it can be argued that investors themselves shared the blame for bloated stock prices. Having missed out on the plastics industry, people get so excited about technology stocks that they have long had a tendency to bid up stock valuations to unsustainable levels, even when they don't really understand a company's business. They found out how unsustainable when the bubble burst.

The perception from the Valley is that some law firms simply found this an extraordinarily rich environment in which to practice their class action suit tactics. "There was a time when you could simply buy one share in every public company in order to become part of class action suits," says Jack Levin, the former director of legal and regulatory affairs at Montgomery. But the companies that profited the most were often the law firms that filed the suits and negotiated settlements. "Shareholders got less than seven cents on the dollar for every settlement," says Levin. Investment banks were often named as defendants in these suits.

And yet, despite the volatility, the rise in technology stocks over the decades has outperformed practically every other investment on the planet. In many cases, everyone but the law firms would have made more money by holding onto the technology stocks until the cycle turned up again.

In the early 1990s, Congress began drafting reform legislation, in part due to complaints from Silicon Valley. A copy of the early proposals came across Levin's desk. He thought it was flawed with loopholes, and decided to draft a letter to key members of Congress to raise his complaints.

But before mailing the letter, he decided he'd better run it by his boss, just so he wouldn't be taken by surprise. Weisel studied the proposal much more diligently than Levin expected and came back to him with two suggestions: to add his own signature to the letter, and to send it to 100 Montgomery clients to see what they thought of it. "He could not have been more supportive," says Levin. "He not only said go do it, but asked how he could help. He is an incredible leader."

The letter was received like a glass of cool water in the Mojave Desert. Within two days, says Levin, over half of the clients had called him asking to add their names as well. So Levin expanded the list of recipients, and the letter spread across the technology community and the country. Levin even got a letter from Ford Motor Co., a company with which he had never had any dealings, asking to be included. "Suddenly, I had an ad hoc committee on securities litigation reform," says Levin.

Instead of mailing the letter, Levin ended up traveling to Washington to present his case in person. Weisel, who was then chairman of Empower America, tapped the organization to get access to key members of Congress. "Every congressman who read it would flip to the back page to see who signed it," recalls Levin. That gave him the inspiration to make a change: listing signatories by region, so politicians could see who from their territories had signed.

Levin ended up helping to draft the 1995 Securities Litigation Reform Act. It still had one flaw. Opponents kept it from including provisions to preempt state laws, enabling litigants to make an end run through state legislatures. Not even sympathetic Republican supporters could afford to try to change that provision, since they traditionally support the idea of states' rights over federal.

Nevertheless, President Clinton vetoed the bill, launching the furor and sense of betrayal in Silicon Valley. Encouraged by top industry executives, especially those in the Valley, Congress easily came up with the votes to override the veto.

Within months, the battle moved to California. An initiative was put on the state ballot to make it easier to file class action securities suits in the state. Levin and Weisel helped to campaign against the bill, which was defeated. Then Levin went back to Washington to testify before Congress that the California initiative proved the flaw of the federal bill. It was successfully altered to preempt state law.

It was an enormous coup for the Silicon Valley business scene, which showed the kind of clout it could have in Washington when it put in the effort.

This whole effort may now seem misguided, given the current environment in which accounting and financial scandals have destroyed both companies and investors' portfolios (see Chapter 13). "Some people will say, 'you changed the law, and now look what happened,'" acknowledges Levin. "But it's not true. I want the fraud-doers locked up as well. Media Vision was one of our companies. I didn't want to stop that case, I wanted to be a plaintiff!"

Levin asserts that the Reform Act was designed only to stop frivolous lawsuits, not legitimate ones. He says it merely tries to define more clearly what constitutes fraud, raises the bar for pleading, and stops people from collecting "bounties" for becoming plaintiffs. "Now you're going to see a lot of cleaning up" of financial accounting, says Levin, with appropriate lawsuits filed against companies that deserve to be sued.

Either way, the issue demonstrated Weisel's political as well as business clout in the nation's affairs.

While Weisel's youthful enthusiasm for politics conflicted with the views of his first wife, his passion for art is actually what led him to his current wife, and it is one source of the bond between them. Weisel collects both modern art and Native American antiquities. In August 1990, when Emily was 24 and he was 49, he walked into an art gallery in Santa Fe, New Mexico, where she was working.

Pete Wilson first met Thom Weisel in the late 1980s. A mutual friend introduced them at a dinner party of about half a dozen people. Wilson recalls that he and some friends had been fishing that day, didn't have time to go home for a shower and change beforehand, and "smelled terrible." But they decided that "instead of being horribly late, we made excuses."

Weisel had no problem with the fishing team's appearance or odor, but found a great partner with whom to discuss business, politics, and sports at great length. "He's very down-to-earth, very smart, and a good listener," says Wilson, who later became governor of California. "He asked very good questions. It was evident that the guy had genuine interest in the conversation, which is as flattering as the converse is not."

Wilson was impressed not only with Weisel's knowledge of the topics and his business success, but with his understated personal demeanor. Wilson never heard about Weisel's own athletic exploits until he was told by others. "He puts you at ease, unlike some people who have been competitive athletes," says Wilson. "I've known some that are a pain in the butt. But I've never heard Thom mention his own accomplishments."

They became (you guessed it) close friends, as well as political allies. Wilson is not involved directly with Empower America, but is friends with several people in the organization, including Jack Kemp, Jeanne Kirkpatrick, Bill Cohen, and Bill Bennett. Wilson has called on Weisel from time to time to help with political causes.

Undoubtedly, Wilson's admiration is enhanced by Weisel's political bent, which Wilson describes like this: "He is a good, strong fiscal conservative. Like a number of Republicans in

California, he has strong social views, is pro-choice, and is interested in protecting the environment, but only when the protections are based on honest science. I share most of these views, so naturally I think he's marvelously rational."

But Wilson also just likes the guy. He recalls when Lance Armstrong won his first Tour de France in 1999. Wilson, Weisel, and some friends were in Europe, watching the race on television before Weisel had the opportunity to catch up in person. Weisel was so excited watching as Lance won a stage of the race that his friends kidded him about his over-the-top enthusiasm. "It was a great joy to watch Thom for an hour as he watched Lance win the Tour de France," says Wilson. "He's really fun to be with."

Emily figured he was maybe 40, had no kids, and was probably an art dealer. She had no idea how wealthy he was. When they met, he was in training for his last major pastime, Masters cycling, where he became a world champion. "He was in phenomenal shape from bike racing then," recalls Emily.

She then found out that he had children about her age. They dated long distance for a while, and after about a year she moved to San Francisco, where they were married. Emily had barely a clue what investment banking was, but she and Thom found they had a lot of other things in common. She has influenced his taste in art, especially in native American antiquities. And she has taken up cycling herself. She's become a better skier. They love traveling to Europe, looking at architecture and art, as long as there's also cycling involved. He's mellowed a little. Plus, she adds, he's very energetic and does not act his age. "He's got a young side to him," she says. "Even today he looks very young."

Weisel approaches art the way he does everything else: by getting intimately involved with the subject and learning everything he can. He likes to meet artists in person if possible. With a few, particularly the California artist Wayne Thiebaud, he has struck a good friendship. Weisel admires artists for their difference from himself: unstructured, creative in a way that he is not, and willing to embrace a risky profession that may never pay a livable wage.

His interest in art goes back three decades. Introduced to modern art by some friends who were part of a San Francisco art group in the early 1970s, he set out to find out as much as he could about modern art. He read books, such as *Systems and Dialectics of Art* by John Graham, an eccentric artist and philosopher (he liked to ride around Paris on a horse, was prone to wearing a large cape, and was into the occult). Graham became an intellectual guru, and his book (published in 1937) a guiding philosophy for many of the Abstract Expressionists. These artists became prominent in the 1950s and 1960s, and some are still painting today.

Weisel talked to experts to learn what they liked. His best source was a New York art dealer named Allan Stone. Weisel found in Stone a source he liked and could trust, and drew as much information out of him as he could. When he felt he had learned enough about the topic, he started collecting a few pieces. Weisel's firm, Robertson Colman Siebel & Weisel, first bought a few pieces from Stone for the office, and all the former partners have gone back to him to buy art. "Thom was the most enthusiastic and adventurous," says Stone. "He's a great student."

Stone has been a strong influence on Weisel, and Weisel developed another friendship. Stone, who also has a house in San Francisco, recalls an important incident in his life. About 10 years ago, he had a heart attack while playing tennis in San Francisco. He was rushed to the hospital where, he says, he "literally died. I had the whole out-of-body experience, the white light, everything."

The doctors brought him back, though, and when he woke up, one of the physicians told him, "I don't know who you are, but people have been calling from all over the country telling me what to do with you. There's a local guy here who says he's taking charge of your case."

"A doctor?" asked Stone.

"No, an investment banker."

Says Stone: "That's just the kind of guy Thommy is."

Stone specializes in Abstract Expressionist art, but also deals in other art and particularly likes finding and showing new talent. One of those new artists was a California painter named Wayne Thiebaud. Thiebaud came to Stone's gallery in 1961 after almost all the other galleries in New York had turned him down. He showed Stone his paintings, which at that time were of things like pies and cakes and lollipops. "I thought, Are you kidding?" recalls Stone. But he decided to take some of Thiebaud's paintings home and live with them for awhile. "The more I looked at them, the more insistent they became," says Stone. "His pictures always make you feel good. They make you smile."

After Weisel met Stone a decade or so later, he became a dedicated collector of Thiebaud's work. Now Thiebaud is one of the country's leading contemporary artists.

Weisel also developed a particular fondness for the New York Abstract Expressionists and the California Bay Area Figurative artists. As his income allowed, he collected more, and now has an impressive collection. Says Stone: "We didn't spend a lot of money on things. Good collecting is all about sharpshooting, not about big expenditures. It's about keeping the aesthetic sense high; finding stuff that makes your hair stand up."

Weisel followed that philosophy. Aside from Thiebaud, Weisel has collected paintings by Willem de Kooning, Arshile Gorky, Franz Kline, Frank Stella, Ellsworth Kelly, Richard Diebenkorn, David Parks, and Nathan Oliveira. He also started picking up sculpture, including works by Barry Flanagan, Aristide Maillol, Henry Moore, Richard Serra, and David Smith. "He's built a very beautiful collection," says Glenn Lowry, director of the New York Museum of Modern Art. "If forced to, I'd take it!"

When Weisel started collecting them in the 1970s, many of the works were relatively cheap—say, $10,000 to $15,000. Following Stone's philosophy, he chooses art for the emotional impact it has on him. But he also acknowledges that he felt these artists' works had huge potential to increase dramatically in value. From his studies of the history of art, he felt that the Abstract Expressionists, in particular, were undervalued when put into the context of the development of painting over the past several centuries.

To Weisel, discerning the value of these paintings was similar to determining the value of underappreciated entrepreneurial companies and athletes. In November 2002, Weisel decided to take advantage of a very strong art market and put 21 paintings up for sale through Sotheby's. The sale brought record prices for three California artists: Thiebaud (over $3 million), Oliveira ($317,500), and Park ($779,500). It also set a record for a Kline painting (over $4.5 million). The lead painting, de Kooning's *Orestes*, sold for over $13 million. Weisel netted over $40 million from the auction. Although not all the paintings sold, indicating a weakening market, Weisel couldn't lose: Sotheby's had guaranteed a minimum price for the lot. The auction house can now keep the unsold paintings or try to sell them again. If they sell for more than the minimum already paid to Weisel, most of the upside will go to him.

Weisel says he hated to sell the paintings but couldn't resist when he realized how much they were worth. His tastes have also evolved, and he's collecting more contemporary art as well as moving into primitive Oceanic art these days.

Weisel also supports the arts. He joined the board of the San

Francisco Museum of Modern Art in 1983. He's a strong contributor to the museum and helped to raise the money for SFMOMA's impressive new downtown museum, which dramatically revived attendance at the museum. A plaque on the second floor of the museum dedicates a wing to him. Weisel also helped SFMOMA buy several paintings, among them works by Wayne Thiebaud and James Weeks, and he and Emily cochaired the capital-raising campaign for the California College of Arts and Crafts, raising $15 million for a new San Francisco building.

Several years ago, New York MOMA director Lowry began looking for a Silicon Valley connection who might help to create a technology advisory board as the museum moved into the electronic arts. "We realized that technology was going to be an integral part of what we're doing at the museum," says Lowry. One of the museum's trustees suggested he try Thom Weisel, who was a collector of modern art himself.

They met over breakfast in 1996, and Lowry was bowled over. "Thom was like a dream come true," says Lowry. "He brings a really fresh perspective to the board, contributes both his time and money, and is always available for advice. He comes to every board meeting he can. He is a genuinely good guy."

Like Emily, Lowry also admires Weisel's energy. "He has two speeds: stop and full blast," says Lowry. Weisel joined the board of New York MOMA in 1996. He helped pull together the technical advisory board, which now includes Yahoo!'s Tim Koogle and venture capitalists Geoff Yang and Mike Leventhal. Weisel has given a number of promised gifts to MOMA, including works by Serra and Gursky. A few years ago, Weisel also helped MOMA create the largest retrospective of the work of Jackson Pollack ever produced. Weisel contributed time and money and brought in some of the biggest sponsors the museum has ever had for a special exhibition.

Adds Lowry: "There's something exhilarating about being around somebody as energetic as Thom. And he has high standards. To be around Thom is to be around somebody who is determined to excel."

Philosophically Speaking

Thom W. Weisel

Politics and art are real passions of mine. I've been interested in political thought since college. I was really challenged by the political courses at Stanford—studying such issues as the Civil Rights Act and Constitutional law, reading Kierkegaard and Heidegger, just being exposed to a lot of material that really stimulated thought on the issues.

Of course, Stanford is pretty liberal, and I was always getting into heated discussions with my professors. I've always leaned toward the more conservative philosophy, and was intrigued with Barry Goldwater. I would debate the value of free markets with my professors, arguing for the merits of a libertarian society versus one where the government promised to take care of everything for you. I didn't have a definite view on it at the time, but was still trying to get my arms around the issue.

My interest in politics lay dormant through much of my adult life as I spent time building my business. But once I was given the opportunity to make a difference, I decided to become involved.

My political philosophy revolves around the need to encourage entrepreneurial capitalism. I always felt the tax code in this country impeded the ability to accumulate capital, which is anathema to entrepreneurs; it's their reward for taking risks, for creating new companies and new industries. The harder you work, the more you contribute to the economy and to society, the more you have to pay. It just didn't seem fair to penalize the most productive part of society with progressive tax rates. And the first thing President Clinton did in office was to jack up taxes and implement a millionaire's tax rate.

I therefore felt Empower America had a very important role to play to counterbalance the liberalism of the Clinton administration. We had to take the viewpoint of the entrepreneur. Empower America is a good pro-growth advocacy group, a perfect fit with my views. At Empower America, we believe in free markets, free trade, lower taxes, and incentives that reward hard work.

Through Empower America, we've been able to take on some important issues. Empower America proved to be key in helping bring about securities litigation reform. Through members' contacts and access, we were able to get to the right people at the right time. Jack Levin and I would sit down with some of the most influential senators and congressmen in the country and explain why this was so important.

The industry groups—including the Securities Industry Association, the National Venture Capital Association, and the accounting industry—did a great job of bringing about changes in issues that directly affected them. But once they got what they wanted, they just didn't care about other things that might improve the situation in the United States. That's perfectly understandable. They had specific goals, and it wasn't their role to take a broad political stance.

It was a pleasure to work with Jack Levin on that issue. We put in an enormous amount of time to defeat Proposition 211 in California. That bill was insidious and destructive to entrepreneurial capitalism. It would have benefited a few lawyers at the expense of companies and shareholders.

I also have great admiration for Jack Kemp. He's an unabashed advocate for capitalism and the free enterprise system. I don't think that capital gains tax relief would have happened without him.

There are still a lot of issues to deal with. It's important to start bridging the gap between the lower and upper financial tiers of society. Government handouts will never help anyone build a strong economic foundation for their families. For that, you've got to offer incentives that reward independence and hard work. When people show they really want to reeducate themselves and build a career, the government should support them in the endeavor. Wisconsin has a system based on this philosophy, and it has worked out extremely well.

Right now, the incentives are backward. If an unwed mother stays home and has more babies, she gets more money. We're offering incentives that encourage people to stay out of the job market, rather than encouraging them to get into the job market.

I'm a big supporter of changes in education in this country. It's at the core of a lot of our problems, the thing that needs the most help. The federal government has not done a very good job with K–12 education. You can't dictate sound educational policy with one-size-fits-all edicts from Washington. This issue should be dealt with on a more local level, as each state sees fit.

There's no quick fix in helping the poorest parts of society get a good education. That requires jobs and economic growth. A strong business environment supports a strong educational system.

There are a whole host of things that local governments could do to help public schools. We must start supporting schools on the basis of their performance. We need to monitor the performance of the students, the educators, and the schools and help to support the approaches that work.

Teaching is a very rewarding profession, and there seems to be an adequate flow of people willing to get into it. But teachers need to make a livable wage, and their salaries haven't kept pace with the cost of living. Here in the Bay Area it's a particularly difficult problem. We should stop compensating teachers based solely on their seniority, a common flaw of a bureaucratic government-run system, and implement merit-based compensation for teachers.

The Education Bill that passed in December 2001, which increases federal spending and requires annual tests in reading and math, unfortunately does not adequately address these issues. The only successful approach to education reform is to introduce market-based incentives at the state level, such as charter schools and private school vouchers, so that every family can have access to the finest education. These are the types of approaches we advocate at Empower America.

I'm not a big environmentalist, but I'm big on trying to get more open lands with access for everybody. I'm obviously interested in cleaner air and purer water. I contribute to the Nature Conservancy to keep lands free and open to the public. But I'm not in favor of shutting down important projects because of a bird that happens to live on a particular piece of property. We tend to go a little overboard on this kind of issue in this country. If it were up to me, we'd be drilling in the Alaska wilderness. It's hugely important to do whatever we can to become energy self-sufficient, so that we don't become more embroiled in the Middle East. The environmental impact is not as great as the alarmists try to lead us to believe.

I'm not a big fan of tax policies aimed at creating alternative energy sources. It's just more government meddling in what people want to do. This approach usually ends up being more trouble than it's worth.

I've been concerned about security and building a strong defense. Jeanne Kirkpatrick and Donald Rumsfeld have been on the board of Empower America and have written a number of very good papers on the issue. I'm worried about how volatile the nuclear situation is, especially in light of terrorism in the world, and I was concerned about Clinton's lack of attention to the situation.

But I'm not a pure Republican, either. Where I part ways with the Republican Party—and with some board members of Empower America—is over social issues. I believe in a woman's right to choose. I differ with Republicans on the issue of admissions policies in universities. I have some sympathy for the idea that the best people ought to be admitted. But it's also important that people with less privilege have access to a good education. It's also better to have a more rounded student body.

I also disagree with many Republicans' stance on illegal aliens. If people have been here for a number of years, I'm not just for kicking them out or denying them medical care or an education. They're generally doing very useful things for this country. In many cases, they're doing jobs that others simply don't want.

I don't even necessarily agree with Kemp on every issue. I don't believe in the gold standard that he promotes, for example. Currencies are fixed when they are tied to the gold standard, but world economies change, and currencies ought to float with those changes. You don't just give everybody a hall pass. Governments have to be held accountable for their own economies and the value of their currencies.

I support politicians who are pro-business and pro-entrepreneurial capitalism. I supported George W. Bush. I have a lot of admiration for Dick Cheney, Colin Powell, Bill Bennett, and Jack Kemp. I also really like Willie Brown, the Democratic mayor of San Francisco. He's a real character, but he's a great politician and he understands entrepreneurship and the role of business in a community. He's very supportive of market forces.

Basically, I feel the government's role is to create rules that ensure a level playing field in business and to provide us with the essential services we need to keep the country running. Other than that, it should stay as small as possible, keeping taxes low and keeping money in the pockets of Americans who work for it.

I still go to Empower America meetings whenever possible, although my new company has kept me pretty busy lately. I also try to give enough attention to my positions at the New York and San Francisco Museums of Modern Art.

My interest in art began some 30 years ago. I took architectural appreciation courses at Stanford, and now I wish I had taken some art appreciation courses as well. The genesis of my interest was probably when my brother and I went to Europe after college. We traveled around looking at the architecture and then started visiting the major museums.

In the early 1970s, some friends and I joined a group called SECA, the Society for the Encouragement of Contemporary Art. Every year SECA chooses a Bay Area artist who has exceptional talent but has not been widely recognized, and awards the artist a cash prize and an exhibition at SFMOMA. I got to know some of the young artists through that program.

With that, I started thinking, Well, art looks pretty intriguing. I really got interested in the intellectual process behind the artists' thinking, and how that philosophy was manifested on canvas. It's kind of a right brain versus left brain thing, with art almost the yin next to the yang of sports and business. It's much more intuitive, not nearly as objective.

I didn't really know anything about art when I started, and I didn't start buying right away. I didn't have the money. For a few years, I would sit down with local artists and talk about art, just trying to learn. I started visiting galleries and reading books.

Friends told me I had to go to New York to see the galleries there. But I was really turned off by the pomp and circumstance of the New York gallery scene. I'd walk in and they'd try to get rid of me as quickly as possible. They had a lot more interesting art in the back room, but I was never invited to go see it. Unless you're a known collector they won't pay any attention to you.

As I learned more, all I saw at most galleries was an ability to gouge buyers. You could drive a Mack truck through the spreads they were asking. I couldn't figure out what anything was worth. It didn't look like there was a clear market for most art.

Then a friend of mine heard I was interested in art and introduced me to Allan Stone. In 1973, I went to Stone's gallery in Manhattan. Instead of a fancy showplace on 57th Street, his gallery was in an old building on 84th and Madison. The place was totally overrun with art, African masks, things from New Guinea, stuff just piled all over the place. Then out comes Allan in casual clothes, sneakers, and a big smile—a real contrast with the stiffs on 57th.

He was terrific. I was full of questions about the current art scene: Color Field painters, new Pop Art, and Abstract Expressionism. I asked who Allan liked and who he did not, and why—nitty-gritty stuff. Our first meeting lasted three or four hours. I was astounded that anybody with Allan's stature would spend that much time with me. Allan has been extremely helpful in guiding me where I had interests. He has had the biggest influence on my understanding of art over the decades.

As my tastes refined, I started getting to know a few artists. So I made a mission of not just getting to know the art, but getting to know the artists themselves. The Thiebauds today are great friends, as is Nathan Oliveira, a Bay Area artist who was a professor at Stanford for 20 years. I didn't know Richard Diebenkorn well, but I knew him.

I got help from people I knew. One of my friends from Stanford, John Eastman, was a great connection. His dad was a lawyer who acted as a confidante to many of the New York School

Abstract Expressionists and was good friends with Mark Rothko and Willem de Kooning. John was good enough to introduce me to de Kooning.

I've always had an affinity for artists. They're people who are dedicating themselves to a totally different world than mine. They're pursuing something that's an absorbing passion for them, creating new ways of expressing themselves, a path that rarely leads to a career or an ability to make much money. There's no end game. They just do it. Perhaps I have a little envy of that ability.

Wayne Thiebaud is probably one of the most insightful, witty, and artistic people you could ever hope to meet. Not only is his art incredible, but it's very eclectic. He doesn't just have one style; over 25 years, his stylistic characteristics have become entirely different, from painting rows of pies in the 1960s to urban landscapes in the 1980s and 1990s to more rural scenes today. He has an incredible depth of knowledge of painting and a wonderful ability to put it into context with history.

But he's also an amazingly humble individual. It's not easy to draw information out of him. He doesn't like to represent himself as an expert. But that doesn't mean he's quiet, and I love to engage him in dialogue about an artist whose show we've both seen. He loves to teach, and he plays competitive tennis every day. Wayne and his wife, Betty Jean, have enriched my life.

My tastes continue to change and expand over time. I like the post-World War II Abstract Expressionists. Their work came out of Cubism and Surrealism, but the Abstract Expressionists found an entirely new modality for themselves. It was a reflection of the changes society was going through at the time, moving into new and uncharted waters both economic and societal. Many of the artists had gone through the Depression. They emerged with a brand-new energy and form of communication, a new poetry. It's leading-edge stuff, beautiful and intellectually powerful. It reflects the enthusiasm and pent-up energy and brilliance that's embodied in entrepreneurial capitalism. They're very intellectual artists. I really responded to this art.

Out of the 90-plus artists painting in the 1940s and 1950s, I particularly gravitated to de Kooning, Gorky, and Kline. I tried to understand their entire body of work, then collected only what I felt was the best work representing the best periods of those artists. In the same vein, the Bay Area has produced its own masters, and from this group I started collecting works by Wayne Thiebaud, Richard Diebenkorn, Nathan Oliveira, and David Park.

These days, Emily and I continue to expand our horizons. Over the past several years, we've enjoyed collecting the more contemporary paintings, photographs, and sculptures of Andreas Gursky, Ellsworth Kelly, Richard Serra, Sean Scully, Sol Lewitt, Michael Craig-Martin, Enrico Castellani, Barry Flanagan, and Jun Kaneko. We're also collecting a few younger California artists doing great work, such as Tony Berlant, Charles Arnoldi, Michael Tompkins, Naomi Kremer, Deborah Oropallo, Dennis Clive, and David Beck.

Art is about formulating your own ideas and getting them to come out in your work. It's mostly replicating other movements in a new and better way. There isn't really anything completely new, unless it's conceptual or video art or one of the new art forms that I've never been interested in. Very seldom do you see breakthroughs.

Andreas Gursky might be an exception. He takes photographs and makes them look like art. His pictures are totally manufactured, done with digital manipulation, cutting and pasting, transforming a scene into something uniquely interesting and different. His most famous picture is one of the Rhine River and the river bank. It's been recut into three powerful horizontal bands of color; sky, river, and land. Unless you look at it carefully, it looks like an abstract painting. If you found that place on the Rhine, you'd see houses and people and garbage all over the ground. Gursky manipulated that to create a beautiful image.

I also met Tony Berlant, who was friends with Thiebaud, Diebenkorn, and many of the Southern California artists. I liked Berlant's own art so much I bought some. His work is all done in metal, but is hung like a painting.

Berlant is also probably the world's authority on Native American weavings and prehistoric pottery. He's been instrumental in helping me to understand the Native American world, as has John Holstein, another trusted advisor.

I've studied and developed an admiration for some of the native American art forms. Navajo blankets look like Barnett Newman paintings. But they were woven in the mid-1800s for the people's own use, not as art. When you see an old image of a Navajo woman on the plains of New Mexico weaving something, it turns out to be a blanket for her chief. It's amazingly well done, all animal-dyed materials, and aesthetically incredible.

Ceramic bowls from between 800 and 1200 A.D. were mainly ceremonial pieces, created for the deceased, and were located at the grave site. The geometry and graphic depictions are very Picasso-esque and show humans evolving from fish or other animals.

Among the most fascinating Southwest tribes are the Hopi. Their ancestors, the Sitaki, created flat ceramic bowls with abstracted kachinas (their many gods) painted on the outside. The most famous painter in the historic Hopi works of pottery was Nanpayo, who memorialized many of the Hopi symbols in her pottery.

The Northwest Indians were best known for their work in wood, especially the Shemshun masks done for the shaman of the village. Their rattles, knives, and totem poles are rich in iconographic material and craftsmanship.

Apache baskets also incorporate a beauty rarely seen in other native peoples' crafts. The Apache created these objects that were never meant to be art. They were to be used.

Emily and I have had some great experiences together in our pursuit of this field. In the Hopi tradition, a bean dance inaugurates the beginning of the growing season. It starts with the dancers representing the kachinas, who have been sleeping and resting in the San Francisco mountain ranges during the winter. They come down from the mountain ranges, traveling under the earth, to the mesas of the Hopi in Arizona just before sunup. The Crow Mother leads this group of kachinas into the village. For two days they go through a ritual, dancing to the gods that are going to give them plentiful crops for the year. These dances only take place in the late afternoon or at 2 A.M.

The men do a ritual dance around the parts of the tribe, go into every home, and bring out every young man. Some are punished because they've been bad, others they give new things to because they've been very good. It's an astounding ceremony. We went down to Arizona, outside of Flagstaff, with Tony Berlant and John Holstein to see one of these ceremonies when my son was three years old. I don't think he'll forget it his whole life.

In the lobby of our company I have a carving of a Haida shaman, a medicine man from the Northwest. These tribes have a lot of ceremonies. The masks and rattles they use in these ceremonies are incredibly magical.

The Haida, from the Queen Charlotte islands 30 miles off the coast of Alaska, had a fascinating culture. An individual would have a potlatch, a ceremony in which he or she would give away most of his or her possessions to the tribe. The Canadian government couldn't figure out why anyone would do that, so the practice was outlawed for decades.

The Haida build totem poles that are graphic depictions of the fish, birds, and animals that are a part of the tribe's ecosystem. A raven is a transforming figure, able to change from a bird into a woman.

Jim Hart, a Haida, designed a totem pole for our home. It took him over three years to make it. Then we had a raising ceremony for it. Hart brought five or six workers from his tribe, his wife, and his kids. They all camped out at our house. We had several dozen people over for the pole raising, complete with masks and dancing.

I wouldn't recommend collecting art as an investment. For an investor, this is the highest-risk category. If an artist falls out of favor, it's just expensive wallpaper, so you'd better like looking at it. Collecting art is a matter of following your passion. Every time you buy a painting, you're stepping out and making an aesthetic statement.

The Big Sale

*Education is when you read the fine print. Experience
is what you get if you don't.*

—*Pete Seeger*

Although the genesis of the Internet was a Defense Department experiment called ARPAnet in 1969, it took a little
while to catch on. By the 1990s, college students, engineers,
scientists, and a few reporters and other geeks knew about and
used the Internet, mostly to send e-mail messages and to join
online chat groups.

At the same time, every company in computer technology or
communications was searching for the elusive Information Superhighway, an über-network that would electronically connect people
all over the world in an entertaining, informative, and valuable
way. In his book *The Road Ahead*, published in 1995, Bill Gates
described the superhighway fairly presciently:

It is impossible to predict exactly what it will be like to use the
network. We'll communicate with it through a variety of devices, including some that look like television sets, some like
today's PCs; some will look like telephones, and some will be
the size and something like the shape of a wallet. And at the

heart of each will be a powerful computer, invisibly connected to millions of others.

There will be a day, not far distant, when you will be able to conduct business, study, explore the world and its cultures, call up any great entertainment, make friends, attend neighborhood markets, and show pictures to distant relatives—without leaving your desk or armchair.[1]

Microsoft and other companies were trying to figure out how to build such a highway. To that end, Microsoft was teaming up with cable companies, while software rival Oracle was linking up with telcos in attempts to merge their software with the physical wiring already running to homes across the country.

The funny thing is, when the book was written in 1994, Gates didn't believe that the Internet would become that highway. It was too esoteric, too difficult to use, and too limited in capability. Gates wanted to start from scratch, an interesting mistake for a man who built an empire by piling more and more software on top of an esoteric, difficult-to-use, limited operating system called DOS. In the foreword to his book, he said: "Some people think the highway—also called the network—is simply today's Internet or the delivery of 500 simultaneous channels of television. Others hope or fear it will create computers as smart as human beings. These things will come, but they are not the highway."

And then came Netscape, which modified the Internet software system to make it graphical and simpler to use (an idea modeled on the Macintosh). In October 1994, Mosaic Communications (renamed Netscape Communications a month later) released its new browser, "Mosaic Netscape," over the Internet, and it became the biggest overnight sensation since Elvis Presley gyrated his way onto the airwaves.

Suddenly the Internet started to look more like a superhighway. Gates was slow to accept the concept, most likely because he wanted to create the highway himself and thus control the standards, as he had done for personal computer operating systems.

The entire computer and communications industry changed course and headed straight for the Internet. The reasoning was simple. There had already been so much hype over the Information Superhighway that once people believed they saw it, they recognized it as the Next Big Thing (NBT), and staking out an early position was of the utmost importance.

Venture capitalists and technologists have long had an obsessive belief in the NBT. It's born of the idea that each generation of technological wonders goes through a bell curve–shaped growth cycle, but before it is spent, it's replaced by the next NBT. Most people only recognize the NBT after the fact. But some of the people who recognize it very early on, the way Bill Gates recognized the potential of the microprocessor and its need for software, can become fabulously rich. The race to be the first to exploit this NBT made sane people as crazy as gold lust had done more than a century before.

Netscape's IPO in August 1995 was a hit before a single share was traded. At first, the underwriters, Morgan Stanley and Hambrecht & Quist, planned to offer 3.5 million shares at $12 each. But the road show demonstrated such interest that the price kept going up. The underwriters finally settled at 5 million shares at $28 apiece. So what if the company had no profits? In fact, since it gave away its browser, it had almost no revenues. But at that IPO price, Netscape would have $140 million to play with. The companies and individuals who actually got to buy the stock at $28 fared just as well. The stock opened at $71 and closed the day at $58.25. Netscape's valuation at the end of the first day of trading was $2.3 billion.

After that, everyone started dreaming up new uses for the Internet—including using it as a trading platform for stocks. Day traders moved in and the Internet phenomenon fed itself as stock speculators used it to invest in other Internet companies. It was the biggest NBT the world had seen since the tulip bulb.

In the latter half of the 1990s, press articles finally stopped describing Montgomery as a powerhouse that nobody ever heard of. In 1996, Montgomery's revenues reached $705 million, with a pretax profit estimated by *Institutional Investor* magazine as $200 million, of which Weisel's personal take that year was "perhaps $20 million."[2] In 1996, Weisel finally decided to break out of the single office in the Transamerica Pyramid and opened offices in New York and Boston.

The criticism that Montgomery was good at acting as an institutional broker, but not at taking companies public, was finally erased as well. Montgomery did 376 IPOs in the 1990s, 169 of them as lead manager. That made Montgomery the 4th-largest underwriter of IPOs, 11th in amount of money raised. And in most of its focus areas, it was in the top five. It was the fifth-largest underwriter of health care stocks, for example, ahead of Morgan Stanley, and it beat out Goldman Sachs in technology and business management services underwritings. *Institutional Investor* now described equity underwriting as Montgomery's "specialty."

Make no mistake, Robertson Stephens and H&Q were serious players on the Silicon Valley stage. With their focus on technology, they still got some of the best tech IPOs. Over the years Robertson had helped finance companies such as Sun Microsystems, Applied Materials, Dell Computer, National Semiconductor, and Pixar. H&Q was involved in offerings from Adobe, Apple Computer, Netscape, and U.S. Web.

Who wanted to worry about retailers, restaurants, or hotels when there was an Information Superhighway to build and exploit? Actually, Weisel did. In the latter half of the 1990s, Montgomery was involved in the IPOs of Dollar Tree Stores, Red Lion Hotels, Ambassadors International, Redhook Ale Brewery, and Il Fornaio

America. Deals like these pushed it ahead of Robertson and Hambrecht.

Probably more importantly, the relationships that Montgomery had built up over the years were paying off with huge repeat business. Montgomery sole-managed large secondary offerings for Lone Star Steakhouse & Saloon ($126 million) and Doubletree Corp. ($76 million), and was the lead manager for many other nontech company offerings, including another $115 million for Doubletree and $160 million for Lone Star, plus offerings for Sunglass Hut, Papa John's, Dollar Tree Stores, Orchard Supply Hardware, and others. And Montgomery was still active in education (Apollo Group and Sylvan Learning), health care (including OmniCare and Oxford Health), and media (Clear Channel Communications, Outdoor Systems).

Montgomery's broader focus and impressive block trading capability made it bigger and more powerful than its San Francisco neighbors. In terms of revenues and employees, Montgomery Securities was several times the size of either H&Q or Robertson Stephens. In the first quarter of 1998, H&Q had revenues of $107 million, while Robertson (after its acquisition by BofA) hit $97 million. Montgomery's revenues that quarter (after its acquisition by NationsBank) were around $300 million.

Weisel didn't do it alone, of course. His top management team included Alan Stein, Bobby Kahan, Joseph Schell, Jerry Markowitz, John Skeen, Kent Logan, and CFO Shaugn Stanley. Weisel even hired Lew Coleman the second-highest ranking executive at BankAmerica when Stein retired at the end of 1995 as head of investment banking.

Still, Montgomery was caught up in the technology tidal wave along with everyone else. And it made quite a bit of money from it. In 1995, Montgomery led a $38 million follow-on offering for a technology company called Uniphase Corp., a maker of optoelectronics equipment for fiber-optic communications. A year later, Montgomery led another $60 million offering for Uniphase, which helped put the firm in a position to make significant acquisitions. It bought IBM's laser operation in 1997, acquired Philips's optoelectronics group in 1998, merged with the Canadian company JDS Fitel in 1999 (becoming JDS Uniphase), and bought IBM's optical transceiver business at the start of 1999 for $100 million in cash and 26.9 million shares of its stock. It then went on to become one of 1999's best-performing stocks, with an 830 percent gain.[3]

Montgomery's other major technology underwritings in the latter half of the 1990s include Affymetrix, Applied Graphics, LSI Logic, Macrovision, Polycom, RF Micro Devices, 7th Level, and a small start-up called 8X8 Inc., founded by Weisel's old friend Joe Parkinson. Few of these companies are household names, although some are important in their industries. Montgomery seemed to specialize in more industrial tech companies rather than consumer technology.

But that began to change as the Internet began to spawn new business. In 1996, Internet mania was growing like a bad debt, VCs kept investing, and companies were tossed onto the public market almost as soon as they had a complete management team together—or perhaps before. The philosophy was that the Internet was like a vast plain of government land suddenly thrown open to homesteaders, and the first one to stake a claim would have the best chance of winning. The search for the Superhighway was replaced by the need to become part of the New Economy, which would be dominated by young new companies that knew how to use the Internet.

Running an Internet company at a loss was not only common, it was practically required in the frenzy to establish a position. At one conference for entrepreneurs, venture capitalist Ann

Winblad, a partner at Hummer-Winblad known for her savvy software investments, told entrepreneurs that if they were making a profit, she would be concerned that they were not reinvesting sufficient revenues into growth. The model seemed to be: Grab the land, set up a store, give everything away until you have enough customers to claim dominance, and only then actually charge for the goods. It worked, at least for a while, because there were always new investors willing to hand over more money for stakes in the New Economy companies.

Weisel made it a point to start introducing himself to some of the promising technology companies. In 1996, Montgomery captured a share of the IPO of a little company called Yahoo! Inc. It was one of those classic Internet stories, started by two Stanford students, Jerry Yang and David Filo, in order to try to help friends find their way around the Net. But Yang and Filo brought in professional managers, and Yahoo! started looking like a real company. It even had advertising revenues, which most experts at that time believed would be the main revenue source for the Internet.

In the spring of 1996, Yahoo! CEO Tim Koogle started the beauty pageant, inviting investment bankers in to strut their stuff and tell why they would be the best choice to handle the IPO. Although Yahoo! only had 30 or 40 employees, all the bankers were interested. Koogle had developed a short list of the most desirable. One of his venture backers, Sequoia Capital, suggested he put Montgomery on the list.

All the bankers sent out teams of analysts and managers carrying their binders with all their statistics proving how great they were. Montgomery was coming in at 7:30 on a Saturday morning. Mike Moritz, a partner at Sequoia who was helping the company evaluate the bankers, walked into Koogle's cubicle and said: "T.K., Thom Weisel is in the lobby." No other firm had sent even a senior executive, let alone the CEO. "It was a wonderful gesture," says Koogle. "The way Thom goes at a business personally is different from everyone else."

Weisel struck Koogle as an impressive businessman who had been in the industry a long time and who had a huge reputation and a broad and balanced business perspective. He was also "really funny and lively and confident," says Koogle.

Koogle chose Goldman Sachs to take the lead, since it was the biggest and most prestigious firm, with Montgomery and DLJ in secondary positions. He had also considered Hambrecht & Quist, which had a strong reputation in technology as well, but, he says, "I just liked the vibes better with Thom."

Weisel developed a personal fondness for the firm, and often showed up himself when a Montgomery team came in with new ideas and suggestions for businesses Yahoo! might wish to enter. He would say, "Is this an area you guys should be getting into? I'll put together the team," recalls Koogle.

Koogle also liked two other things about Montgomery. When joining Internet companies became the latest road to riches, many investment banks and consulting firms started losing top executives who wanted to become CEOs. Montgomery was different. "Thom always has huge loyalty from his people," says Koogle. "I didn't see as much of a revolving door come March after the commission checks were cut." Koogle also felt that Montgomery's research was better than most, not as compromised by attempts to get more investment banking business. "Thom's firm was never one of the bad ones," he says.

Weisel also developed a good relationship with Siebel Systems, a software company that pioneered and leads the category of helping service firms to maintain strong connections with their customers (known as customer relationship management, or CRM). CEO Tom Siebel is actually a second cousin to Ken Siebel, the man who originally brought Weisel in to Robertson, Colman & Siebel.

Despite the fact that Ken Siebel went with Robertson after the split, Tom Siebel says he has never heard his cousin say a negative thing about Weisel.

When it came time for Siebel's IPO in June 1996, Siebel chose all three San Francisco firms to handle the offering. H&Q was the book manager, with Montgomery and Robertson in secondary positions. "I believed that if I called Thom Weisel, Sandy Robertson, or Dan Case (the CEO of H&Q), they would call me back," explains Siebel. "They would be interested in what we were doing. If I called the CEO at Morgan Stanley, there's no chance he would call me back."

After the IPO, Weisel worked the hardest to keep a good relationship going, to establish it for the long haul. "He invested his personal time," says Siebel. "He went out of his way to introduce me to important people. He also bought our software to use at Montgomery."

Like Koogle and others, Siebel has become friends with Weisel and has developed a lot of respect for him. "Thom's almost a force of nature," he says. "There's a lot of energy there. He can almost will things into existence. People like to follow him."

In March 1997, Weisel sold Montgomery Asset Management to Germany's Commerzbank for $250 million in order to use the money to expand its fledgling high-yield (junk bond) business. Junk bonds are basically a form of debt financing for companies without a very high debt rating. Junk bonds are higher-risk and consequently have higher returns. More and more technology companies were starting to use junk bonds as another financing technique. Most Silicon Valley companies are non-investment grade, because they generally have low cash flow, making it more difficult to cover the interest and principal payment.

Markowitz started building the high-yield business from scratch. He hired several traders, salespeople, and researchers with experience in high-yield financing, including a telecom high-yield analyst from Chase and a top trader from Bear Stearns. In all, he hired nearly 50 people for the business, and within six months had mandates for two lead-managed deals. But before the business ever got off the ground, the banking environment began a huge shift.

This was about the time that the prohibitions set forth by the Glass-Steagall Act were dramatically weakened, opening up the potential for mergers between different types of banks. Commercial banks, asset-heavy but lacking any skills in the skillet-hot investment banking business, went on a spending spree.

Alex.Brown, which is actually the nation's oldest brokerage firm at over 100 years old, and the biggest of the HARMs, was sold for $1.7 billion—2.7 times book value—to Bankers Trust in April 1997. In June, BankAmerica paid $540 million for Robertson Stephens. Weisel decided he had to look for a partner.

A partnership could give Montgomery more working capital and access to a much bigger debt financing (including junk bond) business than it could ever achieve on its own. It had never managed a "bought" deal, in which the bank has to put up some money of its own during the transaction, of more than $215 million. Which was too bad, because Doubletree, a longtime Montgomery client, now needed to raise more money and wanted to do an overnight bridge financing. It required a commitment of $600 million. Montgomery couldn't do it, and the deal went to Morgan Stanley.

Weisel now saw the opportunity, through a merger, to end up on a par with the biggest Wall Street banks. This wasn't just an opportunity to become one of the largest specialty banks, but one of the largest investment banks, period. Weisel put together a small team from inside his firm to analyze the alternatives and hired Lazard to help the search.

If any banker epitomizes the strategy of growth through acquisition, it's Hugh McColl. In 1983, when banks were small, regional entities prevented from expanding beyond state borders, he became chairman of a tiny Southern bank with the oxymoronic name of North Carolina National Bank. But he had a strategy to make it big.

Slowly, the federal government started loosening restrictions on interstate banking, and McColl took advantage of the trend. Renaming his firm NationsBank, he set about building a behemoth. One of his first moves was the purchase of Bankers Trust of South Carolina (BTSC), a small bank with a credit card portfolio, in 1986. In 1988, he made one of his best deals when he bought the troubled First Republic Bank of Texas. The deal was orchestrated by bank regulators, which awarded him with extensive tax breaks in order to make the purchase, reducing the price to almost nothing. His timing was good. Soon afterward, the Texas economy recovered.[4] In all, McColl created his empire by buying nearly 60 banks since taking over.

But McColl was never successful in getting into the investment banking business. He bought a small Chicago derivatives firm in 1993 for $225 million, but never got any traction. He also tried to create a securities brokerage partnership with Dean Witter Reynolds but had to close it down in 1994, according to *Business Week*, "after a spate of regulatory actions and customer complaints alleging improper sales practices, which were settled or dismissed."[5] He also began hiring dozens of high-profile Wall Street bankers, but personalities clashed and many quit or were fired. In 1995 he tried and failed to complete a merger with Donaldson, Lufkin & Jenrette. Although McColl had a reputation for heavy-handed, top-down management, he also had a reputation for overpaying for his acquisitions.

In the late spring of 1997, Weisel had conversations with Société Générale in France, Swiss Bancorp, BankBoston, ING, and others. One day in late spring, he flew from Boston to New York to meet with NationsBank. There was a storm raging, and the pilot wasn't sure if he wanted to land the plane in those conditions. Weisel demanded, "Just land the damn plane. We're going to get to that meeting."

Hugh McColl, however, didn't. The storm hadn't stopped Weisel, but it did prevent the NationsBank team from making it to the meeting, which had to be rescheduled for a few weeks later. The two CEOs finally met for the first time in Manhattan on June 10, 1997.

Now the value of a good negotiator (Weisel himself) became obvious as Weisel got NationsBank to commit to a $1.3 billion purchase price, an astounding 13 times book value. Seventy percent ($840 million) was to be paid up front to the partners, including a reported $120 million to Weisel. The rest would vest to Montgomery executives and employees over three years in stock.

Many other bankers and financial analysts were stunned at the price. But Weisel argues that book value wasn't the best way to price the company. That's the information outsiders had available to them, since Montgomery was private. Based on expected earnings for the coming year, the price represented about 15 times earnings, which is the valuation that Alex.Brown went for. Weisel never had to put the money from the sale of his asset management business into his junk bond group, and instead distributed the money to the partners.

Fortunately, Weisel is also a stickler for details, and he knew that NationsBank had a reputation for making promises it didn't keep, so he made sure everything was spelled out unambiguously in writing. Montgomery would remain autonomous, a San Francisco–based subsidiary of NationsBank's corporate banking division. Weisel would become chairman of that division and CEO of NationsBanc Montgomery Securities. Weisel was to oversee all the equity, investment banking, capital markets, and debt business, including the high-yield, high-grade, and distressed trading business. Hugh McColl also agreed to put in $600 million for a private equity group run by a group put together by Weisel.

With NationsBank behind him, Weisel would be able to hire new people for the derivatives business, merge his high-yield group with that of NationsBank, and expand the investment banking business to include some of NationsBank's strengths, such as real estate. The deal was announced June 30. Weisel had exactly what he wanted—at least, on paper.

Hugh McColl and Jim Hance, NationsBank's vice chairman and CFO, both made enthusiastic statements to the press on the benefits of buying Montgomery instead of trying to build the business by themselves. The new subsidiary was called Nations-Banc Montgomery Securities. The other partners were just as enthusiastic. "We went into this deal with all sincerity, intending to do a phenomenal job," says Dick Fredericks, the former banking analyst at Montgomery.

But at least one person did not seem to like the deal. Ed Brown, NationsBank's managing director for global capital raising and global markets, was not the type of guy to give up power so easily—certainly not to these upstarts from California. Weisel believes Brown lobbied against the arrangement to give the public debt business to Weisel from the start.

Weisel began merging the businesses of the two firms. He hired John Sandalman, who was running the equities derivatives business for Salomon, to come in and put together a business plan for the derivatives business. He sent Jerry Markowitz to New York to run the merged high-yield business and hired Jerry Rosenfeld from Lazard to run a private equity group. In order to get back into money management, NationsBanc Montgomery Securities made a $150 million investment to help Tom Marsico, a money manager from Janus, set up his own firm. NationsBanc Montgomery owned 50 percent of Marsico Capital. (Bank of America bought the other half after Weisel left.)

In the first six months after the merger, NationsBanc Montgomery's business was up over 50 percent, according to Weisel.

NationsBanc Montgomery worked on the IPOs of such Internet-focused companies as Exodus Communications, InfoSpace.com, RealNetworks, and Ticketmaster Online and did other stock offerings for online auction site Onsale, Inc. and Preview Travel.

Other technology stocks were swept upward with the dot-com stocks, and NationsBanc Montgomery was involved in underwritings for Applied Micro Circuits, Charles River Associates, Flextronics, Intuit, Macrovision, and Spectra Physics Lasers. It also lead-managed the IPO of Echelon, started by ROLM founder Ken Oshman.

Outside of technology, its underwriting business continued to thrive, with clients such as Avis Rent A Car, Cheesecake Factory, Children's Place Retail Stores, Dollar Tree Stores, Fox Entertainment Group, Lamar Advertising, and SportsLine USA.

Weisel also started expanding his investment banking business into areas where NationsBank was a major lender, such as energy, food and beverages, and textiles and apparel. Weisel still thinks the merger could have worked—if he had been left in charge of the businesses originally agreed upon. "We were a powerful combination," he says.

The most frequently overlooked obstacle to a successful merger is the clash of cultures that might erupt. Turf wars develop, egos butt heads, and consolidating assets and merging the infrastructures of two organizations form huge impediments. Weisel, who had always proved to be skilled at building organizations with great teamwork (even if he first had to fight to take over), thought he could avoid these problems by spelling out the terms in advance and keeping the two organizations apart and autonomous. He was wrong. The situation became too convoluted, especially after NationsBank bought BankAmerica.

Weisel had trouble getting the two high-yield groups together. Weisel's investment bankers were used to dealing with CEOs, while NationsBank's corporate lending officers, he says, were used to dealing with managers further down the ranks. The lending officers wanted to be the ones to call on accounts, even though Weisel felt his contacts were better. Finally, he was told that autonomy wouldn't work after all and that the managers wanted to merge Weisel's organization into theirs. The junk bond business was taken from Jerry Markowitz and merged with the junk bond group at NationsBank under Thomas White, one of McColl's lieutenants. It was almost like Hugh McColl had never read the fine print of his contract with Weisel. While McColl and Hance had made the deal with Weisel, says Markowitz, "It got to chief lieutenants, started to break the deal from day one. One by one, they started taking things back."

Weisel walked out the door in September 1998. This time, instead of McColl or Hance, Ed Brown was the one to comment on the split. In an interview with *The New York Times,* he said that it was important to have "investment banking businesses that are in sync with our whole franchise." He also revealed what it was he thought NationsBank had really gotten out of the merger, which seemed to be everything but Weisel. "If we take a look at the power of our franchise, we will miss him, but we will go forward," he said of Weisel. "He was good at attracting a very successful group of people who are joining our team."[6] Ed Brown took over the investment banking business in June 2000.

Many executives followed, collecting the remaining 60 percent of their three-year incentive payments at once because the terms of the contract had not been met. In January 1999, Weisel announced the formation of Thomas Weisel Partners, and a month later was open for business. It took another month or two for BofA to file a lawsuit.

In fact, all three of the San Francisco stars ran into the same difficulty. When NationsBank bought BankAmerica in 1998, it avoided the obvious culture clash that would arise between Robertson and Montgomery by selling Robertson to BankBoston.

That worked for a while, because BankBoston actually did keep Robertson largely autonomous. But when the BankBoston was bought by Fleet Bank, the relationship started to break down. Sandy Robertson had already left the company he founded. Finally, in 2002, with the investment banking business sucked into the abyss along with the dot-com decline, Fleet shut down Robertson altogether after failing to find a buyer.

Two years after Montgomery was sold, Chase Manhattan paid $1.35 billion for Hambrecht & Quist, a 22 percent premium on its stock price. At the time of the acquisition, H&Q had 970 employees. But the firm did not survive being swallowed by a whale. Sources close to the company say that by the summer of 2002, only 45 of those employees remained.

NationsBank has not been a stellar performer. In terms of number of branches, it is the largest U.S. bank, although Citigroup is larger in terms of assets. NationsBank has been saddled with bad loans, leading to billions of dollars in write-offs, acquisitions that have not been profitable, and a reputation for poor service. When McColl announced early retirement in early 2001 after a year and a half of declining stock (from about $65 to about $45), *The Economist* noted that the new Bank of America (NationsBank adopted the name shortly after Weisel left in 1998) was "widely regarded in the industry as a beached whale."[7]

To make up for its loss, BofA went shopping for new investment banking stars. Many observers feel that the company had to offer too much in salary and options since it was shopping at the top of the market. But the shopping spree has made a difference; finances improved under the control of McColl's successor, Ken Lewis. Net income for the first half of 2002 was $4.4 billion, up from $3.9 billion the year before and $4.3 billion in the first half of 2000. By July 2000, Bank of America's stock had recovered to about $65. Most of the income increase was due to consumer banking, but the company also recorded a 2 percent increase in its investment banking business, now called BancAmerica Securities, in 2002. As far as Silicon Valley is concerned, however, the company's technology investment banking business is dead.

The HARMs are gone. In their place, only Thomas Weisel Partners is left standing.

Why We Merged—And Divorced

Thom W. Weisel

The Book of Montgomery

In the beginning, there was Thom. And Thom knoweth Joseph, and Jeremiah, and Jonathan and Karl and Alan and the man from Kent, and the man known only as Kahan. And for 25 years Thom and his followers slaved in the city far west of the other tribes. And they ploweth their earnings back into the fertile soil. And it was good.

In the 26th year Lewis cameth and joineth the tribe and shared news of the larger tribes. And some of Thom's followers came unto Thom, "We seeth a storm ahead for thy western tribe, thou should seek shelter amongst the larger tribes to the east." And Thom listened politely as he shoeth them out the door. And still Thom and his followers plowed more and more back into the soil. And it was good.

But other tribes, the tribes of Morgan and Dean and Alex of Baltimore believed the stories of storms that cometh to be true. And they had great gifts bestowed upon them as they mergeth. Finally, Thom could take no more. Thom went to his closest followers and spoke unto them, "Findeth a deal for us." And Thom said unto them, "Run they numbers and find thy disciples." And it was good.

Now Thom ruled absolute over his domain. And Thom com-

manded Lewis to take action. And Lewis summoned Shaugn and commanded him, "Shaugn, run thy numbers until I have the answer I need." And behold Shaugn, who ranneth thy numbers day and night for forty days. And on the fortieth day Shaugn came unto Lewis and said, "I have runneth thy numbers and found thy answers. And they are the answers thou want. And Lewis went to Thom and sayeth, "We shall build an even larger kingdom among the tribes of shekels. You shall be a king of a new empire." And Thom looketh at Lewis and said, "What of thy disciples?" And lo, brothers Wilson and Shedlin from the house of Lazard entered and spoke. "Our disciples shall sing your praises from San Francisco to Zurich. And we shall prevail upon our friends and make them better friends, and we shall prevail upon our enemies and make them friends."

So Thom and his closest followers and the brothers from the house of Lazard all came east and ventured to New York, the deepest and darkest place on the earth, and sought to join armies with one of the eastern tribes. And many sought to join them even though they spoke of earnings in a land of book value. And it was good.

And finally there were four armies who seeketh the army of Montgomery: the Dutch Masters, the Brahmans, and La Generales. And there was another, a Charlotte man who spoketh the southern tongue and told of the power of growth. And they meeteth with each of the generals of the other tribes of shekels and invited them west. Once west, Thom and Joseph and Jeremiah and the man known as Kahan and legions upon legions of Montgomery disciples came unto the room and spread the word. But after every meeting Thom was restless. He commanded Lewis after each and every meeting, "Go forth and read from the book of Wilson and speaketh of what it says." But Lewis assured him that all was good. And all was good.

Now this Charlotte man was an unusual man, a man much liketh Thom. And Thom liketh this Charlotte man named McColl. And this man McColl promised to bestow upon Thom and the tribe of Montgomery all that they desired. And McColl would not leave until he joined his army with the army of Montgomery. And they joined armies. And all was good.

—George W. Yandell III,
Montgomery Securities Closing Dinner,
October 3, 1997

In 1997, we got a wake-up call.

That year, Bankers Trust announced it was going to buy Alex.Brown. It was like a shot across the bow: One of our direct major competitors was linking itself up with a larger bank. Sure, we had competed with large banks in the past, but now a bank that focused specifically in our area would be well capitalized with the ability to offer debt financing and other services. We already had questions about our available capital. We now had to start thinking about how we were going to compete.

We knew the global banking scene, because we followed the financial services business. We had Dick Fredericks, our crack bank analyst, now running our financial institution investment banking practice. We had Lew Coleman, who had joined us as a partner from BankAmerica, where he was the number two person. We had probably the best bank analysts in the country. Diane Meridian, who was our analyst then, has now gone on to work at Morgan Stanley. Ken Wilson was our investment banker at Lazard and is now at Goldman Sachs. These were four of the most connected and intelligent financial services experts that existed. So we started contacting potential partners.

Jerry Markowitz, John Skeen, Kent Logan, and myself met with Swiss Bancorp at its office in London. We spent a few days there, meeting and talking to the key executives. On the final dinner with them, they kept trying to poke holes through our business model. They said they didn't think the spreads in underwriting in America could hold up.

Then they asked me what price I was asking. I said $2 billion. They all choked. They asked me how I could justify that price, so I went through all the projections and the criteria for our valuation. And that ended the dinner.

Two days later, I picked up the paper and read that Swiss Bancorp had announced its intent to buy Dillon Reed. When we were meeting with the Swiss Bancorp people in London, they obviously had the Dillon Reed people there as well, probably two doors down from us. As I read that, I turned to Kent Logan and asked, "Well, now what do we do?"

First Alex.Brown was gone, then Dillon Reed. We heard that Robertson was talking to BankAmerica. Dan Case, the CEO of Hambrecht & Quist (who passed away in June 2002), was out shopping H&Q.

At the time, ING owned 20 percent of Dillon Reed. When Swiss Bancorp bought Dillon Reed, it freed up ING for a potential pursuit of another investment bank.

We had initiated discussions with ING, Société Générale, Bank-Boston, and NationsBank. We had a very firm view on a minimum price: $1.2 billion plus a $100 million incentive program to retain our employees.

On paper, NationsBank seemed like the most likely partner for us. Our other choices were two foreign entities and a smaller Northeastern bank, and in my opinion they did not fit with us as well as NationsBank. Hugh McColl was bigger than life. He was on a tear when it came to making acquisitions. He was influential. NationsBank already had a footprint in corporate and leveraged lending, which we needed. It had not yet succeeded in investment banking, and the equity markets capability we had would be a really good fit with its corporate customer base.

When we had our first lunch in New York, Hugh McColl was very friendly. He admitted that NationsBank had made several forays into investment banking and failed. He said they wanted us to drive the bus, and I thought they would appreciate our history and our people. He did not seem to have a problem keeping us as an independent entity. We both felt our equity platform with debt capability would offer a complete set of financing services for companies.

McColl gave me a lecture about how talented Ed Brown was. He was supposed to be one of the best people running corporate banking today.

We signed an agreement within three weeks. During those three weeks Brown came out several times to try to convince us that the debt piece should remain inside NationsBank, not as part of Montgomery. I don't know this for a fact, but I understand that after our deal was consummated, Ed Brown wrote a memo to McColl and Jim Hance, saying he disagreed with the structure that had been agreed to.

We were excited about the prospects of this merger and celebrated at a final dinner in October. But the ink wasn't even dry when I started feeling like the merger was a mistake. We would go to Charlotte and talk to the corporate banking people, and we could see that they thought of us as product specialists, not as relationship bankers.

In June NationsBank acquired BankAmerica. One of the divisions that came along with it was D.H. Shaw, a derivatives operation. In late July or August, with the collapse of long-term capital and of the economies of Asia and Russia, they had to take a big write-off on Shaw. McColl used that as an excuse to fire Dave Coulter, the CEO of BankAmerica. McColl eventually used the BofA acquisition as an excuse to reorganize our relationship with the bank.

After our acquisition, we had a tortured negotiation over how we were going to reorganize, to integrate the organizations.

Most of my interaction was with Jim Hance, an honorable, quality executive. We'd get an agreement with Hance, and then either Brown or Murphy would come back with a totally different iteration.

Eventually, the terms of the agreement were broken. I believe NationsBank never intended to keep them. For example, part of the strategy at NationsBank—now Bank of America—was apparently to try to cut out the basic foundation of the old Montgomery. As an example, they wanted us to port our entire trade processing over to their system, and they were going to charge us egregiously for it. They wanted to control our financial and accounting systems. I felt our individual culture was important. We had our own P&L, so keeping our own infrastructure capability was important to us. And since we paid for it, it should not have mattered to the bank—but it did.

They were taking over every support function, from the CFO to our back-end processing. The Montgomery people became very disaffected. They weren't going to be in charge anymore. We fought it like crazy, because we were supposed to be independent.

Then, as we discussed working in teams to cover individual banking accounts, the talks turned divisive and protective. They also started down the path of private equity as we had agreed, and then shut it down.

But the biggest issue became control of the debt products. They never intended on keeping that part of the agreement. We were supposedly in charge of the debt capital business, including the high-yield business. And yet Tom White, the guy who was running the book in high yield, wouldn't even return our phone calls, let alone open a discussion. We wanted to resolve personnel issues and consolidate all the activities in New York. But we got stonewalled, and were told that we had to keep everyone in North Carolina.

The situation between Brown and myself got so difficult that I finally called up McColl to find out what the story was. He didn't want to hear one word of my whining, of my reasons for wanting to do things differently. His response was simply: "Thom, I thought we bought you."

Under the guise of their acquisition of BofA, NationsBank executives came to me and said they needed to reorganize Montgomery. They said, "We know we said you would be independent, but now we don't think that works." That was the end of the line for me. There wasn't anyplace left to go. Logic was not going to prevail. Ed Brown had spent 26 years at NationsBank, starting right after business school, and it didn't matter what the contract said. I had no choice but to leave—out of principle if nothing else.

At least they were big enough to fess up and admit they hadn't stuck to the terms of our contract. So they had to accelerate the last two payments to our partners and employees and let us out of the noncompete agreement. Lew Coleman was in charge of the transition. At first I had a good relationship with him. Bank of America had unused space up on the 38th floor, so he leased it to us for three months, and we moved up there to start planning our new business.

I wasn't the only one upset. Over the course of the last month I was inundated by partners and others who could see major turmoil at the bank, hated life there, and were asking me what I was going to do. The most disaffected were Derek Lemke-von Ammon and Frank Dunlevy. They were key players at Montgomery leading up to the sale. Derek was caught in the crossfire, and Dunlevy, who is big on culture, couldn't stand what was going on there. They and Sanford Miller were my founding partners for the new firm.

I had a nonsolicit agreement, so I had to be very careful. The minute I had an inkling I was going to leave, I hired a lawyer to give me advice about what I could and couldn't do. He helped to negotiate my extraction. I followed every letter of what he told me to do.

By the first quarter of 1999, Bank of America could see we were going to be a real competitor, instead of this pipsqueak little boutique. Its people had obviously gotten their hands on our offering prospectus. Suddenly, they decided to sue us, claiming that we were stealing their people and clients. When they sued me, they hired the same lawyer I had used to help with my extraction! He apparently thought he could just run the meter forever. It was an egregious conflict of interest. I ended up settling with BofA. There was absolutely no validity to their lawsuit, but the distraction would have taken too much of my time, which is exactly what they wanted. However, I sued the lawyer and won.

The thing is, the merger could have worked. I think Nations-Bank did the right thing by buying something like Montgomery. Bank of America has actually done very well with the acquisition. It truly has a corporate bank, not just a retail bank with the corporate banking bolted on.

We were looking for synergies. We built up the real estate business, an area where NationsBank also had strong capability, with its own contacts inside the real estate world. Immediately after the merger, we did three transactions that raised literally hundreds of millions of dollars for three new real estate investment firms.

I had convinced NationsBank management that we should be in the derivatives business. We had a tremendous distribution system in the corporate and high-net-worth area. We spent months getting their risk management committee comfortable with the business. They authorized me to go ahead and get into derivatives, but then started to renege and said they wanted a guy from Chicago to run that business. Eventually, though, they gave in and said we would do it. We spent months putting together the risk committee. Within two years, that area alone was producing $800 million in revenues, $350 million in pretax profits for BofA.

I liked the money management business a lot, but we had sold our money management unit off six months before the merger. When I saw Tom Marsico leaving Janus, I called him up. We eventually struck a deal to put Marsico in business, and the bank wrote a check for $150 million for 50 percent of Marsico Capital. That turned out to be a good deal as well: A year ago, BofA paid $950 million for the other 50 percent of Marsico Capital.

At the beginning of 1998 we felt we needed to bring in a new head of investment banking who could relate to the bank's calling officers and help in the organization of the new entity. By midyear we had cut a deal with Carter McClelland, who I had known at Morgan Stanley and who had helped DeutscheBank build out its U.S. investment banking operations. Carter was then left with the job of remaking the investment bank. He's done that, with a brand-new set of lieutenants. He has ended up as a key player there, integrating and building out the investment bank. He had to deal with the details of the backlash from losing practically the entire investment banking team—and not just from losing the people to us. Scotty Kovalik at BofA decided now was his time and led an insurrection, getting rid of anybody he could, including Kent Logan. It took him about a year, but then he played his hand too hard and ended up leaving.

I actually think Carter has done a good job of using Montgomery to build out a very credible investment banking business at BofA. He's done a good job of maintaining a presence in the middle markets. BofA is not a top five player yet, but is probably around 10th in the industry, about where it was when I left.

If Chase were still independent, I think the H&Q acquisition would have worked. H&Q was the equity platform for Chase, but since the J.P. Morgan acquisition, it has all but disappeared. Deutsche Bank might be going through its own domestic challenges right now, but clearly it wants to be a global powerhouse.

Bankers Trust's acquisition of Alex.Brown made sense. It gave Bankers Trust a good investment banking arm that focused on middle markets. The one real question was BankBoston acquiring Robertson. There's a question of how serious BankBoston was about building out a true national footprint. It was mainly a regional bank.

But a majority of the acquisitions, the ones that were well thought out, have served the buyers very well.

The Big Boom

Man cannot remake himself without suffering, for he is both the marble and the sculptor.

—*Alexis Carrel*

When Thomas Weisel decided to leave NationsBank and start a new company, most people in the industry were shocked. Observers questioned whether there would really be opportunity for a small, focused firm in this era of merged mega-conglomerates. After all, Weisel himself had orchestrated the merger with NationsBank in order to stay competitive in a consolidating industry.

In reality, setting off on his own was not Weisel's preferred approach. It meant giving up his dream of creating a top five investment bank that could go nose to nose with Merrill or Morgan Stanley or Salomon. He still saw the value of a broad-based firm, and felt the first year with NationsBank had been a success—except for the fact that the good old boys from North Carolina had decided they were in charge.

Besides, could anyone really expect one of the most competitive people on the planet to just walk off with his millions into the sunset of early retirement? His friends and colleagues didn't.

Some of the Montgomery execs, such as Bobby Kahan and Jerry Markowitz, took their money and retired. But Weisel wasn't about to just take his $120 million or so and call it a career. If anything, he had more resolve than ever to build a great new bank, one better than Montgomery. If he couldn't do it as part of NationsBank, he would do it on his own.

"Thom, like any real leader, needs enemies, whether they're real or spurious," says Dick Fredericks. "It gives them something to focus on. It's like the war on poverty, the war on inflation, or the war on terrorism. Thom wasn't declaring war on NationsBank, but it was a bogeyman to be competitive with. He wanted to show he could do it all again."

NationsBank's Jim Hance, acknowledging that the contract had not been honored, agreed to accelerate the final payments from the purchase agreement. Because one year had passed since the acquisition of Montgomery, the partners and employees at Montgomery had been paid $120 million of their $360 million, three-year incentive to stay. The remaining $240 million was now being paid in one lump sum.

In his year at NationsBank, Weisel had come to believe there was room for a focused growth investment bank after all. It might not have as much capital as the large banks for doing bridge loans or offering a lot of junk bonds, but he thought he could put together a company with enough capitalization to still do some fairly large deals. And he felt he could get some of the best talent in the business.

At the end of 1998, Weisel set out to create his new firm. From his base of operations in the Transamerica Pyramid, courtesy of Lew Coleman, he began to put together a new team. He was no longer restricted by a noncompete agreement because his contract was broken, but he was not allowed to solicit BofA employees to join him. That didn't matter, he says, because his former employees flocked to him anyway. Frank Dunlevy, Derek Lemke-von

Ammon and Sanford Miller, who were partners at Montgomery and at NationsBanc Montgomery Securities, joined him as founding partners.

In all, 137 people left NationsBank to join Weisel, from top partners to a cleaning lady. Flush with their new windfall, the partners who joined Weisel were able to contribute considerable capital to the new firm themselves. There were 67 partners at the start of Thomas Weisel Partners, both former Montgomery people and executives from other banks. They contributed $30 million to the new venture. It devastated the investment banking business at NationsBanc Montgomery Securities. By April 1999, the firm had lost so many people to TWP that Sandy Robertson was quoted in *The Wall Street Journal* saying that Montgomery was now probably only worth $400 million,[1] one-third the price paid less than two years earlier. In August 1999, both the names Montgomery Securities and NationsBank disappeared. NationsBank became Bank of America, and NationsBanc Montgomery Securities became Banc of America Securities.

Weisel quickly put together a business plan for his new firm, Thomas Weisel Partners. He was aided by new partners Frank Dunlevy, Derek Lemke-von Ammon, and Sanford Miller. It wasn't really the optimal situation for trying to put together a world-class banking team, but he now had 30 years' experience to help him create as close to an ideal bank as he could. "This was not just going to be Montgomery II," he says.

This time, he wanted to build a full-service merchant bank. A merchant bank, unlike a Montgomery-style investment bank, invests its own money, in addition to helping companies raise money from others. Although Montgomery was more diversified than the other tech-focused banks, with its broader industry coverage and trading capability, TWP was designed to be even more diversified, with private equity and a strong strategic advisory activity.

The business lines at TWP were to include investment banking and institutional brokerage like Montgomery, and TWP would be heavily research-driven, relying on the quality of its industry analysts to help identify new industries and opportunities. Weisel has launched a new conference for growth companies. He also put more emphasis on private client services (for wealthy individuals) and settled his new bank solidly into the private equity business with several investment funds.

With the other tech-centric banks gone, Weisel managed to create stronger ties to the investment community than any bank had done before. He got 22 VC, money management, and leveraged buyout firms to invest directly in his fledgling business, collectively putting up $35 million for a 7 percent stake in the firm (giving it a valuation of $500 million). Some of the most prominent Silicon Valley investment firms are on the list. VC investors include Accel, Bessemer, Brentwood, IVP, Mayfield, NEA, and Oak. Other leading private equity investors include Citicorp Venture Capital, TA Associates, Saunders Carp, Madison Dearborn, and Weston Presidio.

TWP, for example, co-invests with the VC firms. The firm has put some of its money into different VC funds, while some of the VC and money management firms have put money into Weisel's private equity funds.

Weisel also tapped his extraordinary list of luminaries in Silicon Valley and elsewhere to join up as directors and advisors, including Yahoo!'s Tim Koogle, Siebel Systems' Tom Siebel, Jerry Markowitz, politicians Jack Kemp, and Pete Wilson, former Pacific Telesis CEO Phil Quigley, Sun America CEO Jay Weintrob, Wilson Sonsini's Larry Sonsini, and his old friend Erik Borgen, now running Borgen Investment Group. And he created a CEO Founder's Circle of entrepreneurial CEOs who collectively put up about $120 million into one of the firm's venture funds and network with each other.

Weisel ensured that TWP could leave its nest high in the Transamerica Pyramid flying by hiring experienced bankers from such firms as Merrill, Morgan Stanley, and Salomon. With all the mergers in the industry, the cultures of the other banks were changing as well, undoubtedly with huge internal power struggles raging within. Weisel chose people for their skills, connections, and apparent ability to fit into the culture he was building. He tapped his contacts, hit the phone and the road, and began raiding other firms for talent.

Among his key hires was Tim Heekin, a top Salomon trader who Weisel had tried for 10 years to lure to Montgomery. When Salomon merged with Smith Barney, Weisel called Heekin in London, where he was based at the time, and offered him the opportunity to join as head of trading. He brought in Mark Shafir, who was head of global technology investment banking and M&A at Merrill, to head the investment banking business. Bob Kitts was head of M&A business development at Morgan Stanley, now director of M&A at the new firm. Weisel also captured Paul Slivon, a top salesman from Robertson Stephens, who is now head of sales at TWP. They were offered salaries far below what they had been getting, but would be partners sharing in the profits of what they hoped would be a fast-rising firm.

Weisel also organized "tiger teams" around each industry. The teams consist of everyone needed to look at the industries from all angles. These are miniature industry planning groups that meet regularly and provide the analysis of the most promising industries. They look for markets with "tailwinds," or agents of change in the economy or in society that can push certain markets along faster than the rest.

The new industries they picked were similar to those Montgomery had focused on: technology, consumer products, business services, media and communications, health care, and financial services. But with Silicon Valley seemingly taking over the world, TWP slipped into a larger emphasis on technology.

Despite the boom in technology, however, t here were troublesome signs elsewhere at the end of 1998. Russia defaulted on loans and Latin American economies got the flu, while both the European and Asian economies were sluggish. People wondered how long the U.S. economy could continue to soar when most of the rest of the world's economies seemed grounded.

The stock market was retrenching. The IPOs of Inktomi and eBay (both led by Goldman Sachs) in 1998 were stellar, but many tech companies that went public in 1998 found their stocks below their IPO price by the end of the year, and the Dow Jones News Service declared the "End of the IPO."[2]

Weisel built his firm with what he believed was a "realistic but conservative" business plan. It called for revenues of $96 million in 1999, $272 million in 2000, and $569 million by 2003.

And then all hell broke loose. Perhaps fear of the nonexistent Y2K bug boosted spending on technology, which in turn brought in more VC money for new tech firms, or maybe everyone just caught the Internet bug all at once. Whatever the reason, 1999 became the year of the Internet. Venture capital firms began raising billion-dollar funds. Everybody with an ego and a rich friend decided to raise his or her own small funds or angel investing groups. Day traders went wild, although most of them seemed to lose money. Still, like gamblers who couldn't leave the table, they kept going, convinced they were about to strike it rich.

TWP came out of the gate faster than Lance Armstrong soaring down the side of a mountain with the wind at his back. TWP's technology practice included companies making telecommunications equipment and Internet companies setting up online retail business for consumers—a nice match with TWP's other strengths. It opened its doors for business in February, and by the end of March had brought in $9 million in revenues, hitting profitability right from the start. TWP helped issue stock for five companies in March and had five other deals in the works.

A few of the highlights: One month after its founding, TWP orchestrated Yahoo!'s $3.6 billion stock acquisition of GeoCities (by the time the transaction was completed in May, the deal was worth $4.7 billion, due to Yahoo!'s rising stock price). TWP was also co-manager of a $375 million follow-on offering for Jabil Circuit, an electronics manufacturer that builds products under contract for other companies.

In 1999, TWP became an extraordinarily hot IPO machine. It helped with the highly successful IPOs of companies such as Akamai Technologies, Drugstore.com, Fogdog, FTD.com, InfoSpace .com, MapQuest.com, Netcentives, Red Hat, Scient, Stamps.com, TheStreet.com, TiVo, and the ever popular Webvan Group, some of which are still in business today. In most of the stock underwritings it played the secondary role, but the money was just as good.

In its first year, TWP completed 108 transactions (it was the lead bank for 8 of them), collectively worth $23 billion, including 53 IPOs, 26 follow-ons, 11 private placements, 14 M&A deals, and two convertible offerings. It generated revenues for itself of $186 million, nearly twice the amount Weisel had aimed for in his business plan. And in that year Lance Armstrong won his first Tour de France.

Weisel built out his private client services—helping wealthy individuals with investments and other financial services—in March 1999. TWP's second quarter brought in over $31 million in revenues and was again profitable. The firm opened an office in Boston in early June. In the third quarter it opened a London office headed by Otto Tschudi. Weisel also added a convertible securities business to TWP that quarter. By October the press was describing TWP as one of the fastest-growing investment banks in history. In 2000, revenues reached $476 million.

Weisel also continued his fund-raising activities for the firm. One investment firm Weisel had approached when he was starting the company was the California Public Employees' Retirement

System (CalPERS), the nation's largest and most influential public pension fund (with assets of $136 billion). Weisel was told to talk to one of the fund's outside advisors, who didn't express much interest. But toward the end of its first year in business, Weisel revisited CalPERS to see if the firm might be interested in an investment in one of TWP's private equity funds.

One of the executives, Barry Gonder, who was running private equity investments at CalPERS, stopped Weisel two hours into a long presentation and said, "Thom, can I see you outside?" He told Weisel that he didn't know how they had missed TWP in its first round of investing, and added, "You are just the kind of company we've been looking to invest in." CalPERS wanted to partner with a merchant bank that could leverage its research capability for both investment banking and private investments. Weisel suggested they complete the deal to get CalPERS to invest in TWP's fund, then discuss a direct investment in TWP itself. "And that's exactly what happened," says Weisel.

In January of 2000, CalPERS announced it would invest $100 million for a 10 percent stake in TWP, doubling the firm's valuation to $1 billion. CalPERS also committed $500 million as the lead investor in TWP's new investment fund, and allocated up to $500 million more to support new business activity by the firm. Gonder ended up leaving CalPERS after that, but Weisel says the relationship has been great. TWP is now the exclusive manager stock distributions for CalPERS. The deal helps CalPERS to maximize profits as shares of stock are distributed to partners when a particular investment fund cashes out. TWP has also put together a distressed fund—looking for troubled companies with promise—funded by CalPERS. CalPERS also became an early investor in a new money management hedge fund run by TWP.

In early 2000, *Investment Dealers' Digest* awarded Weisel its coveted Banker of the Year award. It was a heady time, and it looked as though Weisel had pulled off the comeback of the century. As

TWP soared, Banc of America Securities faded from the technology investment banking scene, missing the boom of the millennium.

TWP's second year looked just as promising. Its underwriting clients included AT&T Wireless, Harvard Bioscience, Nvidia, and Pets.com. Again, these were companies whose business was coveted by almost every investment bank in the business.

In April 2000, TWP, under the direction of the new head of investment banking, Mark Shafir, helped orchestrate the $41 billion merger between JDS Uniphase and SDL, setting yet another record for a merger between technology companies. Its revenues in 2000 reached nearly $500 million, again almost twice its original target. TWP itself was looking like one of the most successful start-ups in the world. Weisel was elated, although he also started expressing concern about the sustainability of this market, along with many other stock watchers.

So did Federal Reserve Chairman Alan Greenspan, who had been warning of the "irrational exuberance" in the stock market since 1996. The debate raged: Was this a bubble, or was it really a New Economy with new rules? Old valuation methods, such as price/earnings ratios, seemed as antiquated as vinyl records— revered by connoisseurs, but irrelevant to the masses. Accountants and consultants started writing papers that purported to define the new valuation metrics. Nobody understood them.

It's now difficult to recall the environment and the reasons for the exuberance, but in the midst of the excitement, it was difficult not to get caught up in the movement. It gained momentum like a snowball rolling downhill, growing fat with new believers as it sped toward the abyss.

In August 2002, Greenspan defended his record during the bubble in response to critics who have asserted he might have been able to slow or lessen the collapse by raising interest rates or making it more difficult for people to borrow money to buy stocks at the right time. It's a wildly debated topic, because Greenspan actually did increase interest rates several times in 2000, although he said it was not to control the stock market but to prevent inflation. Many people in Silicon Valley, however, complained that the inflated stock market was precisely the reason he was increasing rates, and that he may have helped to burst the bubble—exactly the scenario Greenspan now says would have been the case if he had used interest rates to try to slow the stock market rise.

Looking back, we can now see that 2000 was the year the stock market died. The slide seems to have started in March 2000, but it took too many people too long to see it. Dot-com companies, New Economy magazines, angel investors, and VCs continued to spend like the party would never end through most of 2000, when in fact it was already over. The number of IPOs actually peaked in 1996, perhaps indicating that it was already getting difficult to find good start-ups to take public. Everyone was investing in the Internet, but very few entrepreneurs had any idea how to make money off the new phenomenon.

The beginning and end of the Internet craze was probably best personified by one of the key players in its existence: the brilliant young programmer Marc Andreessen. He was one of the original programmers of Mosaic, the precursor to the Netscape browser, at the National Center for Supercomputing Applications (NCSA) at the University of Illinois, and then joined up with entrepreneur and investor Jim Clark to create Netscape and its browser.

Netscape was the first Internet company to go public, in 1995, starting the dot-com phenomenon in the first place. Andreessen became rich, Clark became richer, and the trend seemed to trickle down to the greenest entrepreneurs and most naïve investors. In the meantime, however, Microsoft stepped in and stomped on Netscape, which was then sold to America Online.

Andreessen went on to cofound a company called LoudCloud (now called OpsWare) to help companies build and operate Web sites. In its last private round of financing in June 2000, it was valued at $700 million. It managed to squeak in an IPO in March 2001, making it one of the last Internet companies to go public. At its IPO, the company's valuation was reduced to $450 million. By April 2002, it was valued at $116 million.[3] The entire dot-com market seemed to rise and fall with the fortunes of Andreessen's companies.

Although Weisel was already concerned about a market correction in 2001, he dramatically underestimated the severity and length of the decline. Suddenly, he found his firm overstaffed and too heavily invested in technology. TWP did 108 investment banking transactions in 1999 and 138 in 2000, but then plummeted to 52 in 2001, and the number will probably be down again for 2002. He had to start retrenching, and his job became a lot less fun. TWP's revenues dropped about 30 percent in 2001 to $323 million, and another 20 percent in 2002. Still, he's been in tougher situations than this. It's just hard to remember when.

Of course, Weisel wasn't the only one surprised by the suddenness and severity of the tech decline. Tim Heekin, for example, had been sitting in his office in London for Salomon in the late 1990s, reading about all these new stars like Yahoo! and eBay, wondering what the magic was, when Weisel called him in late 1998 to convince him to come to San Francisco and join TWP. "I didn't want to miss the wave," says Heekin. Indeed, for the first year, Heekin rode the crest of the Internet tsunami. But two years after he joined, the wave petered out. "Now I feel foolish," he says. "I had hoped the wave would last longer than it did." Still, he hasn't lost all faith in technology, and hopes that the next few years will see the return of an exciting underwriting business.

Since the crash, the Silicon Valley rumor mill has processed a steady stream of speculation about the firm's impending demise: a cash shortage, top executives walking out, huge impending layoffs—all denied by Weisel.

To Weisel, it's just another crisis to work through, and he has been working hard at it. He has reduced the company's head count from about 800 at its peak in March 2001 to about 600 at the end of 2002. But he didn't just reduce staff, he also hired. He cut people who were working in markets that he wanted to get out of (such as telecom and consumer dot-coms) and hired new people to focus on more lucrative lines of business.

The changes began with the research department. Weisel hired Mark Manson from Donaldson, Lufkin, & Jenrette, the firm that had originally started the trend of in-depth research. Manson is a veteran with 28 years experience as an analyst, with expertise in consumer, gaming, industrial, and other nontech businesses.

Manson reorganized research at TWP. He increased the number of health care analysts from two to eight. The number of analysts in consumer businesses rose from 4 to 12. TWP also added coverage in the defense and environmental services, publishing, major pharmaceuticals, and food and beverage industries. In fact, of the roughly 450 companies TWP was following at the end of 2002, about 300 had been added since the beginning of 2001.

TWP now looks like a different company. Technology companies accounted for about 58 percent of the total number of companies in TWP's research universe in 2000. That number is now down to under 36 percent. Telecom companies, TWP's biggest difficulty, have dropped from 11 percent of the companies TWP researched in 2000 to 3 percent now. "We got sucked up in the tech bubble," Weisel acknowledges. "We've had to remake this organization."

Some of the major themes for TWP now include publishing, major pharmaceuticals, beverages, defense, and environmental services. (For other markets in which TWP is now focusing, see Chapter 14.)

In fact, TWP is in surprisingly good shape given the state of the market. The trading business is once again strong as it was at Montgomery, with TWP moving about 60 million shares a day by October 2002, up from 22 million shares a day in 2000. The stock trading business, across all the markets TWP is involved in, accounts for about two-thirds of TWP's revenues. "Even though our overall revenues have come down dramatically, our brokerage business continues to do extremely well," Weisel insists.

Also, in October 2001, he pulled off an enormous coup. Despite the rapidly deflating investment banking business in the United States, Nomura Holdings Inc., the parent company of Japan's largest securities firm, agreed to make a $200 million investment in TWP. It includes a $75 million direct investment in TWP, upping TWP's valuation to $2 billion ($700 million more than Weisel sold Montgomery for in 1997). Nomura committed an additional $125 million into TWP's private equity funds and pledged to help raise up to $500 million more for the funds. Nomura and TWP also agreed to cooperate on cross-border mergers and acquisitions services.

In many ways, TWP seems even stronger than Montgomery was at its peak, when Weisel sold it. Altogether, the company's equity capital (the amount the firm raised from investors) is about $240 million at TWP, compared to just $100 million at Montgomery. And at least $100 million of TWP's capital is still in the form of cash, which it it uses to help out with deals in which TWP has to provide some of the capital itself. TWP runs four private equity funds and its own asset management business (including its own hedge funds and a stock distribution business that helps client investment funds, such as CalPERS, manage distributions of stock from their investments). The private equity and asset management businesses together control $2.7 billion for its clients. Altogether, the firm has about $7 billion in assets, including $5 billion in its private client asset department.

One thing Weisel is particularly proud of is the firm's standing among money management firms and other investment companies. Every year, firms vote on their preferred banks, helping to determine how much business to give the different firms. TWP started its rankings around 35 or 40, but has moved into the top 10 or 15 at several firms. In the top 50 investment firms focused on emerging growth companies, for example, TWP generally ranks number one or close to it.

Weisel believes that he has expanded his firm into growth areas that will be among the first to come back when the stock market recovers. "We're built to last," he says. "By anybody's standard, we've clearly built a sustainable franchise, with high-quality clients in every industry we focus on." TWP has managed to trim its expenses sufficiently to remain profitable at the current run rate.

Even though the firm's investment banking business is down, it's not out. TWP completed over $1 billion worth of transactions for VC-backed companies in 2002. It is the lead manager of 40 percent of the underwritings it does today, leading secondary offerings for such companies as Polycom, Peet's Coffee, and Movie Gallery. In November 2002, it managed to bring IMPAC Medical Systems public in a very tough market.

It also has a strong M&A advisory business. Notable deals it closed in 2002 include selling Crossworlds Software to IBM, eRoom to Documentum, Telera to Alcatel, the tunable laser division of New Focus to Intel, and Ocular Networks to Tellabs. It also represented Accredo Health in its purchase of the Specialty Pharmaceutical Services Division of Gentiva Health Services.

Still, all of this has obviously taken a toll on the company's morale. Bankers who had joined the firm anticipating years of huge profits from the New Age Internet companies found themselves with low salaries and little extra from the firm's profits. Alan Menkes, cohead of Weisel's private equity group, began complaining around mid-2001 that the compensation package for his group was not up to par with the rest of the industry. Weisel hired a consultant to evaluate how their compensation fit into the industry norm, and concluded that private equity partners in a similar position would not only share in profits from the firm overall, but also share in the revenues generated from their funds. So Weisel agreed to add a percentage of the private equity group's profits and fees to their compensation. Despite that, Menkes ended up resigning anyway, which Weisel says indicates that he just did not want to work for the firm. He had come from a small investment firm and wanted to set out on his own.

Obviously, some partners are not happy with the fact that they are making so much less—especially the junior partners, who can sometimes find it difficult to get by in pricey San Francisco these days. But virtually every other investment banking firm is in the same position. Weisel was even able to find a replacement for Menkes who is more likely to fit into the firm's investment capital/ private equity business mix: Larry Sorrel, whose extensive investing experience includes 12 years at Morgan Stanley. The private equity business managed to avoid the dot-com mania (although its one weak spot is about $100 million invested in the depressed telecom industry), and Weisel believes the private equity investments will prove to be profitable when the companies start going public again—soon, he hopes.

"The big issue is compensation. People are making less money now," Weisel acknowledges. "But that shakes out the people who didn't really have the long-term interest and passion for the business."

Weisel is, of course, also watching the scandals shaking the industry with concern, mainly over new regulations that might hurt investment banks' ability to nurture entrepreneurial capitalism. There was still little sign of business picking up again in October 2002.

Rumors of TWP's death will probably persist, but so will Thom

Weisel. Most of the partners are hanging in, hoping for a recovery. They agree with Weisel that the firm is well positioned for that event. Notes Mark Shafir: "We're really the only game left in the growth space."

Besides, Weisel isn't about to give in. Says Ed Glassmeyer, founding partner of Oak Investments: "Thom is like a general in the first leg of the battle, sword in the air. He stands out in front and is willing to take the hits. His magic is this positive belief that he can do what most people find daunting or impossible. I can't think of anyone else who comes close."

In other words, nobody wants to underestimate Thom Weisel.

What Burst the Dot-com Bubble?

Thom W. Weisel

The phenomenon of the Internet bubble is something none of us had ever seen before. We're not likely to ever see anything like it again in our lifetimes. A convergence of events brought it about, and another convergence brought it all to an end.

The first and most important thing that contributed to the speculative bubble was the fact that the cost of capital went almost to zero. It was an extraordinary phenomenon. Venture capitalists had billions to spend. People were buying dot-com stocks like they were gold. Suddenly, it cost almost nothing to raise the capital to start a new company.

Several events created that phenomenon. When the ERISA rules were changed, making it easier for pension funds to put more money into equities and more risky securities, many government and corporate pension funds just indexed their equity allocations, essentially earmarking a certain percentage of their funds for investment in the public stock markets and earmarking other funds for private equity investments. In addition, companies and individuals, believing that the Internet was an extraordinary new phenomenon that could immediately make them rich, poured money into private investment funds as well as directly into private companies.

Two-thirds of all venture capital money invested in the last five years went into the Internet. It's not because the investors were dumb or naive. These were the same folks that brought you many of the past decade's winners. But people were willing to invest in the Internet dream and funded companies throughout the nineties that were, in some cases, based on little more than dreams.

Growth investing was in vogue, and everybody started putting money into technology companies, because that's what had led the growth over the last 20 years.

The trend toward globalization also led some governments to try to build a technology business by helping to finance their industries. The two main areas they put money into were semi-conductors and telecommunications. The global telecom build-out created a huge demand for things like Cisco routers, Sun servers, and EMC storage devices.

The second major factor was the reaction by the so-called old line companies to the Internet phenomenon. Every bricks-and-mortar company thought it was in danger of becoming obsolete, and so invested heavily in new technologies. There was a time when virtually everyone, including our analysts, thought that a large component of retail sales—perhaps 25 percent—would be con-verted to the Internet. I no longer think it's going to be that high.

The third factor was Y2K. Companies were investing enor-mous resources in upgrading computer equipment and networks before the year 2000 came around. With all that investing, the 500 most representative companies, those in the Standard &

Poor's 500, saw a tripling of their growth rates over the last two decades. They went from 7 to 8 percent growth per year to 15 to 20 percent, with profit margins also expanding. Superimposed on that were these hypergrowth technology companies, growing at 40 to 100 percent a year.

All of this investing created a huge tailwind behind technology companies, especially Internet companies, accelerating their growth. The success of some of the early movers, like Amazon .com and Yahoo!, played a role in that. The promise of the Internet looked so good that one could justify the high prices of these companies' stocks. It looked like the gold rush or the creation of the railroads. People thought that the Internet was such a Big Idea that these companies would be able to expand their volume and make money. But the cost of acquiring new customers really hurt. The joke in Silicon Valley was: "I lose money on every customer, but I'll make it up on the volume."

The long boom that people talked about was just an extrapolation of the growth rate of the previous year or two into the future. Every home was going to have a high-speed Internet hookup. The Internet was going to accelerate the growth of the economy over the next three to five years and bring us a Dow of 20,000.

Then it all hit the wall. Y2K came and went, and companies didn't have to make these huge investments in their technology infrastructure any more. Global markets weakened and the telecom industry turned out to be overbuilt. Global Crossing, for example, had invested enormously just on this promise of a need for more bandwidth. Look at all the dark fiber that's been laid all over the world. Half of it may never be lit. The infrastructure build-out was enormous and the cost was very high, but sales are still modest.

And the Internet dreams haven't come true. The applications just aren't there yet to use this massive bandwidth buildup we thought we needed. Look at how long it took PCs to really develop their applications. We have all this memory and computing power, and how many people use an Excel spreadsheet today? PCs are not used for the things people envisioned they would be used for in the early days. They're not personal computers, they're communication devices. It simply takes time for these applications to develop.

We expected all these broadband needs, the convergence of media and telecom and wireless broadband. The use of the Internet for buying and selling consumer goods or for business-to-business exchanges has materialized at a much slower pace than we expected. There's still a question of how useful all this information available on the Internet is to people's lives.

Then, on top of all this, the Federal Reserve policy started tightening up, trying to choke off the capital flow. The Fed raised interest rates, so this nearly zero cost of capital started getting pretty expensive. The Fed was definitely trying to cool all this down. That policy change would have been a pinprick if all this other stuff wasn't in place. But because it was, the psychology of investors turned from greed to fear.

At the time of the build-out, the biggest constraint was a shortage of skilled labor. Now the equation between the availability of capital and intellectual capacity has flipped. The scarcest commodity is capital, and the most abundant is people.

When the Internet boom went bust, the bricks-and-mortar companies realized they didn't have to reinvent themselves or get eaten by the dot-com businesses after all. They pulled back on the technology investments that were designed to rush them onto the Internet.

I misjudged how bad this environment was going to get. I missed how big the impact of this reversal in capital flows was going to be. There were too many companies in too many limited spaces, and the technology companies were creating demand for each other. Companies assumed that advertising revenues would continue strong. But it turns out that the dot-com companies themselves were doing much of the advertising.

During the boom, companies as well as analysts were using different measurements: eyeballs, page views, click-throughs, and things like that. But in the long term, there are three things that drive stock prices: revenues, earnings, and cash flow. Now, the short interest in technology companies is at an all-time high. Most institutions are now underweighted in technology. The small-cap technology companies are selling at rock-bottom prices and are, I believe, the buying opportunity of the century.

I think someone should do a study of the stock-buying habits of the Internet era. It's one of the greatest mass psychology studies any university could ever do. There was mass hysteria. In 1999 and 2000 we saw the most money ever invested, the most money ever made, and the most wealth destroyed. I don't think anybody appreciated at the time how volatile this cocktail was. But, as extended as the market got on the upside, I believe it has overdiscounted the future on the downside. Time will tell if this is right.

Conflicted

[W]hat really distinguishes American capitalism from most other countries' is not that we don't have C.E.O. crooks, but others do, or that we never have bogus accounting, bribery, corruption or other greedy excesses, but others do. No, we have all the same excesses that other capitalist nations have, because fear and greed are built into capitalism.

What distinguishes America is our system's ability to consistently expose, punish, regulate and ultimately reform those excesses—better than any other.
—Thomas L. Friedman

Toughening existing criminal laws and adding new ones might seem the best way to make sure that future Enrons and WorldComs won't happen—and to send a clear message that America will not tolerate dishonesty in corporate boardrooms.

But it won't work. We have gone down this path many times before, and if experience is any guide, new criminal laws are as likely to make things worse as to make them better. The reason is both simple and all too easily ignored: Criminal laws lead people to focus on what is legal instead of what is right.
—David Skeel and William Stuntz

The recession that followed the dot-com mania of the end of the twentieth century also brought with it huge scandals and the biggest crisis in investor confidence since the Great Depression. Executive after executive was shown on the nightly news, in handcuffs, being led to prison for fraudulent accounting. Accounting firms that were supposed to audit the books lost credibility, and investment banks were blamed for helping to inflate the bubble with hype and hot air.

Given Thom Weisel's penchant for aggressive business tactics, and the fact that he was at the center of the tech IPO action as it turned to tumult, the obvious question arises: What role did his firms play in all the fuss?

Neither Montgomery Securities nor Thomas Weisel Partners had been officially charged with any wrongdoing as of publication of this book. But every investment bank, from the most respected Wall Street giant to the smallest boutique, has been scrutinized by the SEC. Press reports have said that TWP is among the firms that the regulators are considering fining. As of publication of this book, it was unclear what practices the SEC considers improper at TWP.

Weisel himself is appalled at some of the business practices that have been uncovered, as well as some of the overreaction of the regulators and plaintiffs. As previously noted, he has always publicly insisted that integrity is vital in business.

Overreaction is a natural side effect of a stock crash. The problem is that, while some of the tactics are clearly illegal and unethical, others fall into a gray zone. Some are questionable from both a legal and ethical viewpoint, some are questionable in only one category or the other, and some are merely potential conflicts of interest being loudly decried with no actual proof that anything improper ever resulted. In many cases, regulators still seem to be experimenting with the appropriate level of regulation and control.

Financial businesses have had their share of scandals since the invention of money. In modern times, accusations of abuse often crop up once the tidal wave of over-the-top speculation ebbs into recession to reveal muddy balance sheets. Just as often, the accusations bring about calls for reform with the idealistic goal of preventing the abuses from ever happening again.

In the United States, for example, the recession of 1837 drove many commercial banks out of business. Regulators and investors criticized the close ties that had developed between the banks and the securities markets. As a result, commercial banks lost much, but not all, of their control of investment banking—for a while.

The stock market crash of 1929, which also followed a recklessly speculative stock market bubble, created an even larger scandal in the banking industry. Some 10,000 banks closed or were bought out over the next few years. People once again criticized the ties between savings banks and investment banks. Commercial banks were faulted for investing their own assets in risky stocks, putting those assets—including individuals' savings deposits—at risk. They were also accused of pushing questionable stocks to their banking customers, even lending them the money that enabled them to buy the stocks. And some of the recommended stocks were those the banks had already invested in themselves, creating a clear conflict of interest.

Early in 1933, at the depths of the Great Depression, Congress held hearings on the abuses of the banking and securities industries. Much of the blame for the Depression was placed on the shoulders of the banks.

A wave of important new legislation followed. Congress passed the Truth in Securities Act of 1933, which required any company issuing new securities, debt, or equity to fully disclose all risks of the offering. The prospectus for every new stock offering today still includes a section titled "Risk Factors," but few investors seem to read that section. Or they assume that since every possible negative has to be reported, the risk factors are the financial equivalent of a warning label on a new set of screwdrivers asserting that you must wear safety goggles when using them or (presumably) you might poke an eye out.

The Glass-Steagall Act, part of the Banking Act of 1933, once again separated the deposit banks from the investment banks. That required breaking up J.P. Morgan & Co. into two separate companies: J.P. Morgan got the banking and lending group, while Morgan Stanley & Co. took the investment banking business. The Banking Act also created the Federal Deposit Insurance Corporation (FDIC) to provide insurance on depositors' funds in the event of bank failure (which came in handy during the S&L crisis of the 1980s but taxed the FDIC's resources). The Securities and Exchange Commission was created in 1934 to oversee these businesses and watch for abuse.

Today, historians, academics, and bank executives still argue over how much responsibility the banks actually held for the stock market crash and the Depression and over the effectiveness of the resulting legislation. Did the banking conflicts cause the market to spin out of control, or was it simply naive and excessive investments of the public? Either way, the Glass-Steagall Act was gradually weakened over the years, allowing banks to start merging again, and was finally effectively repealed in 1999 when President Clinton signed the Financial Services Modernization Act. That act also allows banks to own insurance companies.

The recent dot-com bubble and crash, followed by recession, has become the largest and most devastating financial scandal since the SEC was created. It has also severely tarnished the once shining image of Silicon Valley, although it was not the first scandal to hit high-tech business. In the late 1980s, Oracle Corp. looked into the chasm of bankruptcy when it was discovered that overly aggressive salespeople were booking revenues for products that had not really been sold—or in some cases even built—yet. Oracle restated earnings and CEO Larry Ellison pulled the company back from the edge by replacing almost all of his top management team. The new, more experienced managers put in controls and restored the software company to profitability, prominence, and respect.

Other companies, trying to cover up disappointing earnings with accounting tricks, have acted in a more blatantly illegal fashion and have been prosecuted. Also in the late 1980s, a Colorado disk drive company called Miniscribe fell into bankruptcy for overstating revenues and earnings and using creative techniques to cover it up. Miniscribe will forever be remembered in the technology community as the company that shipped boxes of bricks to warehouses to make it appear as though it were shipping products. The CEO, Q.T. Wiles, was convicted of securities and wire fraud and given a three-year sentence.[1]

That scandal bears several similarities to some of today's accusations. The company was under huge pressure to show strong results—in this case because it was supposed to represent another astounding turnaround by "Dr. Fix-It" Wiles, who was specifically brought in to turn around the ailing company after successfully repairing several other troubled firms. It also sullied the reputations of its financial advisors. Hambrecht & Quist was the company's investment banker and a major investor, and H&Q co-CEO Bill Hambrecht was on Miniscribe's board. It was H&Q that brought Wiles in to save the company. H&Q ended up paying $21.4 million as its part of a settlement to end a shareholder suit. And even though the trial revealed that Miniscribe employees broke into the records of its auditor, Coopers & Lybrand, in order to make a few adjustments, the accounting firm ended up paying $95 million as its part of the $128 million settlement.[2]

At any given time, there are probably a certain percentage of companies fudging their balance sheets in order to look like they're more profitable than they really are. And at times—most of the time these days, it seems—some auditors aren't as diligent at catching these errors as they should be. And there is nothing like an outrageously bullish market to tempt people's greed. When every other company is breaking records and seeing stock prices that turn college students and fresh MBAs into instant multimillionaires, it's hard to accept mediocre results for one's own company. When fortunes are made overnight, everyone wants to join the party, and some of the partiers are not as scrupulous as others.

Microsoft, which might be accused of many things, but could never be described as a hollow dot-com exploiting a rabid market, was recently chastised by the SEC for its financial reporting. But the problem wasn't overstating earnings but understating them. Microsoft is so rich it didn't need to pump up earnings, but the accusation is that the company kept Wall Street happy by using some of the earnings that were held in reserve during good quarters to boost results when there was an unexpectedly bad quarter. Microsoft executives asserted that they never thought their technique illegal, but have promised to refrain from the practice in the future.

Many obvious illegal acts were uncovered after the crash, and it's easy for the investing public to feel as though all corporations are corrupt—especially when all investors have lost money. Consider the enormity of some of the post-dot-com scandals that were making the news in 2002:

- The executives of Adelphia Communications were accused of looting the company for their own gain and investigated for allegedly neglecting to mention billions of dollars of liabilities on their balance sheet. Several executives were arrested, and the company was delisted from the NASDAQ in June 2002.
- Enron executives admitted that the company had overstated earnings by $600 million over the last few years, and

that losses were hidden in off-balance-sheet partnerships. The company was delisted from the NYSE in January 2002. The common public perception seems to be that Enron executives acted without morals, although there has been considerable debate over how many of its actions were actually illegal.

- WorldCom admitted to some $6 billion in fraudulent accounting that even the new management team acknowledges was illegal. Former executives were arrested, and WorldCom filed for the largest bankruptcy in U.S. history. The company was delisted from the NASDAQ in July 2002.

- The accounting firm Arthur Andersen was found guilty of obstruction of justice for shredding documents related to Enron, a clear violation of the law, and a former executive turned states' evidence. The firm, founded in 1913, may not survive the scandal.

- Merrill Lynch agreed to a $100 million fine and changes in its structure to settle charges that it sold dot-com stocks to investors with strong buy recommendations from Internet guru Henry Blodget, knowing they were lousy bets. Estimates of Merrill's liability from lawsuits run as high as $5 billion, and its stock price dropped nearly 20 percent in one month.[3]

- Citigroup Salomon Smith Barney and its telecommunications analyst, Jack Grubman—who was possibly the country's leading telecommunications analyst—were sued by investors claiming to have lost money following Grubman's recommendations on scandal-ridden Global Crossing, which was also one of Salomon's big investment banking clients. WorldCom CEO Bernie Ebbers, another big Salomon client, earned $11 million on IPO stock from other companies the brokerage made available to him. Grubman testified before Congress that he was so close to the company he was supposed to be judging that he had attended meetings of WorldCom's board. Both Grubman and Salomon CEO Michael A. Carpenter lost their jobs over the scandals, and Citigroup, Salomon's parent, faces lawsuits that could cost it up to $10 billion in damages.[4]

- Goldman Sachs, one of Wall Street's most respected firms, was accused of offering hot IPO stocks to top executives at some of its client firms, who then "flipped" the stocks, immediately selling them at a huge profit after prices soared on opening day. Allegedly, these were essentially payoffs to executives in return for ensuring that the clients did more business with Goldman.

- Credit Suisse First Boston agreed in January 2002 to pay $100 million to settle separate investigations into kickbacks of stock-trading profits that the firm had demanded and received from customers. The following October, the Commonwealth of Massachusetts filed fraud charges against CSFB for allegedly using positive stock ratings to reward companies for hiring the firm to underwrite their stocks and bonds. They also contend that bank executives offered IPO shares to executives of companies whose business they wished to attract.[5]

That's just a small sampling. Over a dozen companies have been hit with headline-making scandals, and many more are being investigated. Despite the fact that there are still thousands of companies that have not been accused of any wrongdoing, and that most CEOs have conformed to the new policy of vouching for the credibility of their financial statements in writing, distrust is now rampant. Even if only a tiny percentage of corporations are guilty, how can an ordinary investor know which one is next? It could be one of the trusted companies in your portfolio.

How did this happen? Did corporate executives suddenly become as corrupt as G. Gordon Liddy?

Sadly, the answer is no, not suddenly. It's likely that many of the practices started small, in the gray zones, and progressed slowly, like Alice falling down the rabbit hole—an easy slide down the clichéd but eminently accurate slippery slope. There are also undoubtedly executives who jump onto that slope without hesitation. And in a stock market feeding frenzy, the slope turns into a free fall.

There have been warning signs for years, and the scandals indicate that the financial industries have been largely incapable of policing themselves well enough to prevent them (although many argue that they police themselves well enough to catch the abusers after the fact). The accounting scandals, which essentially stem from rubber-stamping financial statements, were a self-inflicted wound waiting to fester. Every time an American corporation has been caught cheating over the decades, regulators have asked why the auditors did not catch the problems, and investors have often included the auditors in their lawsuits.

In the early 1990s, enough financial tinkering slipped past the auditors to get the attention of the Public Oversight Board (POB), the auditing industry's self-policing watchdog. But while the POB condemned the practices, it also tried to stem the flow of lawsuits by urging Congress in 1993 to limit accountants' liability. The limits would have applied even in cases where shareholders could show that they lost money on audited financial statements that turned out to be false. (Congress did not comply.)

In return, however, the POB had conceded that auditors needed to be more skeptical when examining their clients' books, and backed some proposed reforms. The POB chairman, for example, endorsed a bill by Rep. Ron Wyden (D-Oregon) that would require auditors to report corporate fraud to the SEC if management does nothing to correct it. Melvin R. Laird, a member of the POB and former congressman and secretary of defense, was quoted by *Bloomberg News* in 1993 as saying, "Accountants had better support these reforms before it's too late."[6]

The *Bloomberg News* article also noted that all of the Big Six Accounting firms (Arthur Andersen, Coopers & Lybrand, Deloitte & Touche, Ernst & Young, KPMG Peat Marwick, and Price Waterhouse) had recently had adverse court judgments regarding their audit work. But they did wait too long, and now it's difficult for them to make amends.

The investment banking business faces the same kind of conflicts as the accounting firms. Most investment banks are in multiple businesses, and what is good for one (like an investment banking client getting a glowing research report) may be bad for another (like the banks' investment clients, who want skeptical scrutiny). A conflict of interest increases the likelihood of abuse, but doesn't mean the abuse actually took place.

Investment bank analysts made stock recommendations that now appear to have had as much credibility as Bill Clinton's definition of sex. But a stock recommendation is by nature a subjective thing, and a bad recommendation is not necessarily illegal. Even if an analyst feels that a stock is overvalued by historical standards, it could still rise during a boom and could be fairly recommended as a buy. It's hard to have faith, however, in analysts who privately disparage stocks in internal e-mails as "dogs" or "pieces of crap" while publicly still recommending them as a buy—even if the firm does say the comments were taken out of context.

The press must share some of the blame for echoing questionable recommendations. Every financial reporter knows that an investment bank that took a company public is about as likely to rate the company poorly as the CEO's mother. But, until the scandal broke, few even bothered to ask if the bank did any other business with the company it was recommending.

Another ambiguous area: writing off purchases made in the normal course of business. Some expenses must be accounted for in the current quarter, while others (generally, only big-ticket physical assets such as buildings or machinery) can legitimately be written off over several years as capital expenses. The rules defining which expenses can be written off over time are often vague. One can easily imagine companies with earnings pressure giving themselves the benefit of the doubt in the most questionable areas, leaving the issue of legality in question. However, if the accountants take more and more liberties until, as with WorldCom, the liberties amount to billions of dollars' worth of items that clearly do not fit the rules, they have crossed the line into fraud.

Investors are also quite reasonably incensed over executive pay that has reached absurd and unprecedented heights. In many cases, that lofty position has apparently made some executives feel they are above the law, especially when it comes to insider trading. But the salaries are not illegal, just unjustifiable.

Some of the excessive payments come from stock options. The stock options themselves are sometimes awarded with appalling lack of sense. But these options, along with low-interest loans, have been used to lure executives for decades, especially by technology companies. It would seem to make sense to tie a CEO's compensation to the performance of the company's finances, and hence its stock price. Such incentives are critical in an environment as competitive for talent as it was in the dot-com boom. Reform is needed, but what's the best approach?

In fact, 50 years ago, top executives were accused of acting too much in their own interests, rather than those of shareholders, because they did not own a significant part of the companies they ran. Stocks were volatile, and executives were criticized for not doing enough to raise and stabilize the stock prices of their companies.

None other than Adam Smith was concerned about companies

that were run by executives who did not have a significant ownership of their corporations. He expressed a preference for locally owned and run companies, especially partnerships in which the partners were the primary shareholders, rather than "joint stock" companies owned by shareholders who had no say and little interest in how the companies are run. In *Wealth of Nations,* Smith wrote:

> The directors of such [joint stock] companies, however, being the managers rather of other people's money than of their own, it cannot well be expected, that they should watch over it with the same anxious vigilance with which the partners in a private copartnery frequently watch over their own . . . .Negligence and profusion, therefore, must always prevail, more or less in the management of the affairs of such a company?

The widely proposed solution to this problem was to encourage executives to own more stock in their companies, on the theory that they would be more responsive to shareholders' needs. This was known as the "principal agent" theory.[7] Now that executives and board members are commonly rewarded with stock, they are accused of the opposite flaw: focusing exclusively on short-term stock prices, to the point of illegally boosting earnings to drive the prices up. (Maybe the ultimate solution is to require all executives to use their companies' products in order to ensure their sympathy lies with their customers.)

Stock options and allocations have been abused. When Internet stocks were doubling, tripling, and quadrupling on their first day of trading, everybody wanted to be among the select group that got the stock at the IPO price. That decision is made by the "book manager" at the lead investment bank, who wants to reward the firm's best clients with the best IPO stocks. But the book manager is also put in a position to get kickbacks or make other demands in return for allowing certain buyers access to hot IPO stocks, something the general public rarely gets.

One accusation of IPO abuse, for example, is called "spinning." In this scenario, the book manager allocates hot IPO stock to CEOs or CFOs who may want to float some stock from their own companies soon. The accusation is that the executive gets the hot IPO stock in return for hiring the investment bank to underwrite his or her own company's offering later. This abuse is particularly egregious because the individual executive benefits by directing the company to pay for services from the book managing firm. The cost goes to the company, and the benefits to the individual.

Now consider this: A book manager wants to reward good clients. Theoretically, the idea is to reward clients that are steady stock buyers and long-term investors who might hold onto a stock for years, helping to ensure some price stability. Those are reasonable justifications. But spinning often had the opposite effect during the boom because executives getting the IPO stocks regularly flipped them on opening day, or soon thereafter, taking huge profits. Where is the line of propriety between the statements, "You've been a great customer over the years, so you get some IPO stock," and "Sorry, but you're going to have to start giving us more business if you want some IPO stock. When are you next planning to issue more stock yourself?"

On the other hand, the question may not even have to be asked to violate regulations. The NASD bars investment banks from selling such shares to "any senior officer" of an "institutional-type account" who "may influence or whose activities directly or indirectly involve or are related to the function of buying or selling securities" for such institutional-type accounts. The rule, however, apparently only applies to institutional investors, like mutual funds, and not to corporate executives at client companies who may find themselves in a similar position. That, however, may change soon.

Weisel's companies have been in a position to allocate IPO shares to friends and clients, and have done so. A 1997 *Wall Street Journal* article, which apparently helped start investigations into the practice, listed Montgomery, Robertson Stephens, and Hambrecht & Quist as firms known to allocate IPO stocks to favored clients, and questioned the legality of that practice. In Montgomery's case, the *Journal* specifically named Jamie Coulter, CEO of Lone Star Steak House & Saloon, a long-time Montgomery client, as having been given shares in several other Montgomery IPOs.[8] Weisel points out that Coulter had been a great client long before getting any IPO allocations, and that there was never any agreement to give Montgomery more business as a result.

There do not seem to have been any official charges against any of the San Francisco firms, but a recent *Wall Street Journal* article reported that the NASD was investigating accusations of spinning at Hambrecht and Robertson as recently as April 2002.[9] Montgomery managed to get a class action suit alleging improper spinning thrown out of court.

Another practice investment banks have been alleged to participate in is known as "laddering," or "pay for play." The accusation is that the book manager may agree to give a particular institution (or individual) IPO stock if the institution or individual also agrees to buy more stock after the IPO at a higher price. On one hand, this would seem to deal with the problem of flipping and help provide price stability. The problem is that this can also artificially drive up the price of a stock after the IPO, making it appear as though institutional investors think the stock is actually worth the higher price. And the investors can then sell the stock after it has been driven up even further. It's also illegal to try to artificially boost a stock price. Weisel says he has never allowed this type of deal at his companies, and thinks it would actually be very difficult to make work: Few institutional investors are willing to tip their hands and reveal how much they're willing to pay for a stock. It's bad poker.

Nicholas Maier, a former manager with the hedge fund Cramer & Co., has written a tell-all book claiming that Goldman Sachs specifically told him to agree to buy certain stocks in the aftermarket at higher prices in order to keep getting allocations of hot IPO stocks.[10] Maier said he has cooperated with the SEC in its investigations of Morgan Stanley, Smith Barney, and Goldman Sachs, and claimed that the SEC showed him an investment banking book that detailed how much aftermarket stock companies like his former employer had agreed to buy. James Cramer, the former senior partner for the hedge fund, denied the charges, as do Goldman executives.

Maier's credibility has also been thrown into question because of other allegations in his book: that Cramer himself engaged in insider trading by touting stocks in his broadcast programs and instructing his fund managers to immediately sell the stock when prices rose on his recommendation. Maier and his publisher, HarperBusiness, have since issued a retraction to that allegation and reissued the book with the reference deleted.

There are other accusations of illegally allocating stock to companies or individuals in return for kickbacks. Credit Suisse First Boston was accused of unfairly profiting from hot IPOs by allocating stock to investors who agreed to pay higher brokerage fees for other stock trades. Since the SEC mandated an end to the standard broker fees of 35 cents a share in 1975, the fees have remained less than a dime per share of stock sold. But in the dotcom boom, some investment banks were allegedly charging as much as $1 or $2 per share to clients that were allocated IPO stock. So much for driving prices down with negotiated fees. Again, Weisel says this practice does not take place at his firms.

Weisel definitely has more supporters than detractors on the issue of business integrity. Says Dick Moley from Stratacom: "I have always found Thom to be very honorable." Jack Wadsworth, the former Morgan Stanley investment banker who worked with Montgomery on Micron's IPO, says, "Thom is honest beyond question." Wadsworth also thinks that "By now, the executives without integrity have been discovered and are either in jail or are on their way there." A reasonable observer without inside information, at least, would have to put Weisel on the side of the honest bankers.

In all fairness, it may also be noted that Weisel's two firms faced less temptation, at least in the peak years of the boom, for one simple reason: Weisel's departure created inner turmoil. After he left in 1998, Banc of America Securities lost its strength in the technology and emerging growth categories, and it still has not recovered. And although TWP had an outstanding first year in 1999, it was still new and small enough that it mostly came in as a secondary bank in stock underwritings. Neither firm was the book manager of very many dot-com IPOs, so neither was in a position to frequently allocate shares, properly or improperly.

Obviously, something has to be done to fix the problems in the industry. These abuses have been widely reported, and very many of them are egregious misuses of the trust put in the executives who committed them. The question is how. Should new laws and regulations be passed to try to prevent the abuses from happening again? Should the banks once again be separated into different lines of business in order to avoid the temptation? Or is the fact that so many problems have been uncovered proof that the system actually works, and dishonesty is uncovered in the end?

These questions are tough to answer. Anyone is susceptible to temptation, and the industry watchdog organizations were caught napping, or worse. There needs to be oversight and regulation of the accounting and investment banking industries. If we rely on market forces to eliminate the bad apples, can we justify the suffering, recession, and losses due to fraud as an acceptable price to pay while waiting for market forces straighten out the problems? If we do create new rules and regulations, are we in danger of doing more harm than good in the rush to destroy the villains and raise the political standing of those calling for reform?

Both approaches have been working their way through the system. Everybody from President George W. Bush and SEC chairman Harvey Pitt to California State Treasurer Phil Angelides called for substantial reforms after the WorldCom accounting tricks were revealed in June 2002. Angelides, who oversees $50 billion in California state funds that's invested in stocks and other securities, called for investment banks to completely sever ties between analysts and other parts of the investment banking business.

The investment banks also became proactive by promising their own reforms. Merrill Lynch, stung by its own analysts, bought two-page newspaper ads promising strong reform, including more oversight of its analysts, separating their compensation from other parts of the bank and switching to a simple "buy, neutral, sell" stock rating system.

If that doesn't work, there are plenty of research firms that have analysts but no brokerage or underwriting business, and brokers who have no underwriters or analysts. David Pottruck, co-chief executive of Charles Schwab, has been railing for years against the conflicts of the big brokerage houses that underwrite stocks and then have their analysts recommend them. More recently, Schwab has been taking out full-page newspaper ads asking, "If all anyone is telling you to do is buy, how do you know when to sell?"

Most people agree with some of the changes. The accounting business clearly needs reform, although outright fraud can be difficult for even accountants to detect. They must work with the numbers they are given, although there should be some incentive or control to make them look at the books with a bit more skepticism. CEOs should be held more accountable for their financial statements, under threat of criminal prosecution. Corporate boards should be held more accountable for a corporation's moves and not act like a backup chorus to the CEO.

But many proposed reforms are hotly debated. Should companies be prevented from handing out loans to executives? Should analysts be prevented from being at all involved in the banks' other businesses? That's tough, considering that research reports are a cost center and do not generally produce any revenues. Plus, many banks, such as Weisel's, were designed specifically to use their analysts not only to decide which companies to recommend to clients but to spot the promising companies that need underwriting services. Will researchers now be prevented from helping to find promising private companies or identifying possible merger candidates? Should investment banks be prohibited from allocating IPO stock to long-standing brokerage clients, when wooing clients is a long-standing tradition in both business and politics? Should investment banks be prohibited from investing in private companies, or developing too close ties to private investors, even though that is a natural extension of their services? These relationships and traditions have been established over decades for legitimate reasons. It's only when they're abused that there's a problem—such as offering clients IPO stocks specifically in return for business from the client's company.

Probably the most despised issue of all among corporate executives is how to account for stock options. Stock options can boost the recipient's compensation by millions of dollars a year. So why not expense them along with salaries and bonuses? The law currently allows companies to avoid the write-offs until the options are actually exercised. Opponents point out several problems with changing that law. It's difficult—sometimes impossible—for a company to determine what the options will be worth when they're finally exercised, so how does one determine the write-off up front? The options actually do not cost the company anything until exercised, so why list them as an expense before then? When they are exercised, they do not change the company's net earnings, but lower earnings per share because more shares are placed on the open market. Shareholders, therefore, not the company, actually end up paying for the options. That's a good argument for taking measures to make sure they are not abused, but expensing them up front may not be the best approach. Furthermore, the start-ups of Silicon Valley say they have no other way to offer competitive salaries without options. And start-ups are a huge growth engine in Silicon Valley. If they expense options up front, they are likely to suffer disproportionately relative to larger firms.

While some prominent corporations have announced they will expense stock options from now on, others have made it clear they will not. Intel has been one of the most vocal, saying that it will now offer more detail about option grants in quarterly statements so shareholders can decide whether to approve them. This is the approach favored by most businesses in correcting abuse: enough transparency in the numbers to enable shareholders to make informed decisions or exercise their voting power to prevent the move. But Intel executives say adamantly that they will not list options as current quarter expenses.

Investor confidence is at an appalling low. Some measures must be taken to restore that confidence, or we will damage an extraordinary stock trading system that plays an undeniably critical role in creating new companies, jobs, and economic growth. Even the current prosecutions may not be sufficient to make small investors happy, because the laws are limited. Tom R. Tyler, a psychology professor who studies popular conceptions of justice at New York University, noted in an analysis in *The New York Times:* "A simple application of the law is not going to produce what people will perceive to be justice, because many of the things that have been happening are not necessarily illegal, even if the public considers them immoral."[11]

That may be the impetus for dramatic changes in the law. Some of those changes may not be beneficial. And not every CEO and CFO is a candidate for Leavenworth just waiting to be caught. It's just that right now, too many of them are.

At the very least, business has to lay out its financial cards more clearly and openly if any semblance of confidence is to be restored.

And investors must remember that it is not a game to be taken lightly. But it's not a zero-sum game. Let's hope the final solutions benefit honest people on both sides of the stock-trading business.

It Ain't All That Bad

Thom W. Weisel

As we write this, we're sitting in a very challenging postbubble environment. Pessimism is pervasive. There's a crisis of confidence in corporate leadership, and this psychology is weighing heavily on the stock markets. We have experienced a two-year bear market so far, which destroyed much of the growth we saw in the previous several years. Certainly that's true of the stock market. The NASDAQ dropped from its peak of about 5,000 to as low as 1,200, below its prebubble peak. In July, mutual fund redemptions reached a record $50 billion. Nobody knows when business will pick up again.

A number of industries have an uncertain future economically. One problem with technology stocks is that the capital flow for both public and private companies was so great it created a tremendous overcapacity in certain industries. There are roughly 10,000 private companies in need of capital, trying to compete with each other for capital and customers.

Most of the capital during the bubble flowed into technology companies. In the last five years, 13,000 companies were created by venture capitalists, and only 2,000 of them have had an exit. Many died, and roughly 500 have gone bankrupt. We have to work through the inventory of the companies that this bubble created before the survivors have the pricing power and market traction to compete with the entrepreneurial leaders.

There's terrorism around the world with only the United States to defend against it. We're not certain if we'll end up in another war soon. We have a few systemic problems as well. Our university system is world-class, but our public education system is woefully broken.

And finally, financial scandals have rocked the business world, shattered investor confidence, and deepened an already depressed stock market. A few people are looking for scapegoats for the broken bubble, lashing out at anybody they can see, from CEOs to accounting firms to lawyers and even to the president of the United States. This is a dark hour for entrepreneurship.

In this environment, I would like to add a voice of optimism, to state what is good about America and positive about our future. Let's step back a moment and look down from a 40,000-foot view.

I see a lot that's positive. I still see a highly entrepreneurial culture with an incredible work ethic. We have a culture of risk taking, of adventure, and of wanting to do new things. It's one of the things that made, and keeps, us great.

We have free and open markets. That alone is going to keep American companies competitive. We will continue to have a large and transparent market. Statistics bear out the fact that most public companies have ready access to capital. We have low inflation and low interest rates. That benefits consumers who are borrowing for a car or a mortgage or a business.

Our banking system is in great shape compared to 1989 or 1990, or compared to other economies where the banking systems have failed completely. Outside of technology, the economy continues to gain momentum. Even in technology, overall spending isn't down, it's just not growing. Spending on information technology is down from its peak, but it hasn't collapsed.

When the global economies start to rebound, we could have a global resurgence. Not only the United States, but the economies of Europe and Asia, could bounce back and provide a turbo boost to our markets.

We have the finest military in the world, and we have the finances to pay for it. It's not going to break us economically. Even though there's a terrorist threat, we're going to make it.

Silicon Valley cares deeply about the issue of our badly suffering public schools. This country cannot compete in the information age without education. The best potential solution is in applying free market forces to education. I find the adoption of vouchers and charter schools to be very encouraging trends for trying to fix that.

The average stock is relatively cheap. Large-cap stocks are more expensive than small-cap. Large-cap technology companies are still well off their historic lows. But durables and health care companies are selling where they did at the trough of the market over the past 15 years. Stocks are cheap relative to inflation and interest rates, which should moderate any downside from current levels. Nobel laureate economist Milton Friedman was recently asked to compare the current crisis of confidence with past bouts of doubt, and was quoted as giving the following response:

> It's trivial, the American economy will weather today's troubles just fine—if the government doesn't make a muddle of things as it did in the Depression. Federal Reserve passivity in the face of widespread bank failures and bankruptcies in the 1930's turned a garden-variety recession into a global disaster. The biggest risk now is that overzealous regulators could frighten honest chief executives into ducking legitimate risks. The system doesn't work unless business is willing to take risks.[12]

Federal Reserve Chairman Alan Greenspan added an important point that the public tends to forget. In allocating capital, he said, "losses are just as important as profits."

Entrepreneurial capitalism—the reemergence of young, growing companies—will need to lead the next recovery. This is where job growth will come from. Let's hope the current climate in Washington does not go overboard in regulation and witch hunting, forcing the entrepreneurs who create young companies and the firms responsible for capital flows to shift to the sidelines of this much needed risk-taking segment of our economy.

The New Age and Old Age

Thom W. Weisel

We are confronted with insurmountable opportunities.
—*Pogo (Walt Kelly)*

The turn of the twenty-first century was not kind to American business. Technology companies went through their worst recession in memory. Stock markets went into a protracted decline, much worse and more broadly felt than anyone expected. Between March of 2000 and the fall of 2002, the stocks of the Standard & Poor's 500 lost 50 percent of their value. In the technology sector, things were even worse. Many entrepreneurial companies lost 90 percent or more of their value, and many others went out of business entirely.

The first two years of the millennium have been characterized mostly by fear. First is the lingering fear following the loss of so much money in the dot-com collapse. Trillions of dollars in capital was misdirected during the boom, and the capital markets have been slowly shutting down since then. There is also alarm and anger over corporate malfeasance, and concern that more charges and lawsuits are to come. Some people are worried that the process cannot be fixed, others that new legislation might hurt the process of capital formation. We're wary of more terrorism and the possibility of war with Iraq. Everybody has been hunkering down for a long storm.

It all sounds frightening, doesn't it? And it is. But we should also be aware of the fact that fear itself can debilitate the stock market. The best response is not to retreat, but to find a better path. This is the time to remember the basic wisdom that's always proved right but is so hard to believe until it happens: Out of adversity comes opportunity.

We're not talking about returning to the status quo, although we do need a return to the basic metrics of good investment strategies: diversity, profits, and growth. We're talking about emerging from the other side better, stronger, wiser.

Again, we can't find a better model than Lance Armstrong. When he had cancer, he had no choice; it was either fight for life or accept death. But once he was cured, he did have a choice: What happens now? He looked back at his cycling career and said, "I can do better." He realized that he had been coasting more than he knew. He reevaluated how he pursued his goals. He had to rededicate himself and refocus, and he decided to take his game up a serious notch. He then found out he had a lot more potential than he had ever realized.

Now everyone wonders what the ultimate impact of all these problems devastating the economy will be. What does this mean to corporations, to the stock market, to investors, and to the very quality of our lives? In other words, what happens now?

Changing Business

Every company and every individual should reset their goals the way Lance Armstrong did. This is the time for leadership, the

time to challenge corporations and employees. This is the time
when massive changes take place in the marketplace. There will
be huge winners and a like number of losers, and those that face
the environment head-on and change course, rethink strategy,
and become more realistic about the future will prevail.

In this environment everyone needs to analyze how to greatly
improve their game. Companies will have to reevaluate their models and make some dramatic changes. They will have to carefully
set their priorities and be willing to accept more risk than they
would otherwise.

Good companies have always been able to reevaluate their
strategies when the markets turn bad, sometimes exiting markets, sometimes entering new ones. There is no one solution, no
universal advice to focus or to diversify. Every company must evaluate its own strengths and weaknesses, the competition, and the
markets.

Two classic cases are Intel and Micron Technology. Intel is the
company that invented semiconductors, memory chips, and
microprocessors. When competition in memory chips became
fierce in the 1980s, Micron decided to continue to pursue that
market with intense focus, creating a better product. Intel
decided to focus on a more promising product instead: the
microprocessor. Many people criticized Intel for retreating from
a huge market in tough times, but it proved to be the right decision for Intel, just as Micron's decision was the right one for that
company.

Another thing companies should consider: Stock prices, in the
long run, are always driven by earnings and dividends. If earnings
growth at a company is slowing, then that company should seriously consider offering a dividend. That's especially true of a company like Microsoft, which has large free cash flow and no need
for most of the cash it is throwing off anyway.

There is even one advantage to the current malaise: There is more time to work on the character of a company. Building a unique and positive culture takes time, and that's one of the few commodities we have available to us now. For example, I believe that in many industries, but especially ours, the star system is dead. We don't need superstar analysts or prima donna executives now. This is the time to build a cohesive team and to encourage strong team efforts.

In a period of change, entrepreneurial executives need to convey a strong message to their employees: It's all right to fail. You can't try new things without allowing some level of failure.

One day last September, we took a large client out of its investment in a company after the market closed. We had no buyers, so we had to put the block on our balance sheet. We bet that we would be able to sell the stock again in the morning near the trading price. It was a risky trade, using our own capital, but it turned out fine.

Allowing people to fail doesn't mean allowing them to be less rigorous. If anything, more rigor is required. At our company, for example, before our analysts recommend that clients buy or sell a particular company's stock, they typically independently verify that company's business model and earnings estimates by also checking on their customers' demand and their suppliers' shipments. This mitigates the level of risk. Our analysts bring a thought process and a level of scrutiny that adds significant value for our clientele.

Survivors will have the advantage when the economy picks up again. When business was zooming along like a freight train, many people jumped on for the fast buck, but didn't really have the passion or long-term interest in their business. As one of my venture friends said, this period is shaking all the "tourists" out of the business. Only people who truly enjoy their work and are really good at it will be left. Many industries will emerge from the recession stronger as a result.

The Next New Old Future

The stock market is changing as well. For the next few years, returns on all financial assets will be lower than they have been for the last 15 years. The growth drivers and the circumstances will be more muted and diversified than they have been over the last several decades.

The economy and the stock market will most likely return to the growth rates of the early 1990s rather than those of the latter half. The latter part of the 1990s was characterized by 4 to 5 percent annual GDP growth and expanding profit margins, resulting in 15 to 20 percent annual growth in the profits of the Standard & Poor's 500 companies. Stock multiples reflected these high growth rates.

The early 1990s were more muted, with 2.5 to 3 percent GDP growth and profit growth of 5 to 8 percent for the S&P 500. This is the more likely scenario going forward. With overcapacity in almost every industry, margins will continue to be under pressure.

There are plenty of drags on the stock market. As we stated earlier, stock prices are reflecting extreme fear. The uncertainty of war with Iraq, of a double-dip recession, and of more corporate blowups; a lack of confidence in our corporate and financial institutions; and fear of more terrorist acts are all heavily discounted into stocks.

Money managers are also worried about the heavy debt loads of the consumer. The inflated housing market more than likely must undergo a correction. Therefore, the ability of the consumer to carry the economy much further is limited. In addition, the balance sheet risk of some of our financial institutions and larger corporations is being called into question. And finally, some economists are calling for global deflation because of the overcapacity created over the past decade.

The three main determinants of stock prices are fundamentals, psychology, and supply-demand. All have turned negative. We have had the lowest rate of companies going public in decades.

That's the bad news. The good is that most of these elements have already been factored into stock prices—in some cases, too aggressively. There are good techniques for finding stocks that have been too heavily discounted.

It is not sufficient to simply look at the price/earnings ratio in order to determine whether a stock is over- or undervalued. You must also take into account how quickly a company's earnings are growing. A company with faster growth should have a higher P/E multiple.

A good measure of a stock's valuation is to compare the price/earnings ratio to the growth rate of the company's earnings. The S&P 500 has a P/E of about 15, which is about 2.5 times its growth rate of 5 to 8 percent, based on 2003 recovery earnings. That's a high multiple, indicating the stock prices will remain under pressure as well.

On the other hand, the real value in this market is the small- to mid-cap companies, whose proxies are the S&P 600 and the S&P 400. Both of these indexes also have P/Es of about 15. But earnings of the companies in these groups are growing at about 12 to 18 percent a year. That means the P/E is roughly equal to the growth rate, a P/E/G multiple of about 1. So even if there is no multiple expansion for these companies, the stocks should at least perform in line with their earnings growth.

Stocks also must be evaluated relative to inflation and interest rates. Currently the 10-year bond is selling at a 44-year low, reflecting slower economic growth and little inflation. On the Fed discount model, which compares the earnings yield on the S&P, discounted to the present, versus the yield on the 10-year bond, stocks are selling at roughly a 50 percent discount to bonds. This should provide a floor for stocks at some level: about 700 to 750 for the S&P 500.

The average stock on the Nasdaq is down over 85 percent and is now selling at $10 per share, with 40 percent of the stocks selling at $5 or under. That is where incredible value resides. Dozens of companies are selling at a market cap that's less than the cash positions those companies have. These are positive cash flow companies with substantial revenue, customers, and the ability to grow once the economy starts to pick up.

There are several signs that we are at or near the bottom of the market. We are currently 2.5 years into the bear market, similar to the 1973 to 1974 bear market. The longest bear market in history was 1929 to 1932. We will match that record in March of 2003. And yet, we are not in a depression, we do not have stagflation with 20 percent interest rates, and I do not think our financial system is on the brink of collapse as it may have been during the S&L debacle in the 1990s. Further, there is over $2.5 trillion in cash sitting in money funds. Some of this should flow back into the market as confidence returns.

Another indication of a bottom is the Market Volatility Index (VIX), which tracks market volatility based on options. When VIX is high, it indicates that investor sentiment is pessimistic. VIX was very low through most of the 1990s, but hit high points toward the end of 2001 and the summer of 2002, when the stock markets were bottoming out. The volatility index has risen to 50 recently, as it did on July 23, when the stock market hit a low. This indicated a maximum amount of fear in the market, and possibly a trough in stock prices. Mutual fund redemptions, another signal of pessimism, also hit an all-time high in July—over $50 billion. In addition, credit spreads have widened to record levels. This could also indicate we have already passed the bottom of the market.

Some economists are worried about a *double dip*, a second low in the economy. We believe that danger is past. Furthermore, the possibility of a double dip in the economy has already been factored into stock prices. What has not been factored into stocks is the other side of that double dip, when the economy rises again on much stronger fundamentals. Usually, stocks will discount the future 6 to 12 months in advance. So if the recovery starts in 2004, stocks will most probably reflect this by mid-2003 at the latest.

Today, most money managers are looking for the catalyst that will reignite the next bull market. It might be invading Iraq, as it was in 1991 when we invaded Kuwait. It might be favorable earning surprises in the fourth quarter of 2002 or the first quarter of 2003. It might be the newly elected Congress, in sync with the administration in enacting several pro-growth economic packages—such as lowering taxes, eliminating double taxation on dividends, lowering capital gains tax, and accelerating deprecation and research and development amortization.

The bottom line: Start looking at stocks again. Think about dollar cost averaging. About going slowly. Stock investing should see a return to basics. If investors are diversified, with a good mix between stocks and (short-term) bonds (because interest rates are so low now), and if they concentrate on small- to mid-cap stocks, they ought to see reasonable returns of 10 percent plus over the next 5 to 10 years.

The leadership will come from younger, more entrepreneurial companies across the economy's spectrum. The previous decade's market leaders will most probably not lead the next market. Too much capital flowed into these sectors, creating too many companies and thus commoditizing many of these industries. On the other hand, the pace of innovation has not slowed down. Therefore, truly next-generation companies that are addressing sizable unserved markets with quality management teams will be the future winners. The engine for job growth has to come from small entrepreneurial companies, because big business will continue to cut costs to generate the earnings necessary to justify its multiples. So look to the emerging growth sector, which has been torn apart by the bear market, to emerge as the leader over the next several years.

The New New Things

This is a new era of growth investing. New sectors of market leadership are emerging to displace the old ones.

The big issue is that we can no longer solely rely on technology as the growth driver. U.S. technology will play a role in the stock market, but not the extraordinary role it has played recently. It will not have the same absolute sector dominance that it had in the late 1990s.

The positive catalysts, the growth drivers, in the near term will be in the consumer, health care, defense, and industrial growth sectors.

In the longer term, demographic-driven trends will determine the winning growth sectors. The 2000 U.S. census showed that 13 percent of the population—35 million people—are 65 or older. There are 38 million Baby Boomers, aged 45 to 54, who will start retiring in a decade, and those numbers will increase dramatically. The companies that benefit from that demographic change, such as those in health care products and services, will be the leaders. Being ahead of the sector trends can lead to big returns. For instance, the information technology component of the Standard & Poor's 500 went from a $154 billion market capitalization in 1990 to roughly $1 trillion today—and that is after the market crash drove this sector down 70 percent from its peak in the boom years.

Catching these sector moves can lead to above-average gains. It will, however, require active portfolio management, because not all companies in the sectors are created equal, and new competitors are emerging all the time.

Here are some of the highlights we see coming, including projected compound annual growth rates (CAGRs) in revenues for each industry, where possible.

Consumer Products and Services

- **Specialty retailing:** The demographic trend lends itself to a "stay at home" investment theme. Consumers will be looking for high quality and distinctive merchandise and services. They will be looking for value. We look for specialty retailing to grow 15 percent a year for the next five years.

  The Baby Boomer and Echo Boomer generations are big consumers of interactive, high-fidelity, rich media in new technology formats, such as the Internet, DVD, and high-definition TV. We expect entertainment software to grow at 22 percent annually over the next five years.

- **Media:** We also see a recovery in media advertising, especially in cable TV and online advertising. In 2001 advertising spending was down 7 percent, one of the worst years in several decades. We expect advertising spending to be up 1.7 percent in 2002, then up another 4 to 5 percent in 2003. That could help these stocks become leaders over the next 12 to 18 months. A great sub-tailwind theme is the growing Hispanic population, giving a boost to Spanish-language programming.

- **Financial services:** Low interest rates are a positive catalyst here. Ten-year bonds, at under 4 percent, are at a 40-year low. That has spurred the refinancing of $5.9 trillion in U.S. mortgage debt and extensive new home purchases. The 2.5-year decline in the stock market, plus the collapse of major companies like Enron and WorldCom, have heightened the fear and anxiety of retirement planning, an area where people will be looking for help.

- **Restaurants:** Dining out is shifting from a special event to potentially an everyday occasion. Consumers are more time-starved and are looking for convenience. Restaurants are not much more expensive than cooking meals at home these days, and not many people like washing dishes! This sector should grow at about 17 percent annually over the next five years, with the highest growth in high-quality, quick, and casual chains.
- **Education:** There are three factors indicating that higher education will continue to provide a compelling investment opportunity. First, there is solid demographic expansion: The total number of U.S. enrollments will grow by an estimated 8 percent each year for the next decade. Second, state universities and community colleges across the country are facing significant budget shortfalls, limiting their ability to meet the growing demand. This provides the opportunity for proprietary schools to offer swing capacity and increase market share. Third, for-profit higher education business models provide solid revenue visibility, superb returns on equity, predictable earnings growth, and consistent fundamentals.

Other growth areas include food and beverages, hard-line retail, and hospitality and leisure.

Health Care

Health care in the United States already accounts for $1.4 trillion in spending annually, or 15 percent of the GDP. Per capita spending on health care in the United States grew 7.1 percent annually from 1990 to 2000. National health expenditures should grow at 7.5 percent annually over the next five years. And yet, as a group, the stock multiples in the health care sector are selling at or near their trough levels over the last 15 years.

- **Biotechnology:** It took 20 years for scientists to sequence the first 10 percent of the human genome. The recently completed human genome project took 18 months to sequence the other 90 percent. Biotechnology is moving rapidly from medical theory to business reality. Genomics (the study of the genome) and proteomics (the study of proteins produced by the genome) are active areas of research that will identify targets for new drugs and treatments. Cancer therapies will top the list. We foresee 45 percent annual growth rate in biotech.

- **Diagnostics:** Traditional diagnostics is the study of fluids and tissues, a $32 billion market growing in the single digits. Genomic diagnostics—tests to decipher gene activation—is a $1 billion industry growing at 30 to 50 percent a year. We're on the cusp of a whole new world of diagnostics and medical treatments, with better instruments and technology. Projection: 78 percent annual growth.

- **Health care information technology and IT services:** Providers of hospital-based software and services offer more efficient operations and the ability to reduce errors. The sector is growing as overall hospital profitability improves. Despite the pessimism over e-health stocks today, the Internet remains the ideal medium to connect providers, payers, and consumers.

- **Medical devices:** Cardiology and orthopedics show the most promise with about 15 percent growth. In orthopedics, we have targeted spinal disc repair and replacement, minimally invasive surgery, and regeneration technology.

- **Pharmaceuticals:** Large-cap pharmaceutical companies have been driven down for several reasons: The pipelines for new drug developments are lean. There is a lot of talk from the government about controlling drug costs, because they have contributed the most to health care cost increases.

And there are a lot of drugs coming off patent. Companies that have to start competing with generic versions of their drugs will suffer, but investors have penalized the entire sector. The large drug companies are spending $500 billion in R&D over the next 10 to 15 years. That will put new products in the market. We anticipate 8 percent growth a year.

- **Specialty pharmaceuticals:** There are over 10,000 investigational new drugs in the biotech drug pipeline. That bodes well for specialty pharmaceuticals, with 31 percent anticipated growth annually.

Defense and Environmental Services

U.S. defense and homeland security is the new national priority. The U.S. government will accelerate its spending on defense because of the threat of terrorism. Department of Defense modernization will drive military spending over the next five years at 7 to 7.5 percent annual growth.

Companies that are directly or indirectly involved in the management of an environmental resource or hazard make up a $100 billion business. This includes waste management, water utilities, filtration technology, infrastructure, and consulting. Hospitals, utilities, and industrial companies are increasingly outsourcing their environmental tasks, creating demand for the service companies.

Technology

Information Technology spending, industry-wide, will grow 3.5 to 4 percent annually over the next five years.

- **Network storage:** The explosive growth in data makes storage an increasingly vital and strategic resource. By moving data from local to networked storage, sharing resources becomes more efficient and reliable. Storage area networks (SANs) use high-speed switches to create a networked "fabric" connecting many servers to many external storage devices. This is done in a way that makes the networks more scalable, reliable, and ultimately more cost-effective. Cisco has entered the SAN market for those reasons. We forecast 29 percent annual growth in SAN switching over the next five years.

Software to manage these networks is also promising, but future revenues are more difficult to quantify. The major software segments are backup and archiving, storage resource management (SRM), storage replication, and utilities/other. International Data Corp. predicts revenue growth of 17 percent annually for the overall software sector, with SRM experiencing the highest growth of 22 percent per annum.

- **Wireless applications:** Wireless communications stocks are a tough bet for the near term. A lot of investors bid them up, anticipating the Next Big Thing, but the economy knocked the business down. Funding has dried up, and carriers, especially in Europe, are saddled with huge debt from buying spectrum licenses. We're optimistic for the longer term, however, especially as regards the infrastructure buildout. Demand for PDAs, third-generation wireless devices, and networks will grow as the economy recovers. The wireless revolution represents a profound, worldwide socioeconomic change as people become untethered from their desks or homes while staying connected to whichever networks they choose. We anticipate 10 to 15 percent annual growth.

- **Web services and infrastructure software:** Web services represent the next architectural shift in computing after the client/server model. Adoption will be slower, because there is no urgency to start using the new technologies until given a proven return. That gives some advantage to larger players like Microsoft and IBM, but there are some niches open to entrepreneurs. Web security and management services are two good candidates.

- **Business outsourcing:** The three main categories are information technology, professional services, and payroll processing. These industry segments are huge, fragmented, and growing. Right now, their performance is driven by cyclical characteristics. But secular growth is becoming more prominent as companies increasingly find outsourcing to be a more efficient and cost-effective approach to dealing with processes that are not their core competency. The need to save money and time is not affected by business cycles. Growth rates will range from 15 to 20 percent.

- **Electronics manufacturing outsourcing:** The fundamentals for electronics manufacturing services have clearly bottomed. Corporate restructuring has made the EMS value proposition more compelling. When companies like Hewlett-Packard or Sony restructure their whole businesses, they can get rid of their manufacturing by outsourcing. Again, it is not core to what they do: designing, marketing, and selling electronic products. Japanese companies are now starting to outsource as well. Even a deep decline in the end markets for the products has not reversed the outsourcing trends.

Return to Sanity

We've gone through an insane period. There wasn't anybody who was not infected by the promise of the tech bubble gold rush to some degree. But we've now either seen the bottom of the market or are within several quarters of the bottom.

We live in a great country. We will survive and flourish once we get the current environment behind us. The postbubble era will see a return to basics, where the road we travel on will be more important than the destination. We can take the first steps now.

Chapter 4

1. Jack Wilson, *The New Venturers: Inside the High-Stakes World of Venture Capital.* Reading, MA: Addison-Wesley, 1985, pp. 15–16.
2. Ibid, p. 19.
3. Ibid, p. 36.
4. Ibid, p.51.
5. Newsday.com, "From New Amsterdam to Wall Street," March 17, 2002.
6. Ira Unschuld, "The House that Morgan Built," *Financial History*, August 1981, pp. 3–6.

Chapter 5

1. Frederick J. Dory, "The Man Who Invented the Biotech Business," *The Wall Street Journal*, December 14, 1999.
2. "A Research Firm Transforms Itself," *Business Week*, October 2, 1978.

Chapter 6

1. Sarah Bartlett, *The Money Machine.* New York: Wagner Books, 1991, p. 237.
2. Jason Manning, "Wolves on Wall Street: The Eighties Club," http://wolfstories2.tripod.com/id34.htm.
3. Robert A. Bennett, "Team Montgomery," *U.S. Banker*, June 1988, pp. 15–20, 68.
4. "Sweat Stocks," *Time*, November 25, 1985.

Chapter 7

1. Victor F. Zonana, "Montgomery Gets on Fast Track in Securities Field," *Los Angeles Times*, January 4, 1987.
2. Harvard Business School case study N9-800-215, March 13, 2000.

3. Geoffrey Colvin, "Maxim Velocity," *Fortune*, May 8, 2001.
4. Rita Koselka, "Riding the Wave," *Forbes*, May 23, 1994, p. 70.
5. Scott McMurray, "What Makes Montgomery Run?" *Institutional Investor*, February 1997.

Chapter 9

1. Richard Brandt, "Sound Blaster Hears the Blare of Competition," *Business Week*, April 12, 1993, p. 88A.
2. Herb Greenberg, "Herb on the Street," TheStreet.com, August 29, 2000.
3. Reynolds Holding, "Dark Side of the IPO Frenzy," *San Francisco Chronicle*, March 28, 2000.

Chapter 10

1. Paulina Borsook, "Cyberselfish: A Critical Romp through the Terribly Libertarian Culture of High-Tech," *Public Affairs*, 2000, p. 4.

Chapter 11

1. Bill Gates, *The Road Ahead.* New York: Viking Penguin, 1995, pp. 4–5.
2. Scott McMurray, "What Makes Montgomery Run?" *Institutional Investor*, February 1997.
3. Phil Weiss, "JDS Uniphase Revisited," Fool.com, January 5, 2000.
4. "Deal-making Done," *The Economist*, January 27, 2001 [U.S. edition].
5. David Greising, "NationsBank-Montgomery: Love among the Heavyweights," *Business Week*, July 14, 1997.
6. Peter Truell, "Montgomery Chief Quits in Dispute with Nationsbank Parent," *The New York Times*, September 22, 1998, p. C4.
7. "Deal-making Done," *The Economist*, January 27, 2001 [U.S. edition].

Chapter 12

1. Gregory Zuckerman and Rick Brooks, "In New York: Staff Departures at Montgomery Prove Educative," *The Asian Wall Street Journal*, May 4, 1999, page 15.
2. Julie Greenberg, "Burn Rate Olympics: 1998's IPOs," *Wired*, January 1999.
3. Elizabeth Corcoran, "Growing Up Is Hard to Do," *Forbes*, April 29, 2002.

Chapter 13

1. "Where Are They Now?," *Forbes ASAP*, June 2, 1997.
2. Kathleen Pender, "H&Q Will Pay $21 Million to Resolve Suits," *San Francisco Chronicle*, June 23, 1992.

3. Patrick McGeehan, "Brokers Caught in Cross-Fire in Client Suits against Merrill," *The New York Times,* May 25, 2002.

4. Patrick McGeehan, "Salomon Smith Barney Chief Ousted in Shuffle at Citigroup," *The New York Times,* September 9, 2002.

5. Patrick McGeehan and Norm Alster, "First Boston Faces Another Fraud Charge from a State," *The New York Times,* October 22, 2002.

6. "Audit Overseers Call for Legal Relief, Promise Better Quality," *Bloomberg News,* March 4, 1993.

7. Paul Krugman, "Greed Is Bad," *The New York Times,* June 4, 2002.

8. Michael Siconolfi, "Spin Desk Underwriters Allocate IPOs for Potential Customers," *The Wall Street Journal,* November 12, 1997.

9. Patrick McGeehan, "I.P.O. Boom Is Over, But the Inquiries Aren't," *The New York Times,* April 25, 2002.

10. Nicholas Maier, *Trading with the Enemy: Seduction and Betrayal on Jim Cramer's Wall Street.* New York: HarperBusiness, March 2002.

11. Kurt Eichenwald, "Even If Heads Roll, Mistrust Will Live On," *The New York Times,* October 6, 2002.

12. Sylvia Nasar (compiled by Rick Gladstone), *The New York Times,* September 29, 2002, sec. 3, p. 2.

1941
- Thomas Weisel born, Mayo Clinic, Rochester, Minnesota.

1948
- Weisel starts to speed skate in local races at age 7.

1952
- Goes skiing in Sun Valley on 10th birthday.
- Wins Midget Boys Wisconsin State Championship.

1955
- Wins first National Speed Skating Championship and sets national record (220 yards in 19.9 seconds), Juvenile Boys, St. Paul, Minnesota.

1956
- Wins National Speed Skating Championship, Junior Boys.

1957
- Wins National Speed Skating Championship, Junior Boys.
- Sets two national records (440 yards in 36.7 seconds; 1 mile in 2 minutes, 53.3 seconds) in Minneapolis, Minnesota.

1958
- Wins National Speed Skating Championship, Intermediate Boys.

- Wins Class A seniors 1-mile bike race in Wisconsin against national field.

1959
- Holds eight Wisconsin State records.
- Takes third place in 500 meters at the Winter Olympic trials (43.8 seconds, 0.8 seconds out of first), ahead of Terry McDermott, who goes on to win the gold medal in 1964, and Bill Disney, who wins the silver medal in 1960.
- Wins National Championship, Intermediate Boys. Sets national record (440 yards in 36.2 seconds).
- Enters Stanford University in the fall.

1960
- Fails to make U.S. Olympic Team.
- Spends winter in Alta, Utah.

1963
- Graduates Stanford with Distinctions and Honors in Economics.
- After spending three months in Europe, works for Reid Dennis and
- Vic Parakeni at Fireman's Fund for six months.

1964
- Enters Harvard Business School in the fall.

1966
- Graduates from Harvard Business School in June.
- Starts work at FMC Company in San Jose in the fall.

1967
- In September, starts work at William Hutchinson Co. as securities analyst.

1968
- Son Brett is born.

1970

• Daughter Heather is born.

1971

• Son Wyatt is born.
• Leaves William Hutchinson in the spring, and joins with RSC in August as equal partner to build institutional brokerage business. (Hutchinson employees Karl Matthies, John Gruber, Reb Forte, and Steve Mittel join as well.)

1972

• RSC changes name to RCSW.
• Weisel buys condo in Snowbird with Michael Bloomberg, Erik Borgen, and Bill Wilson.
• RCSW takes Victoria's Station and Applied Materials public.

1973

• First annual SROG. Weisel wins 100-yard dash, 880, and bicycle race (first place overall). Transitions back into serious training.

1974

• Buys condominium in Sun Valley.
• Joins U.S. Ski Team board.
• Tours Europe with U.S. Ski Team.
• Places second in SROG.
• Hires John Tozzi to build trading in advance of negotiated commission rates in May 1975.

1976

• RCSW helps take ROLM public.
• Meets Boone Lennon and starts to change skiing technique to become a downhill ski racer.
• Ken Siebel leaves RCSW to start his own money management firm.

1977
- RCSW helps take Tandem Computers public.

1978
- RCSW name is changed to Montgomery Securities after Sandy Robertson and Bob Colman leave.
- Revenues go from under $1 million to $10 million in the 1970s.

1980
- Weisel competes in Corporate Challenge in track, taking third in nationals, 37:58 in 10K Pacific Sun, at age 39.
- Finishes Dipsea Race in 60 minutes.

1981
- Runs 50.6-second quarter mile and 2:02 half mile in local meets.
- Finishes Oakland half marathon in 1 hour, 19 minutes.
- Montgomery helps with follow-on offering for Denny's.

1982
- Places third at National Masters Ski Championship, Anchorage, Alaska (third overall, third in slalom, third in giant slalom).
- With son Brett, attends World Championships in Schladming, Austria, where Steve Mahre wins World Championship in giant slalom.
- Recruits Will Weinstein, Alan Stein, and Bobby Kahan to strengthen management and build out both brokerage and investment banking.

1983
- Elected president of U.S. Ski Team.
- Buys a bicycle and starts riding.
- Joins SF MOMA board.
- Montgomery helps take Amgen public.

1984
- Attends Sarajevo Olympics (U.S. Ski Team wins three gold medals, two silver, and one bronze).
- Montgomery helps take Micron Technology public.

1985
- Starts Montgomery Cycling Team with Steve Johnson and Boone Lennon.
- Goes to national training camp in Fresno conducted by Eddie Borysewicz.
- Competes in first bicycle race, Elephant's Perch in Sun Valley; stage race, time trial, criterium, and road race.

1986
- Will Weinstein leaves to join Pritzker organization as a partner. Pritzker invests $10 million in Montgomery for 12.5 percent equity stake.

1987
- Weisel competes in first National Cycling Championship, Houston, Texas (third in 1K, men aged 45 to 49).
- In spring, a rogue trader loses millions in convertible arbitrage, wiping out half of Montgomery's capital because Montgomery made Pritzkers whole on losses in the account.
- Montgomery helps take Teradata public.
- Stock market crashes in October.
- Montgomery Sports, Inc. formed in October.

1988
- Weisel competes in Masters Track Nationals in Indianapolis (second in 1K and sprint).
- Starts Montgomery Avenir Team.
- Montgomery lead-manages Maxim Integrated Products IPO.

1989
- Weisel and the Montgomery team take the AT&T Four Man National Championship.
- Takes fourth place in Master Criterium Nationals, Long Island.
- Wins silver medal, 1K nationals, men ages 45 to 49, Portland, Oregon.

- Competes in World Masters Game, gold medals in match sprint and 1K, Finland.
- Montgomery revenues go from about $10 million in 1980 to about $100 million by 1990.
- Weisel sets national record for 1K (1 minute, 10.79 seconds) in Colorado Springs for senior men ages 45 and older.

1990
- Establishes first pro cycling team with backing from Subaru.
- In San Diego Nationals, ages 45 to 49, wins gold in criterium, gold in sprint, silver in 1K time trial.
- Lance Armstrong joins Subaru Montgomery along with Nate Reis and Steve Hegg.
- Meets Emily Carroll, Sante Fe, New Mexico.

1991
- In San Diego Nationals, ages 50 to 54, Weisel wins gold in criterium, gold in sprint, gold in 1K time trial, silver in points race.
- Sets two national records in one day (1K and 200 meters).
- Wins Master World Cup, gold 1K, San Diego.
- Named Masters Athlete of the Year by U.S. Cycling Federation.
- Lance Armstrong wins U.S. Amateur Road Championship.
- Subaru-Montgomery takes bike team to Europe.

1992
- Weisel attends Albertville Olympics. U.S. Alpine Team wins four gold and three silver medals.
- Lance Armstrong leaves team to join team Motorola.
- Montgomery sole-manages IPO for Lone Star Steakhouse & Saloon.
- Montgomery lead-manages Strathcom IPO.

1993
- Cycling team wins first U.S. Pro Championship, with Bart Bowen as lead rider.

- The team is offered a coshare Tour de France team with French team Chazal and turns it down.
- Weisel joins board of Empower America.

1994

- Attends Olympics at Lillehammer. U.S. Ski Team wins two gold and three silver medals, rewarding after hard work.
- Steps down as chairman of U.S. Ski Team after four Olympics; remains on board.
- Montgomery lead-manages Doubletree IPO.

1995

- Youngest son is born.
- Weisel becomes chairman of Empower America after Steve Forbes steps down to pursue U.S. presidency.
- Weisel hires Mark Gorski to build new and better cycling program.

1996

- U.S. Postal Service signs on as lead sponsor of cycling team.
- Montgomery helps take Yahoo! public.
- Montgomery helps take Siebel Systems public.
- Cycling team wins second U.S. Pro Championship.
- Emily Carroll and Weisel cochair capital campaign to raise $15 million for new San Francisco building for California School of Arts & Crafts, on whose board Emily sits.

1997

- Weisel sells Montgomery Asset Management for $250 million to Commerzbank.
- Weisel sells Montgomery for $1.3 billion in September. (Revenues went from $100 million in 1990 to $700 million at time of sale.)
- Weisel joins NY MOMA board.
- Weisel-backed team enters Tour de France for first time. All nine riders finish. Jean Cyril Robin is top rider for team, in 15th place overall.

1998

- Youngest daughter is born.
- Weisel resigns from Nationsbanc Montgomery on September 18th. (First six months of 1998 saw investment banking revenues double from previous year.)
- Weisel forms Thomas Weisel Partners LLC in October.
- Lance Armstrong rejoins cycling team. All nine riders finish Tour de France. Jean Cyril Robin is top rider, in sixth place overall.

1999

- Doors open at Thomas Weisel Partners in January. Trading desk opens in February.
- Firm starts with 136 employees including 53 partners.
- 22 strategic investors put in $35 million for 7 percent of firm.
- TWP is exclusive advisor to Yahoo! for its acquisition of GeoCities.
- Lance Armstrong wins first Tour de France, becoming the first American on an American team and an American bike to win the Tour.
- Weisel is behind Lance in the follow car as he climbs the mountain on Sestriére and asks, "How do you like them apples?" Weisel takes victory lap with team down Champs Elysées.
- Weisel receives Investment Banker of the Year Award from *Investment Dealers Digest*.
- TWP shows $186 million revenues in its first year.

2000

- In January, CalPERS invests $100 million for 10 percent of TWP, with an additional commitment of $1 billion for TWP private equity investments.
- Weisel closes $1.3 billion private equity fund.
- Weisel steps down as Empower American Chairman in order to focus on TWP. Remains on Empower America's board.
- Weisel establishes U.S. Cycling Foundation to develop sport at the youth level. Joins USCF board with 2 other members from the Foundation.
- Lance Armstrong repeats victory with Weisel riding shotgun in pace car at Mont Ventoux.

2001

- Weisel begins refocusing TWP on growth sectors in the beginning of the year. Mark Manson from DLJ hired to help expand TWP's research in order to diversify the firm.
- Brings San Francisco Grand Prix to the city; 400,000 spectators attend.
- TWP represents SDL in sale to JDS Uniphase.
- In November, Weisel announces strategic alliance with Nomura Securities, which pays $75 million for 3.75 percent of TWP, $125 million commitment for private equity, agreement to pursue cross-border mergers and acquisitions between Japan and United States.
- Lance Armstrong wins Tour de France with Weisel riding shotgun in pace car at the decisive l'Alpe d'Huez.

2002

- Larry Sorrell brought in to expand private investment business.
- Lance Armstrong wins fourth Tour de France. Weisel in pace car in Pyrenees when Lance pulls away from competition.
- TWP reduces head count from 800 to 600 and brings cost structure in line with current revenues.
- Weisel sells 21 paintings from his collection at Sotheby's.
- TWP manages successful IPO for Impac Medical Systems during IPO drought in November.

Printed in the United States
55590LVS00002B/231

9 780471 214175